NATURAL MENU COOKBOOK

JANE SUMMERFIELD

Avery Publishing Group

Garden City Park, New York

Cover Design: William Gonzalez and Rudy Shur
In-House Editor: Linda Stern
Typesetting: Elaine V. McCaw
Text Illustrator: John Wincek

Avery Publishing Group
120 Old Broadway
Garden City Park NY 11040
1-800-548-5757

Library of Congress Cataloging-in-Publication Data

Summerfield, Jane.
       The natural menu cookbook : imaginative recipes from America's
natural food restaurants / Jane Summerfield.
              p.   cm.
       Includes index.
       ISBN 0-89529-757-4
       1. Vegetarian cookery. 2. Vegetarian restaurants—United States.
I. Title.
TX837.S913 1997
    641.5'636—dc21   97-4289
                                                              CIP

Printed in the United States of America

10 9 8 7 6 5 4 3 2 1

Contents

This book is dedicated to the Creator–Being within each of us that guides us to design and create, grow and develop to our highest potential and fulfill our highest purpose on earth. May that Creative Spark allow us to discover new joys and delights in cooking and in all our endeavors.

Acknowledgments

As with many projects, the energy and cooperation of many people have helped bring this book to completion. I would like to express my deep gratitude to my teachers and guides, both seen and unseen, who have helped me every step of the way with their wisdom, guidance, encouragement, and abundance of blessings and energy from the inception of the idea to its final manifestation.

Thank you to my husband, David, for his abiding love and encouragement, computer assistance, and super recipe-testing skills. Thank you to our children, Leif and Jelica, for helping to test and taste all those recipes! And thank you to my Urbaska family for my first experiences with good food and family fun around the table!

Thank you to Store Manager Ruel Brown and Assistant Store Manager Tom Murphy of the Bozeman Safeway Store for generously donating food to the Test Kitchen so that we could verify the accuracy of each recipe. The cheerfulness and helpfulness of the checkout clerks made my weekly trips to the grocery store a pleasure.

Sincerely, "Thank you, dear hearts" to the Recipe Testers—Christine Atkin, Boston, Massachusetts; Jerri Balsam, Missoula, Montana; Maureen Carey, Phoenix, Arizona; Daphne Gillam, Bozeman, Montana; Margaret Hower, Corvallis, Oregon; Linda Kaholokai, Kawaihae, Hawaii; Linda Klenn, Great Falls, Montana; Tina Lancione, Albuquerque, New Mexico; Robert Smith, Columbus, Montana; Maile Urbaska, Billings, Montana; and Ruth Urbaska, Billings, Montana—all of whom are great cooks and whose skills and judgment I value and trust.

Once the work on my end of the manuscript was completed, the work began for the good folks at Avery. Thank you to Rudy Shur, Managing Editor, for saying, "Yes, we'll publish it." Thanks to Joanne Abrams for her careful, congenial, and steady hand to guide the project along from editor to editor. Thanks abundantly to Linda Stern, editor, for her in-depth knowledge and abilities in cooking and editing. Thanks to Lisa James, editor, for her meticulous attention to detail right up to the end. And with a sweep of the pen, a graphic artist can capture the essence of a recipe. Special thanks to John Wincek, illustrator, for his lovely drawings.

Finally, I wish to thank all of the restaurant owners, managers, and chefs who have generously contributed their recipes. Your efforts to create wonderful vegetarian foods and offer them to the public speaks of your conscious and conscientious commitment to help make this world a better place. These owners, managers, and chefs represent the following restaurants:

Alabama
Golden Temple Natural Foods and Café, Birmingham

Alaska
Marx Bros. Café, Anchorage

Arizona
Dara Thai, Flagstaff
Le Méditerranée de Sedona, Sedona

Arkansas
Beans & Grains & Things, Little Rock
Dairy Hollow House Country Inn and Restaurant, Eureka Springs

California
Alisan Restaurant, Anaheim
Café For All Seasons, San Francisco
Indian Paradise, Newport Beach
Joy Meadow, Redwood City
Lotsa Pasta, San Diego
Lucky Creation Vegetarian Restaurant, San Francisco
Nan Yang Rockridge, Oakland
Restaurant Keffi, Santa Cruz
Tipps Thai Cuisine, Ventura

Colorado
Adam's Mountain Café, Manitou Springs
Creative Vegetarian Café, Boulder
Rio Grande Mexican Restaurant, Fort Collison

Connecticut
Bloodroot, Bridgeport

Delaware
El Sombrero, Dover

Florida
Hyatt Regency Westshore, Tampa
Pineapples Natural Food Restaurant and Market, Miami Beach

Georgia
Bluebird Café, Athens

Hawaii
Chiang-Mai Restaurant, Honolulu

Idaho
Jimmy D's, Coeur D'Alene

Illinois
Chicago Diner, Chicago

Indiana
Benvenuti, Indianapolis

Iowa
The Greatest Grains on Earth, Davenport
The Pizza Kitchen, Ames

Kansas
Cornucopia Restaurant, Lawrence
Paradise Café, Lawrence

Kentucky
Everybody's Natural Foods, Lexington
Rainbow Blossom Natural Foods & Deli, Louisville

Louisiana
Nature Lovers, Metairie

Maine
Bagel Works, Portland
Kingsbury House, Belfast

Maryland
Mela Restaurant, Columbia

Massachusetts
The Raw Carrot, Amherst

Michigan
Seva Restaurant, Ann Arbor

Minnesota
Delites of India, Minneapolis

Mississippi
High Noon Café, Jackson

Missouri

Sunshine Inn, St. Louis

Montana

Bagel Barn, Bozeman

Black Dog Café, Missoula

John Bozeman's Bistro, Bozeman

Madison River Inn, Three Forks

The Community Food Co-op, Bozeman

Nebraska

McFoster's Natural Kind Café, Omaha

Nevada

Blue Heron Natural Foods Restaurant, Reno

New Hampshire

Café Chimes, North Conway

New Jersey

The Garden Vegetarian Restaurant, Red Bank

New Mexico

Artichoke Café, Albuquerque

Natural Café, Santa Fe

New York

Angelica Kitchen, New York

North Carolina

Pyewacket Restaurant, Chapel Hill

North Dakota

Green Earth Café, Bismarck

Ohio

Parma Pierogies, Cleveland

Oklahoma

The Earth Natural Foods & Deli, Oklahoma City

Oregon

The Higher Taste, Ltd., Portland

Pennsylvania

Cherry Street Chinese Vegetarian, Philadelphia

Walnut Acres, Penns Creek

Rhode Island

Extra Sensory, Providence

South Carolina

Angel Fish, Charleston

South Dakota

The Body Guard, Yankton

Tennessee

Slice of Life Restaurant, Nashville

Texas

A Moveable Feast, Houston

Utah

Honest Ozzie's Café and Desert Oasis, Moab

New Frontiers Natural Foods, Salt Lake City

Vermont

Horn of the Moon Café, Montpelier

Virginia

The Mediterranean Bakery, Alexandria

Washington

Doe Bay Café, Olga

The Old Town Café, Bellingham

Washington, D.C.

Fasika's Ethiopian Restaurant

West Virginia

Mother Earth Natural Foods, Parkersburg

Wisconsin

Beans & Barley Café, Milwaukee

Wyoming

Franca's Italian Dining, Cody

Preface

Have you ever dined at one of your favorite vegetarian restaurants, enjoyed their veggie crescent, tofu roast, or Thai curry stir-fry, and wished you could have the recipe? I have. Writing *The Natural Menu Cookbook* has provided me the opportunity to collect the recipes of gourmet chefs from some of the best restaurants around the country. They have perfected their specialties and agreed to share these magnificent delights so we may prepare them at home.

How did this book come about? It started after I chose a vegetarian diet as the result of a spiritual journey that began in the early 1980s. I found that not eating meat made me feel better both spiritually and physically. At that time, there weren't many vegetarian cookbooks. But I was single, and it wasn't difficult to top some veggies with cheese, throw together a salad, and call it dinner. However, once I started a family of my own, I found that I wanted to expand my repertoire of vegetarian recipes in order to add interest and vitality to our dinner-time menus. We also like to entertain family and friends, and I wanted to prepare delicious and exciting meals that all of us, vegetarians and nonvegetarians alike, could enjoy. Thus,

the idea of writing a cookbook started to rattle around in my head.

In the meantime, I moved from Washington State back to my home state of Montana, where I started the Madison River Inn and Conference Center with a group of friends. It was at that time that a friend, May Kay Williams, knocked on our door and handed me a copy of *The Vegetarian's Guide to Natural Food Restaurants* by Avery Publishing Group. One day I perused its pages, and I vividly remember asking the question, "What am I supposed to do with this book?"

The answer came from my intuition: "Here's where you'll get the recipes for your cookbook." That idea struck a chord. Of course! Here were all sorts of restaurants that I could contact for recipes.

I wrote a query letter to Avery and received a call from Managing Editor Rudy Shur. He said it was a great idea, but that there were all sorts of roadblocks I was likely to encounter, from too-busy chefs to closed restaurants. He then asked if I still wanted to do the book. I took a deep breath, and said I did.

Rudy was right about the roadblocks. But they were all surmountable, and doors continued to open all along the way. I worked to make this book happen with the chefs and restaurant owners who sent their recipes to me, and benefited from their good natures and diligent efforts. After accumulating the recipes —at least one from every state in the country— we went on to test the recipes and render them suitable for home use. This involved reducing the amounts to accommodate servings of four to six people. For some particularly labor-intensive recipes, we decided to allow for more servings because we knew that most people would want to get more than one meal out of their efforts.

Because many of these recipes originate from ethnic restaurants that use authentic, natural ingredients, I have indicated where to locate unusual ingredients and how to make appropriate substitutions. Certain methods, such as washing and preparing fresh spinach and leeks, are explained. Many of the recipes call for eggs or dairy products, which are not part of all vegetarians' diets, so I also offer alternatives and substitutions for these ingredients.

Overall, these recipes are not necessarily low-fat or nonfat. I believe that most of the restaurants submitted recipes that were their most popular dishes. When we treat ourselves to a restaurant dining experience, we often splurge on calories. With today's awareness about fat content in foods, however, I feel it appropriate to offer a few suggestions for turning a recipe into your own low-fat on nonfat creation. For instance, in most cases you can reduce the amount of oil called for in a recipe by half. If the recipe calls for $1/4$ cup olive oil, use 2 tablespoons. When a recipe instructs you to sauté onions or garlic in oil, you can substitute water or vegetable stock for the oil. You can also replace the oil with other ingredients. That is, you can substitute fruit purées such as applesauce for vegetable oil in most baking recipes. Sour cream can be replaced with low-fat on nonfat yogurt, and so forth. Experimenting with various alternatives will offer an opportunity to see what works best for you.

I also wanted to provide recipes for both special occasions and for everyday dinners. Some of the recipes are elegant, company fare. Others are simple, quick-to-fix, "everyday" items. Both elegant and simple dishes are well-tested and perfected recipes that you know you can trust the first time you try them.

The pleasure of eating a delicious meal, elegantly or simply presented, borders on being a sacred event. For most of us, mealtime is that rare moment in the day when the whole family gathers. We take time to nourish ourselves and share our stories. The love and joy that goes into preparing the meal, the delight from those who receive it, and the satisfaction our whole being feels throughout the dining experience nourishes us on all levels. May you find *The Natural Menu Cookbook* a refreshing addition to your cookbook collection—one that offers you delightfully new alternatives for your mealtime gatherings.

Appetizers

From Benvenuti *INDIANAPOLIS, INDIANA*

Portabella Mushroom Sauté
with Scallions, Tomatoes, and Garlic

Bellissimo! This dish is easy to prepare and elegant to serve as an appetizer or, when accompanied by a crisp, green salad and French bread, as a lovely, light luncheon entrée. Portabella mushrooms, the meatiest "beefsteak" of the brown cap mushroom variety, are great for grilling on the barbecue, too.

1. Place the oil in a medium-sized sauté pan, and place over medium-high heat. Add the mushroom, and sauté, turning regularly, for about 5 minutes, or until golden and tender.

2. Add the garlic and tomato to the skillet, and gently stir. Then add the wine. To deglaze, continue to gently stir the mushroom and tomato, allowing the liquid to reduce only slightly, by about one-fourth.

3. Add the scallions to the sauté pan, season with salt and pepper to taste, and sauté for 1 additional minute.

4. To serve, place the mushroom cap in the center of the plate. At the bottom right edge of the plate, spoon out the tomato with a slotted spoon, and cover the entire plate with the garlic, scallions, and wine reduction. Serve immediately, accompanied by slices of French bread.

ABOUT THE RESTAURANT

Located in the Century Building on South Pennsylvania Street, Benvenuti is an elegant and distinguished restaurant in Indianapolis. The menu offers gourmet vegetarian dishes as well as exquisite, classical Italian cuisine.

Yield: *1–2 servings*

Preparation Time: 15 minutes

Cooking Time: 10 minutes

$1/4$ cup extra virgin olive oil

1 portabella mushroom, wiped clean and stem end trimmed

1 clove garlic, minced

1 Roma tomato, skinned, seeded, and coarsely chopped

$1/2$ cup sauterne or other sweet white wine

1 scallion (green onion), green part only, finely sliced

Salt, to taste

Black pepper, to taste

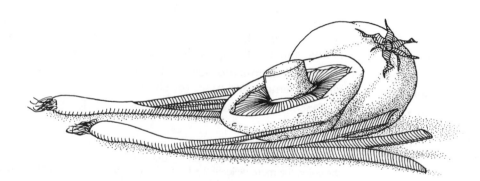

From Angelica Kitchen   NEW YORK, NEW YORK

Mushroom Phyllo Turnovers
with Mushroom Glaze

A delicious beginning to a dinner, these turnovers would also make a perfect luncheon entrée served with a salad and dessert. The creation of Myra Kornfeld and Peter Berley, the dish is a very popular appetizer on the restaurant's autumn-winter menu.

Yield: 6 servings

Preparation Time: 30 minutes for the mushroom glaze; 45 minutes for the turnovers

Cooking Time: 1 hour 45 minutes for the mushroom glaze; 10 minutes for the turnovers

MUSHROOM GLAZE

2$\frac{1}{2}$ pounds white or brown mushrooms

1 large yellow onion, quartered or roughly chopped

4 cloves garlic, separated, skins left on

2 tablespoons canola oil

4 sprigs fresh thyme or $\frac{1}{4}$ teaspoon dried

Water

2 tablespoons olive oil

MUSHROOM PHYLLO TURNOVERS

1 pound fresh spinach (See "Preparing Fresh Spinach" on page 29.)

1 tablespoon umeboshi paste*

1 tablespoon light miso*

1 teaspoon balsamic vinegar

1 teaspoon fresh lemon juice

To Make the Glaze:

1. Preheat the oven to 375°F.

2. In a large bowl, toss the mushrooms, onions, and garlic with the canola oil. Empty the mixture onto a baking sheet, and place the baking sheet in the oven. Roast the vegetables for 45 minutes, or until they turn a deep brown, stirring every 10 to 15 minutes.

3. Remove the baking sheet from the oven. Place the roasted, browned mushroom mixture in a medium-sized saucepan. Add the thyme and enough water to cover the mushrooms. Bring to a boil over medium-high heat. Turn the heat down to low, and simmer uncovered for 1 hour.

4. Remove the pan from the heat, and strain the juice from the mushroom mixture into a sauté pan, pressing down the mushrooms with a large spoon or small plate to extract as much juice as possible.

5. Place the sauté pan over medium-high heat, and boil the extracted juice down to a syrup consistency, about 15 minutes. Remove the pan from the heat, and whisk in the olive oil. Set the glaze aside until the final presentation of the turnovers, and if necessary, gently warm the glaze over low heat, whisking, for 2 to 3 minutes.

To Make the Turnovers:

1. Preheat the oven to 450°F.

2. Lightly oil a large baking sheet and set aside, or use a nonstick baking sheet.

3. Place the spinach in a large pot or steamer with sufficient water for steaming. Steam the spinach over high heat for 1 minute. Rinse the steamed spinach under cold water to arrest the cooking. With your hands, squeeze the spinach dry and chop it coarsely.

4. In a medium-sized bowl, whisk together the umeboshi paste, miso, vinegar, lemon, and mirin (or sherry).

5. Place the mushrooms and garlic in a food processor, and mince together.

* *Umeboshi paste* is Japanese pickled plum paste. *Miso* is a thick brown paste made by fermenting soybeans, rice, or barley under pressure. It may be light or dark. The lighter the color, the more delicate the flavor. Miso is found in most natural food stores.

6. In a small bowl, mash the tofu to medium-fine consistency, with no large lumps.

7. In a medium-sized sauté pan, heat the olive oil over medium-high heat. Add the onion and the salt, and sauté until the onion is translucent. To the pan, add the mushroom mixture, sage, and pepper. Cook until the mixture is almost dry, about 5 minutes.

8. Add the tofu and spinach to the pan, and stir. Add the umeboshi paste mixture to the pan. Stir well, and cook 5 minutes longer, until almost dry. Set the mixture aside to cool to room temperature.

To Assemble and Bake the Turnovers:

1. Cut the phyllo dough in half lengthwise. Cover the phyllo with a clean, damp dish towel or moistened paper towels so the dough will not dry out.

2. Remove a single phyllo sheet from under the damp cloth, brush one side with oil, and fold it in half, oil side in. Place 2 tablespoons of the spinach filling in a lower corner. Fold the dough into a triangle, like a flag, being sure to use all the dough. Tuck any remaining dough into the folds of the triangle. (See the diagram.) Brush the top of the turnover with olive oil.

1 tablespoon mirin* or sherry

12 ounces button mushrooms, quartered

4 cloves garlic, peeled

1 pound firm tofu, rinsed and patted dry

2 tablespoons olive oil

1½ cups finely chopped onion

1 teaspoon salt

1 tablespoon chopped fresh sage or about ¼ teaspoon dried

Pinch of black pepper

12 phyllo dough sheets*

Olive oil to brush the phyllo dough sheets

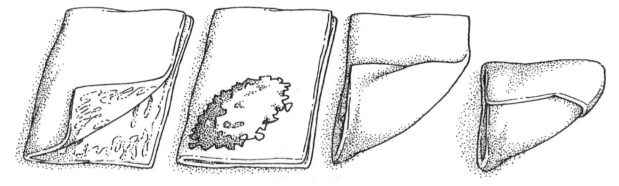

(a) Oil sheet, fold in half   (b) Place filling on dough   (c) Fold up from point   (d) Fold down to seal

Assembling the Turnovers

3. Place the triangles 1 inch apart on the prepared baking sheet. Bake on the lowest rack of the oven for 10 minutes, or until golden brown.

To Serve the Turnovers:

1. Spoon 2 to 3 tablespoons of the glaze in the middle of each individual plate, place a turnover on top of the glaze, drizzle a little glaze over the turnover, and serve immediately, while the turnovers are warm.

ABOUT THE RESTAURANT

Using organic, seasonal ingredients, Angelica Kitchen likes to promote the local farmers and their organic produce. The owners are especially proud of encouraging the creativity of each chef.

* Mirin is a Japanese sweet cooking rice wine used for cooking. It can be found in most grocery stores. Phyllo dough is a light, flaky pastry dough most commonly found packaged as sheets in the grocery frozen food section. Phyllo must be handled carefully, as it tends to break apart easily.

From Pyewacket Restaurant   CHAPEL HILL, NORTH CAROLINA

Southwest Caponata Appetizer

Eggplant is enjoying a well-deserved success these days, as you'll see in this tasty appetizer.

Yield: 6 servings

Preparation Time: 30 minutes

Cooking Time: 30 minutes

2 large eggplants, peeled, ends trimmed, and cut into 3/4-inch cubes

1 tablespoon sea salt

3 1/2 tablespoons olive oil

1 cup celery (about 2 large or 3 medium stalks cut in half lengthwise and sliced very thin across)

1 1/2 cups diced onion

4 large tomatoes, peeled, seeded, and cut into 1-inch cubes (about 4 cups)

1/2 cup fresh orange juice

1/4 cup balsamic vinegar

2 teaspoons finely minced chipolte chilies*

1/2 tablespoon lemon juice

1/2 cup chopped fresh cilantro (coriander)

GARNISH

6 lettuce leaves

18 squares Parmesan cheese, sliced very thin

6 lemon wedges

6 sprigs parsley

1. Place the eggplant cubes in a colander, and toss them with the salt. Let the eggplant sit for at least 30 minutes to drain off the bitter liquid. The salt extracts some of the bitter juices of the eggplant, which then drain away. Rinse the cubes with cool water. Pat and squeeze them dry a little before cooking.

2. In a large sauté pan, heat 1 tablespoon of the olive oil over medium heat for about 30 seconds. Add half of the eggplant. Sauté the eggplant until golden brown and soft. Remove the eggplant from the pan onto several thicknesses of paper toweling to drain. Repeat the procedure for the remaining eggplant.

3. Add the remaining 1 1/2 tablespoons of olive oil to the pan, and allow to heat for 30 seconds. Sauté the celery and onions on medium heat for 10 minutes.

4. Add the tomatoes, orange juice, and balsamic vinegar, and cook for another 10 minutes. Return the cooked eggplant to the pan, and add the chilies. Cook, uncovered, for 15 minutes. Add the lemon juice and cilantro, and cook for 1 additional minute.

5. Serve the caponata warm or chilled. To chill, place the caponata in a covered container in the refrigerator for about 30 minutes.

6. To serve, place a lettuce leaf on each plate. Scoop 1/2 cup of the warm or chilled caponata onto the lettuce, and add the remaining garnishes. Serve with French bread.

ABOUT THE RESTAURANT

Pyewacket is known throughout the region for its salad dressings, which are bottled and sold commercially in the restaurant and in area stores.

*Chipolte *chilies* are dried, smoked jalapeño peppers. Soak them in warm water for 1/2 hour to soften them. Be careful when you are handling chilies because they can burn the skin of your hands, eyes, and mouth. It's best to wear rubber gloves. If the chilies touch your skin, wash carefully with warm (not hot or cold) soapy water to reduce the heat from the chilies.

Madison River Inn THREE FORKS, MONTANA

Hot Mushroom Canapés

Hot stuffed mushrooms are always a favorite as an appetizer. These mushrooms are especially delectable and are neither too filling nor too spicy. They are a great accompaniment to a variety of meals, such as an Italian pasta dinner or a soup and salad luncheon.

1. Preheat the oven to 350°F.

2. Remove the stems from the mushrooms, and set aside the caps. Finely chop the stems.

3. Heat 3 tablespoons of the butter in a large sauté pan over medium heat, add the onions, and sauté until the onions are translucent.

4. Add the chopped mushroom stems, bread crumbs, and water chestnuts to the pan. Remove the pan from the heat, add the parsley and lemon juice, and season the stuffing mixture with salt and pepper, stirring to blend well.

5. Melt the remaining butter in a small saucepan. Brush the mushroom caps with butter, fill them with the stuffing mixture, and place them with the filling side up on a large baking sheet. Sprinkle the mushrooms with Parmesan cheese, and place in the oven to bake for 12 to 15 minutes.

6. Remove the mushroom canapés from the oven and serve hot.

ABOUT THE RESTAURANT

Along the banks of the beautiful Madison River, the Inn presents a stately picture against a Montana landscape of golden wheat fields and purple snow-capped mountains.

Yield: 6–8 servings

Preparation Time: 45 minutes

Cooking Time: 15 minutes

16–20 large, fresh white
  mushroom, washed and dried

5 tablespoons butter

1 small onion, finely chopped

3/4 cup dry unseasoned bread
  crumbs (See "About Bread
  Crumbs" on page 23.)

1/4 cup chopped water
  chestnuts

2 tablespoons chopped fresh
  parsley

1 tablespoon fresh lemon juice

Salt, to taste

Black pepper, to taste

1/4 cup grated Parmesan cheese
  (about 1 ounce)

From Angel Fish   CHARLESTON, SOUTH CAROLINA

Artichoke Heart Eggrolls
with Honey Dijon Sauce

Eggrolls extraordinaire! You'll love the Honey Dijon Sauce!

Yield: 6 servings

Preparation Time: 5 minutes for sauce; 30 minutes for eggrolls

Cooking Time: 2 minutes per eggroll

HONEY DIJON SAUCE

1/2 cup honey

1 cup mayonnaise (See "Alternatives to Regular Mayonnaise.")

3/4 cup Dijon mustard

ARTICHOKE HEART EGGROLLS

2 cups vegetable oil, approximately, for frying

1 large head nappa or savoy cabbage, shredded

1 cup alfalfa bean sprouts (about 1 1/2–2 ounces)

4 scallions (green onions), chopped

To Make the Sauce:

Put the honey, mayonnaise, and mustard in a food processor, blender, or small bowl, and blend well. Pour the sauce into a serving bowl. Refrigerate any remaining sauce in a covered container for up to several weeks.

To Make the Eggrolls:

1. In a large sauté pan, place enough oil to cover half of an eggroll at one time (a depth of about 2 inches). Preheat the oil over medium-high heat. Or if you have a deep fryer, fill with oil and preheat to medium-high.

2. In a large bowl, mix together the vegetables, basil, salt, pepper, and ginger.

3. In a small bowl, combine the flour and water to make the paste to seal the eggrolls.

4. Take one wrapper out of the package, keeping the remaining wrappers in the plastic bag to prevent them from drying out too much. Place about 2 tablespoons of the veggie filling on a corner of the eggroll wrapper. Spread approximately 1 teaspoon of the flour-and-water paste along the edge of the eggroll wrapper in the upper right corner. Wrap tightly, and press the ends together to seal the edges. (See the diagram.)

Forming an Eggroll

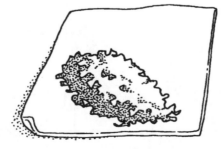

(a) Place filling on dough

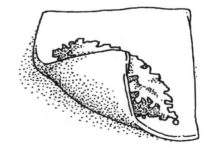

(b) Fold up bottom corner

Alternatives to Regular Mayonnaise

A variety of alternatives to regular commercial mayonnaise are readily available at grocery and natural food stores. You can find mayonnaise made from tofu and canola oil, and some that are eggless and cholesterol-free. Typically, they are lower in calories and have less fat. The texture of alternative mayonnaises is nearly the same as that of regular mayonnaise; however, you may find that the tastes of the alternative mayonnaises vary. We especially like the Blue Banner brand name of eggless mayonnaise distributed by Spectrum Natural, Inc. This eggless mayonnaise has close to the same taste as a regular mayonnaise, is cholesterol-free, is low in sodium, has 75 percent less fat, and has no sugar. When a recipe refers to mayonnaise, you may substitute any alternative mayonnaise and the recipe will work just fine. If you wish to make your own eggless mayonnaise, try the recipe for Excellent Eggless Mayonnaise on page 156.

2 cups artichoke hearts, drained and sliced (about 2 jars, 14¾ ounces each)

2 tablespoons chopped fresh basil or 1 tablespoon dried

Salt, to taste

Black pepper, to taste

1½ tablespoons freshly grated ginger

1 teaspoon flour

2 teaspoons water

1 package eggroll or spring roll wrappers*

*Eggroll wrappers are found in the refrigerated case in the produce section of most grocery stores. There are twenty wrappers in a 1-pound package.

5. To test the oil, dip a corner of the eggroll into the oil. If the oil sizzles and the corner begins to cook, the oil is ready. If the oil doesn't sizzle, allow the oil to heat a few more minutes and then test it again.

6. Place 1 or 2 eggrolls in the hot oil, depending on the size of your pan. Fry until golden brown on both sides, about 1 minute per side.

7. Remove the eggrolls from the pan, and allow them to drain on several thicknesses of paper toweling. Serve immediately, while they are hot, with the honey Dijon mustard sauce.

ABOUT THE RESTAURANT

Fragrant aromas fill the air, as do the staff's lovely Southern drawls, promising a leisurely dining experience at Angel Fish.

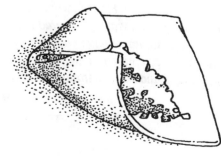

(c) Fold in left corner

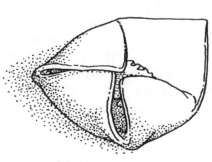

(d) Fold in right corner

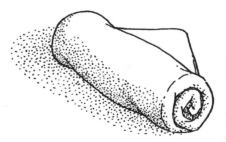

(e) Roll towards top corner

Antipasto of Grilled Vegetables & Cheeses

The succulent flavor of grilled vegetables combines with the cheeses to make a sensational appetizer perfect for a summer party or a light romantic dinner at home.

Yield: 4 servings

Preparation Time: 20 minutes

Cooking Time: 2–3 minutes

1 baby zucchini

1 baby yellow squash

1 baby eggplant

1 baby fennel, bulb only

2 scallions (green onions)

1 red bell pepper

1 yellow bell pepper

$1/4$ cup plus 1 tablespoon virgin olive oil

Salt, to taste

Black pepper, to taste

4 thin slices aged provolone cheese

4 slices goat cheese

8 –10 kalamata olives

1. Preheat the grill or charbroiler.

2. Slice each vegetable on the bias (diagonally) into slices approximately $1/4$-inch thick. Brush all sides with $1/4$ cup of the olive oil. Season the vegetables with salt and pepper.

3. Grill vegetable slices until tender, about 45 seconds on each side. Remove the vegetables from the grill, and set aside to cool. Then place the cooled vegetables in the refrigerator to chill for 30 to 45 minutes.

4. On a large serving plate, fan the grilled vegetables in an alternating fashion in the center of the plate. At the top of the plate, center the cheeses in the middle of the plate, and arrange the olives at mid-bottom of the plate. Or you may arrange the vegetables spoke-style around the plate, fan the cheeses spoke-style inside the vegetables, and place the olives in the center. Sprinkle the vegetables with the remaining olive oil and serve immediately.

ABOUT THE RESTAURANT

J. P. Moraldo, the proprietor of Benvenuti, chose his mother's maiden name for his restaurant. His mother was born in the south of France to a family of vegetable growers. She helped her mother sell their farm produce in the marketplace at Cannes. After marrying an Italian, she moved with her husband to the Italian Riviera. Later, she returned to France, where she opened a small restaurant. Because of the freshness and variety of ingredients used, and her special style of cooking, the restaurant immediately became an enormous success. "The joy of Italian cuisine is celebrated at Benvenuti in tribute to a great lady and her reverence for food and its preparation," states Mr. Moraldo.

From High Noon Café   JACKSON, MISSISSIPPI

Antipasto

Artichoke hearts turn any ordinary dip or spread into a special event. You'll love hearing the rave reviews when you serve this antipasto!

1. Heat 1 tablespoon of olive the oil in a small sauté pan over medium heat, add the onion, and sauté for 2 minutes.

2. Place the sautéed onion in a food processor. Add the rest of the ingredients, including the remaining olive oil, and finely chop to your desired consistency.

3. Scoop the antipasto into a serving bowl. Use as a spread on sandwiches, as a dip with French or pita bread, or as an additional garnish for salads. Store in a covered container up to two weeks in the refrigerator.

4. To store longer, place small quantities of the antipasto in plastic freezer bags and freeze for up to three months. To defrost, bring the antipasto to room temperature and allow to thaw for 1 to 2 hours. Serve with French or pita bread.

ABOUT THE RESTAURANT

All of the recipes from High Noon Café are adapted from Chef-Manager Regina Glass's cookbook, "The Basics of Vegetarian Cooking." Her cookbook is available from Harvestime Farm, P.O. Box 39, Puckett, MS 39151.

Yield: 4–6 servings

Preparation Time: 15 minutes

Cooking Time: 5 minutes

1/4 cup olive oil

1 medium yellow onion, chopped

1 (15-ounce) jar artichoke hearts, packed in water or oil

1 (6-ounce) jar green olives

1 medium carrot, peeled and grated

1 cup medium black olives, whole and pitted (about 6 ounces)

3 cloves garlic, peeled

Rind of 1 lemon, chopped, with white pith removed

Juice of 1 lemon (about 2 tablespoons)

1/2 teaspoon Vege-Sal seasoning salt

1/2 teaspoon dried oregano

From Bloodroot   BRIDGEPORT, CONNECTICUT

Mushroom Walnut Paté

The Bloodroot Collective, which owns Bloodroot, developed this recipe as a dairy-free spread for bread. Bloodroot serves the paté as a salad, though you could serve it as a dip by thinning the paté with $1/8$ to $1/4$ cup vegetable stock. The paté can be frozen and defrosted with no change in texture, and of course, it is delightful spread on bread—especially rye, fresh out of the oven. The recipe is really easier and less complicated than it looks, and the result's well worth the time and effort. The paté is perfect for an elegant, special occasion or as an appetizer on the holiday buffet table.

Yield: 2 cups

Preparation Time: 45 minutes

$1/3$ cup raw sunflower seeds (about 2 ounces)

2 tablespoons raw sesame seeds

2 tablespoons chia seeds,* if available

$2^1/2$ cups coarsely chopped white mushrooms (about 6 ounces)

3 tablespoons shallots, peeled and finely chopped (about 2 shallots)

$1/3$ cup plus 2 tablespoons vegetable oil

Salt, to taste

Freshly ground black pepper, to taste

$1/2$ cup chopped walnuts (about 4 ounces)

1 clove garlic

$1/2$ teaspoon dried oregano

$1/2$ teaspoon dried tarragon

$1/3$ cup olive oil

$1/4$ pound firm tofu, rinsed, squeezed, patted dry, and cubed

2 tablespoons lemon juice

1. Place the sunflower, sesame, and chia seeds in a small coffee mill or food processor, and pulverize into a powder. Remove to a bowl.

2. Place the mushrooms into a food processor, add the shallots, and chop finely by turning the machine on and off several times.

3. If desired, place the mushroom mixture into a clean, lint-free dish towel. Fold the towel over to cover the mixture. Hold the towel over a small bowl, and twist the ends of the towel slowly in opposite directions to extract the mushroom juice. Reserve this liquid. You should have about $1/4$ to $1/2$ cup.

4. Place 2 tablespoons of the vegetable oil in a medium-sized sauté pan over medium-high heat for 30 seconds to 1 minute. When you can place your hand over the oil and feel the heat, put the mushrooms into the pan. Sauté over high heat, stirring until the mushroom mixture is browned and separated or dry. (If you omitted optional step 3, the mushrooms will have to sauté longer to achieve the right texture.) Season the mushrooms with salt and freshly ground pepper. Set aside.

5. Pour the ground seeds into the unwashed food processor, and add the walnuts, garlic, oregano, and tarragon. Turn the processor on. Using the feed tube, very slowly begin to drizzle in the olive oil and the remaining $1/3$ cup vegetable oil. This process should be much slower than the one for making mayonnaise. Alternate adding pieces of tofu, lemon juice, and the oil as the machine runs, until the mixture becomes a very stiff paste. The process should take about 10 minutes. The mixture might become so stiff as to turn the machine off. If that happens, add a little lemon juice to start the machine up again and continue processing.

6. Add the soy sauce and the prepared mustard. Continue to blend until the mixture is completely smooth and all the oil is incorporated. If the paté seems too stiff, add a little of the reserved mushroom juice or water. If the oil was added too quickly, you may see the oil separating out of the mixture as the food processor works. If this

*Chia seeds are small, flat dark brown seeds available at natural food stores.

happens, turn the machine off, pour the excess oil back into a cup, and turn the machine on. After a minute or two, begin drizzling in the oil again until it is completely incorporated.

7. Pour the walnut mixture into a medium-sized bowl, and combine with the mushrooms. Cover the bowl with plastic wrap, and chill in the refrigerator for at least 1 hour before serving. The paté will keep well in the refrigerator for several days, or you may freeze it in an airtight container for up to three months.

8. To serve, arrange the Boston lettuce on a serving plate. Place the green pepper ring on the lettuce, and mound the paté into the center of the ring. Surround the paté with the cucumber slices. Lightly sprinkle with paprika and drizzle with vinaigrette. Finally, top the paté with the fluted raw mushroom.

1½–2 tablespoons shoyu or tamari soy sauce (See "About Soy Sauce.")

⅔ teaspoon prepared mustard

GARNISH

Boston lettuce

Green pepper ring, ½-inch thick

1 cucumber, cut into slices

Sprinkle of paprika

Vinaigrette, 1–2 teaspoons per serving

1 raw mushroom, fluted, with stem removed and edges trimmed

About Soy Sauce

China and Japan have used soy sauce in their cooking preparations for centuries. A richly flavored, slightly salty liquid, soy sauce may be found in most grocery and natural food stores. The soy sauces found in most grocery stores may not be the most natural ones available; shopping at a natural food store will provide a selection of naturally fermented soy sauces without added caramel or sodium. Tamari has the strongest flavor and the darkest color, while shoyu is lighter. Soy sauces also come in wheat-free and low-sodium varieties. Soy sauce adds flavor and color to stews, casseroles, marinades, and sauces.

ABOUT THE RESTAURANT

This recipe is adapted from "The Second Seasonal Political Palate" by the Bloodroot Collective (Sanguinaria Publishing in Bridgeport, Connecticut).

Keffi Seed Paté

The addition of canola oil makes this paté smooth and creamy. However, the dish can be made without the oil for a great-tasting, low-fat spread.

Yield: 1¹/₂ cups

Preparation Time: 15 minutes plus 8–10 hours to soak the seeds

1 cup raw sunflower seeds (about 5 ounces)

1 cup raw, shelled pumpkin seeds (about 5 ounces)

4 cups water

¹/₂ cup diced yellow onion

1–2 tablespoons soy sauce (See "About Soy Sauce" on page 13.)

1 tablespoon dried basil

¹/₄ teaspoon ground black pepper

2 tablespoons canola oil, optional

GARNISH

5–6 green or red leaf lettuce leaves, washed and shaken dry

1. Place the sunflower and pumpkin seeds in a medium-sized bowl with the water. Soak the seeds 8 to 10 hours. Drain and rinse well with fresh cold water, letting any excess water drain completely.

2. Place the drained seeds in a food processor. Add the onion, soy sauce, basil, black pepper, and the optional canola oil. Blend until smooth, stopping the processor occasionally to scrape the sides of the blender jar with a spatula.

3. To serve, arrange the green or red lettuce leaves on a serving plate and spoon the paté on top. Serve with a basket of crackers or pita bread, or use as a sandwich spread.

4. The paté may be kept in a covered container in the refrigerator for 2 to 3 days.

ABOUT THE RESTAURANT

Restaurant Keffi offers gourmet vegetarian dining in lovely Santa Cruz, California. This paté is one of the restaurant's most requested recipes.

From Black Dog Café   MISSOULA, MONTANA

Olive Cilantro Salsa

There are all kinds of salsas on the market, and this is one of the best. It's a refreshingly different, south-of-the-border appetizer.

1. Place the olives in a food processor. Chop, using short pulses, until the olive pieces are about the size of lentils.

2. In a medium bowl, combine the rest of the ingredients. Add the chopped olives. Stir to blend well. Use immediately as a filling for burritos, a condiment to top off beans or sandwiches, or as a dip with tortilla chips.

3. To store, place the remaining salsa in a covered jar. It keeps well in the refrigerator for up to 2 days.

ABOUT THE RESTAURANT

Tucked away on a corner of Broadway Street in Missoula, Montana, the Black Dog Café produces big-time flavors.

*Be careful when you are handling *chilies* because they can burn the skin of your hands, eyes, and mouth. It's best to wear rubber gloves. If the chilies touch your skin, wash carefully with warm (not hot or cold) soapy water to reduce the heat from the chilies.

Yield: 1 quart

Preparation Time: 15 minutes

2 cups pimento-stuffed Spanish olives, drained (2 jars, 6 ounces each)

1 large green bell pepper, minced

1 cup finely chopped red onion

1 jalapeño chili,* seeded and finely minced, optional

1/2 cup chopped fresh cilantro (coriander)

2 tablespoons extra virgin olive oil

2 tablespoons lemon juice

From La Méditerranée de Sedona   SEDONA, ARIZONA

Baba Ghanouj

Easy to prepare, baba ghanouj spread on a bagel, a slice of pita, or crackers is a delicious party dip or satisfying lunch. Tahini may be purchased at your local natural food store or food co-op.

Yield: 4 servings

Preparation Time: 20 minutes

Cooking Time: 15–20 minutes

2 large eggplants

1/2 cup tahini (sesame paste)

Juice of 1 lemon, plus more to taste

2–3 cloves garlic

Salt

1/2 cup olive oil

GARNISHES

Green lettuce leaves

Greek olives

Pita bread, cut into triangles

1. Preheat the broiler.

2. Pierce the eggplants with a fork on all sides, and place the whole, unpeeled eggplants on a broiler pan. Charbroil under the broiler, turning on all sides until the inside is cooked soft, about 15 to 20 minutes. Remove the eggplants from the oven, and allow to cool in their skins.

3. To remove the pulp, cut the eggplants in half and scoop out the pulp with a spoon, or peel the eggplants with a paring knife under cold running water. Discard the eggplant skin, and place the pulp and the tahini in blender. Add the lemon juice, 1 tablespoon at a time, to your desired taste. Add 2 cloves of garlic, and depending on your taste, add more garlic and salt to taste. Blend the mixture on the purée setting until smooth.

4. Slowly drizzle the olive oil into the blender. Continue to blend until all the oil has been incorporated, and the baba ghanouj is smooth and creamy.

5. To serve, line a medium-sized bowl with green lettuce leaves or pita bread triangles. Spoon the baba ghanouj into the bowl. Add olives to the center of the baba ghanouj. Serve baba ghanouj as a dip with raw carrots, celery, pita bread, and crackers.

ABOUT THE RESTAURANT

You might have to blink twice to remember you're not on the Mediterranean when you dine on the terrace and sip your Greek or Turkish coffee under the bright blue umbrellas at La Méditerranée.

From Black Dog Café MISSOULA, MONTANA

Marinated Feta

The herbes de Provence, which you can find in most grocery or specialty food stores, and the red pepper flakes add that special zip to this very easy appetizer.

1. In a small bowl, whisk the oil together with the herbes de Provence, basil, and chili pepper flakes. Cover the bowl with plastic wrap, and let the mixture stand in a warm place for several hours or overnight.

2. In a medium-sized bowl, cover the tomatoes in warm water, and soak for 3 to 4 minutes to reconstitute them.

3. Arrange the sliced cheese, sundried tomatoes, and olives on a large serving plate or platter.

4. Drizzle the flavored oil with seasonings over the cheese, tomatoes, and olives. Drizzle the lemon juice over the platter. Garnish with lemon wedges, and serve with a baguette that has been sliced into $1/2$-thick rounds and toasted.

ABOUT THE RESTAURANT

The Black Dog Café derives its name from two black dogs that the owners, Nancy Randazzo and David Zinger, had as pets. Hailing from New York, both Nancy and David worked for other restaurants for four years and dreamed about opening their own some day. In 1992, their dreams came true when they completed the construction of their own restaurant, most of which they did themselves. Designing, concocting, and building is their forte, as they design wonderful appetizers, entrées, and desserts at the Black Dog Café each day.

*Herbes de Provence is an aromatic combination of dried herbs—including thyme, rosemary, savory, tarragon, and basil—from the Provence region of France.

Yield: 6–8 servings

Preparation Time: 20 minutes for the dish; several hours to overnight to allow the oil to marinate with the herbs and seasonings

1 cup extra virgin olive oil

1 tablespoon dried *herbes de Provence**

1 tablespoon dried basil

2 teaspoons red chili pepper flakes, or to taste

$1/2$ cup sundried tomato halves

1 pound feta cheese, sliced

1 cup black Greek olives

Juice of $1/2$ lemon

GARNISHES

Lemon wedges

From High Noon Café   *JACKSON, MISSISSIPPI*

Marinated Tomatoes

Regina Glass, manager of the High Noon Café at the Rainbow Whole Foods Co-op, likes to use this delicious condiment as a spread on sandwiches, a party dip with pita bread, a topping on beans and rice, and an addition to salads.

Yield: 4 servings

Preparation Time: 20 minutes

4 cups fresh chopped tomatoes or 2 (16-ounce) cans chopped tomatoes

1 small yellow onion, thinly sliced

1 clove garlic, pressed

3 tablespoons chopped fresh parsley or 1 tablespoon dried

1/4 teaspoon dried oregano

1 teaspoon dried basil

1/4 teaspoon salt

2 teaspoons lemon juice

2 tablespoons olive oil

1. Combine all the ingredients in a medium-sized bowl, and stir together. Scoop the mixture into a serving bowl and serve. If you are not going to serve the dish right away, place the mixture in a covered glass container and keep in the refrigerator. If you use fresh tomatoes, they will keep for 2 to 3 days in the refrigerator. Marinated tomatoes made with canned tomatoes will store well for one week in the refrigerator.

ABOUT THE RESTAURANT

This recipe and other Regina Glass recipes are published in her cookbook, "The Basics of Vegetarian Cooking," Harvestime Farm Publishers, P.O. Box 39, Puckett, MS 39151.

Salads

From Beans & Barley Café   MILWAUKEE, WISCONSIN

Indian Basmati Rice Salad

This sunny-golden rice with bright green, red, and orange is one of the prettiest and most festive salads I've ever seen. It's absolutely delicious, plus quick and easy to fix. I would serve it as a hot entrée in the winter and chill it for an equally delicious summertime salad.

1. Place the oil in a medium-sized, heavy-bottomed saucepan, and heat over medium-high heat. When you place your hand over the oil and it feels warm, but is not smoking, the oil ready. Add the cumin and mustard seeds. They will "pop" like popcorn in the hot oil.

2. Lower the heat to medium, stir the seeds, and add the boohna. Stir again to mix well.

3. Add the water, salt, turmeric, and optional cayenne pepper. Bring the mixture to a boil, and add the chickpeas, currants, carrots, and bell pepper.

4. Return the mixture to a boil, and add the rice. Bring to a boil again and stir. Lower the heat to medium-low, cover with a lid, and simmer about 15 minutes, until the rice is cooked.

5. Turn the hot rice mixture into a large bowl. Add the peas, cilantro, and parsley. Stir to mix thoroughly and serve hot.

6. To serve chilled, spread the rice mixture on a cookie sheet to cool for 30 minutes; then place in a covered container, and refrigerate until chilled. Serve the chilled rice salad on a bed of green leaf lettuce.

ABOUT THE RESTAURANT

While dining at Beans & Barley Café, you might see a few famous people in your midst. Anthony Hopkins, Def Leppard, the cellist Yo-Yo Ma, George Winston, Wendy O. Williams, Manhattan Transfer members, David Byrne, and Corbin Benson are just a few who have dined there.

*Boohna is a curry paste made by sautéeing red onion, garlic, ginger, curry, and fresh hot peppers (such as jalapeño or serrano chilies) with oil and chickpea cooking liquid. Prepared red curry pastes from Asian specialty stores or food co-ops are readily available. Boohna and cayenne pepper are hot spices that you will want to use according to the degree of hotness you like. *Basmati rice*, from India, is a particularly aromatic long-grained rice. Be sure to rince it according to the package directions.

Yield: *6–8 servings*

Preparation Time: 25 minutes

Cooking Time: 25 minutes

2 tablespoons corn oil

1 1/2 teaspoons whole cumin seed

1 1/2 teaspoons brown mustard seed

1/2–1 tablespoon boohna,* depending on the degree of hotness that you like

4 cups water

2 teaspoons salt

1/2 teaspoon turmeric

Pinch to 1/4 teaspoon cayenne pepper, optional

1/2 cup cooked chickpeas

1/4 cup currants

1/4 cup peeled, chopped carrot (about 1 carrot)

1/2 medium red bell pepper, chopped

2 cups uncooked white basmati rice*

1/4 cup frozen peas, thawed

3 tablespoons chopped fresh cilantro (coriander)

1/4 cup chopped fresh parsley

GARNISH

Green leaf lettuce leaves

From Dairy Hollow House Country Inn and Restaurant
EUREKA SPRINGS, ARKANSAS

Spectrum of Summer Salad
with Herbed Croquettes of
Oklahoma Goat Cheese and Beet Vinaigrette

This salad has flavors to match its vividly colorful presentation. Baking the beet rather than boiling it makes for a nonsoggy texture and a wonderfully concentrated flavor in the vinaigrette. "The secret of a great salad is to use very fresh, tender lettuce that is well washed and well dried. Wet lettuce dilutes the dressing, and then things go from crunchy and clear-tasting to soggy," says Crescent Dragonwagon, owner-chef of Dairy Hollow House. For a vegan variation of this salad, substitute eggplant slices, either grilled or crumbed and fried, in place of the goat cheese croquettes. Red-oak leaf, also called red leaf, lettuce makes for a colorful presentation. Other lettuces may be substituted throughout if the listed lettuces are not available.

Yield: 8 servings

Preparation Time: 20 minutes for the vinaigrette; 15 minutes for the croquettes plus 1 hour to chill; 15 minutes for the salad

Cooking Time: 35 minutes for the vinaigrette; 10–15 minutes for the croquettes

BEET VINAIGRETTE

1 medium raw beet, unpeeled and washed, or 4–5 small canned beets

$1/3$ cup freshly squeezed lemon juice (juice of about $1^1/2$ lemons)

1 teaspoon freshly grated lemon rind, yellow part only without the bitter white pith

$1/2$ teaspoon salt

Several grinds of fresh black pepper

1 tablespoon honey

1 cup olive oil

To Make the Vinaigrette:

1. Preheat the oven to 350° F.

2. Cut off the beet greens and discard. Wrap the beet in a small sheet of oiled aluminum foil, and bake until tender, about 35 minutes.

3. Let the beet cool, and slip off the peel. Coarsely chop the beet.

4. Put the chopped beet, lemon juice, lemon rind, salt, pepper, and honey in the food processor or blender, and blend until smooth.

5. With the processor on, drip the oil gradually through the feed tube until the mixture is emulsified, about 5 minutes. Taste and adjust the seasonings. You may store the dressing for up to three days in a covered container in the refrigerator.

To Make the Croquettes:

1. Combine the goat cheese, garlic, rosemary, and basil in the food processor. Add a generous grinding of black pepper. Process until smooth.

2. Form the herbed cheese into small (about 2-ounce) balls. Then flatten the balls into disks, about $1/4$ inch thick by $2^1/2$ inches wide. Don't worry if the mixture is soft. Place the croquettes on a sheet of waxed paper, cover with plastic wrap, and chill deeply, until they have become firm, about 1 hour. You can prepare the croquettes up to this point several hours or even days in advance.

3. Just before serving, bread and brown the croquettes as follows. In a small bowl, place the flour and season with a dash each of salt, paprika, cayenne pepper, and black pepper. Stir to blend well. Dip each croquette first in the seasoned flour, then in the beaten egg, and finally in the crumbs. Heat as little vegetable oil as possible, starting with about 2 tablespoons, in a nonstick skillet. Carefully brown each croquette, turning once. Drain on paper towels, blotting well.

About Bread Crumbs

You may purchase prepared bread crumbs in the grocery store. To make your own, place 4 to 5 slices of dried bread (a variety, including perhaps white, whole wheat, and rye, makes a tasty combination) in a food processor. Blend until the crumbs reach a fine-texture consistency. Make sure your processor and blade are completely dry or your crumbs will turn to mush.

To Make the Salad:

1. Chill 6 to 8 large plates in the freezer until ready to assemble the salad. At that time, divide the lettuces among the plates, laying down a bed of whole red-leaf lettuce covered with a mound of the torn green lettuces.

2. Place a small amount of roasted peppers on each plate. Add several slices of fresh tomato, overlapped, with a leaf of basil between the slices.

Roasting Peppers

Roasted bell peppers are often found in the deli sections of grocery or natural food stores. You may also prepare your own. Preheat the broiler. Wash the pepper and place it whole on a lightly oiled baking sheet. Place the baking sheet under the broiler for 5 to 10 minutes, until the peppers begin to darken. Turn the pepper so all sides will roast. Remove the pepper from the broiler, and set it aside to cool. Once it is cool enough to handle, peel the skin from the peppers and discard the peel. Dice or cut the pepper if necessary, and proceed with the recipe.

3. Place one croquette, still warm, at the side of each salad. Gently spoon a little vinaigrette over each salad. Then sprinkle slices of purple onion. Serve immediately, with additional vinaigrette on the side.

ABOUT THE RESTAURANT

Dairy Hollow House Country Inn and Restaurant is nestled in the wooded green valley one mile outside Eureka Springs. For more information about this lovely inn or Crescent Dragonwagon's two cookbooks, "The Dairy Hollow House Cookbook" (Eureka Springs, Arkansas: Cato and Martin Publishing) and "Dairy Hollow House Soup and Bread: A Country Inn Cookbook" (New York: Workman Publishing, 1992), you may call 1-800-562-8650.

CROQUETTES

1 pound Oklahoma goat cheese (or other soft, fresh, creamy goat cheese or Montrachet)

3 cloves garlic

Leaves from 1 bushy, 1½-inch sprig of rosemary or ¼ teaspoon dried rosemary

1 basil leaf

Freshly black pepper

1 cup flour

Dash of salt

Dash of paprika

Dash of ground cayenne pepper

Dash of black pepper

1 egg or egg replacer, beaten

2 cups soft, fine fresh bread crumbs (See "About Bread Crumbs.")

2 tablespoons vegetable oil, and more as needed

SALAD

2–3 small tender heads of red-oak leaf lettuce, washed and dried, with leaves left whole

2–3 small tender heads of green lettuce (limestone, butterhead, or a combination of the two) washed, dried, and torn

3 fresh yellow bell peppers, roasted, peeled, and diced (See "Roasting Peppers.")

3 ripe red tomatoes, sliced

Fresh basil leaves

½ purple onion, peeled and sliced paper-thin

From Artichoke Café   ALBUQUERQUE, NEW MEXICO

Mixed Greens, Oranges, and Fennel Salad
with Orange-Balsamic Vinaigrette

Pat Keene, owner of the Artichoke Café, suggests, "This salad is especially nice to serve in the fall, when the fennel and oranges are in the height of their season. It's great for a festive meal or as a light luncheon salad served with a delicious soup."

Yield: 6–8 servings

Preparation Time: 10 minutes

SALAD

3 small navel oranges peeled and sectioned

4 cups mixed greens (green-leaf lettuce, red-leaf lettuce, radicchio, escarole, sorrel, and spinach)

4 cups romaine lettuce, washed, dried, and torn

1 small purple onion, thinly sliced

1 fresh fennel bulb, sliced

ORANGE-BALSAMIC VINAIGRETTE

1/4 cup fresh orange juice (juice of 1 to 2 oranges)

2 tablespoons balsamic vinegar

1 tablespoon minced shallots (about 1 small shallot)

2 teaspoons grated orange zest, rind only without the bitter white pith

1 teaspoon Dijon mustard

1/2 teaspoon salt

1/2 teaspoon freshly ground black pepper

2 tablespoons extra virgin olive oil

1. In a large bowl, combine the salad ingredients and gently toss.

2. In a small bowl or food processor, whisk the juice, vinegar, shallots, orange zest, mustard, salt, and pepper. Next, slowly whisk in the oil until well blended.

3. Pour the dressing over the salad and toss gently to mix well. Arrange the salad on individual serving plates or serve the salad in the large salad bowl.

ABOUT THE RESTAURANT

Business people crowd the chic Artichoke Café during the noon hour: The upbeat conversations mingle with the savory aromas from the kitchen.

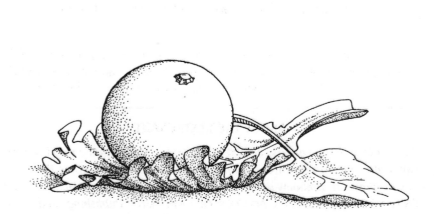

From Café Chimes   NORTH CONWAY, NEW HAMPSHIRE

Mandarin Orange-Almond Spinach & Pasta Salad & Café Chimes House Dressing

This dish is a wonderful change from ordinary pasta salads. The Café Chimes House Dressing offers a unique combination of flavors that gives the salad a nutty, rich, and full-bodied flavor. This dressing would go nicely on other salads and on steamed veggies. Tahini may be purchased at a natural food or specialty food market.

To Make the Dressing:

1. Place all the ingredients in a blender or food processor. Blend for several seconds, until smooth. Use ¹/₂ cup for the pasta salad and store the rest in a covered glass container in the refrigerator for several weeks.

To Make the Pasta Salad:

1. In a large pot of boiling, salted water, cook the rigatoni al dente (until the pasta is done but not soft). Rinse with cold water, and drain well.

2. While the pasta is cooking, place the arame in a small bowl and add enough fresh, cool water to cover. Let soak for 15 minutes: the arame will double in volume. Pat dry after soaking.

3. Combine in a large bowl ¹/₂ cup of the mandarin orange pieces, the spinach, the rigatoni, and half of the arame.

4. Toss the salad with ¹/₂ cup dressing.

5. Line individual salad plates or one large salad bowl with the green leaf lettuce, and spoon the salad on top. Decorate the salad with the remaining mandarin orange pieces, the slivered almonds, and the remaining arame. Serve with a loaf of French bread.

ABOUT THE RESTAURANT

Kathleen Etter, one of the owners of Café Chimes, believes that whole and balanced vegetarian foods are the choice for optimal health. In support of the restaurant's philosophy, the menu quotes Albert Einstein: "Nothing will benefit health or increase the chances of survival of life on Earth as the evolution to a vegetarian diet."

---

*Arame seaweed is a sea vegetable that has been enjoyed by the Japanese since ancient times. It is mentioned in Imperial documents dating from the seventh century. Arame has a sweet, nutty flavor and crisp texture. You can find arame at most natural food stores or Asian grocery stores.

Yield: 6 servings

Preparation Time: 5 minutes for dressing; 10 minutes for salad

Cooking Time: 20 minutes

CAFÉ CHIMES HOUSE DRESSING

¹/₂ medium yellow onion, chopped

¹/₂ medium green bell pepper, chopped

1 clove garlic, chopped

¹/₃ cup cider vinegar

¹/₂ cup tahini (sesame paste)

¹/₂ cup tamari soy sauce (See "About Soy Sauce" on page 13.)

1 tablespoon dried dill

¹/₄ cup canola oil

SALAD

3 cups uncooked rigatoni, white, whole wheat, or Jerusalem artichoke

¹/₂ cup arame*

1 cup mandarin oranges, drained (2 cans, 7.5 ounces each)

8 cups loosely packed, fresh spinach (See "Preparing Fresh Spinach" on page 29.)

6–8 large green leaf lettuce leaves, washed and shaken dry

¹/₂ cup slivered almonds

From A Moveable Feast   HOUSTON, TEXAS

Chef Carl's Zen Pasta Salad
with Peanut Sauce

The garlic, ginger, and peanut butter flavors form a tangy combination that is not too strong for the young ones in your crowd. The bright green snow peas, the deep red peppers, and the playful bow tie pasta make for a sensational salad, dressed and ready for a picnic, potluck meal, or fancy dinner party.

Yield: 6–8 servings

Preparation Time: 30 minutes

Cooking Time: 10–20 minutes

PEANUT SAUCE

3 tablespoons sesame oil

$1/2$ cup water

3 cloves garlic, minced

1 heaping teaspoon peeled, chopped fresh ginger

1 vegetable bouillon cube

2 tablespoons smooth peanut butter

$1/4$ cup soy sauce or liquid aminos*

1 tablespoon honey

1 teaspoon dry mustard

1 tablespoon black sesame seeds

1 teaspoon barbecue sauce

SALAD

1 pound bow tie pasta

1 cup chopped red bell pepper

2 cups snow peas (About 6–8 ounces; if frozen snow peas are used, thaw and wipe dry.)

GARNISH

Fresh lettuce greens

To Make the Sauce:

1. Place 1 tablespoon of the sesame oil and the water in a small sauté pan over medium-high heat. Add the garlic, ginger, and bouillon cube, and bring to a simmer, stirring frequently for 2 to 3 minutes.

2. In a small bowl, mix together the peanut butter, soy sauce, honey, dry mustard, black sesame seeds, barbecue sauce, and remaining sesame oil. Add the garlic, ginger, and bouillon mixture to the peanut butter mixture, and blend well. Set aside.

To Make the Pasta Salad:

1. Bring salted water to a boil in a large, covered pot. Add the pasta, cover, and cook al dente (until done but not soft) over medium heat. Drain and set aside.

2. In a saucepan, bring water to a boil. Add the red pepper and snow peas. Blanch by boiling for 1 minute. Drain and add to the pasta.

3. Pour the dressing over the pasta and vegetables, and combine gently. Line a large serving bowl with lettuce leaves. Scoop the salad into the bowl. Serve the pasta salad at room temperature.

ABOUT THE RESTAURANT

A Moveable Feast, is named after a Hemingway novel. Like the Parisian cafés of its namesake novel, A Moveable Feast is a place where people gather to socialize and to freely discuss art, philosophy, and life. According to the owners, the patrons have included Edward Albee, Greg Allman, Eric Johnson, Ashley Judd, Carl Lewis, Jason Patrick, John Robbins, Ben Stiller, Richard Thomas, Rudy Tomjonavich, and Forrest Whittaker.

Liquid aminos, consisting of purified water and sixteen amino acid proteins from soybeans, may be substituted for soy sauce. This product, with its rich, savory flavor, is not fermented and is naturally low in sodium.

From Hyatt Regency Westshore   TAMPA, FLORIDA

Summery Watermelon Salad
with Raspberry Vinaigrette

An absolutely heavenly salad! Slightly sweet and savory, this salad bursts with summertime flavors. It's perfect as a first-course salad for a brunch or a finishing touch for a dinner.

To Make the Vinaigrette:

1. Pour the olive oil into a small mixing bowl. Using a wire whisk, whisk in the raspberry vinegar. Add the salt, pepper, and sugar. Taste to check seasonings. Adjust accordingly.

To Make the Salad:

1. Place the watermelon cubes in a large mixing bowl. Add the raspberry vinaigrette, and toss gently.

2. Cover the bowl with plastic wrap. Place in the refrigerator to allow the watermelon to marinate for 1 hour, gently stirring one or two times to coat the watermelon.

3. Arrange the lettuce leaves on individual serving plates.

4. Remove the watermelon from the refrigerator, and spoon the watermelon onto the lettuce leaves.

5. Dip the onion slices in the raspberry vinaigrette remaining at the bottom of the watermelon bowl, and arrange several slices on top of each plate of watermelon. Top with sprigs of radicchio. Serve the salad chilled.

ABOUT THE RESTAURANT

Located on the edge of a magnificent bird sanctuary, the Hyatt Regency Westshore offers a sanctuary to its guests. The staff strives to make every guest feel pampered and will prepare menus to suit special dietary requirements.

Yield: 6 servings

Preparation Time: 20 minutes

RASPBERRY VINAIGRETTE

$1/4$ cup extra virgin olive oil

$1 1/2$ tablespoons raspberry vinegar

$1/4$–$1/2$ teaspoon salt

$1/4$ teaspoon black pepper

$1/4$ teaspoon sugar

WATERMELON SALAD

$1/2$ small watermelon, cubed, rind removed (about 6–8 cups)

Leaves from 1 small Bibb lettuce, washed and dried

1 small purple onion, thinly sliced

Several sprigs of radicchio, optional

From Bluebird Café   ATHENS, GEORGIA

Magnificent Meal Salad

A fully satisfying salad in every way! The whole grains and cheeses combine to make a complete protein. For those who prefer not to use dairy, substituting legumes such as chickpeas, lentils, peanuts, or adzuki beans for the cheese will also result in a complete protein.

Yield: 4 servings

Preparation Time: 20 minutes plus 30 minutes to chill the tabbouleh

Cooking Time: 20 minutes

TABBOULEH

1 1/2 cups water

1 cup bulgur*

1/3 cup chopped fresh parsley

3 tablespoons olive oil

1 teaspoon garlic granules

3 tablespoons lemon juice (juice of 1 lemon)

Salt, to taste

Black pepper, to taste

SOY SESAME DRESSING

1 cup soy oil

2 tablespoons tamari soy sauce (See "About Soy Sauce" on page 13.)

4 tablespoons white vinegar

2 tablespoons sesame oil

2 tablespoons molasses

SALAD

2 cups baby romaine lettuce, leaves washed, dried, and torn (approximately the core of 1 head of romaine)

2 cups red-leaf lettuce, leaves washed, dried, and torn (about 1 head)

To Make the Tabbouleh:

1. In a medium-sized saucepan, bring the water to boil over high heat. Add the bulgur, stirring, to blend well. Then remove the pan from the heat. Set aside for 10 to 15 minutes to allow the bulgur to absorb the water.

2. Chill the bulgur in an ice bath by setting the pan of bulgur in a bowl of ice and stirring frequently. Or place the bulgur in the refrigerator until cool, about 30 minutes, stirring frequently.

3. Add the parsley, oil, garlic, and lemon juice to the chilled bulgur, and mix well. Season with salt and pepper to taste.

To Make the Dressing:

1. In a medium-sized bowl, place the soy oil, soy sauce, vinegar, sesame oil, and molasses. Whisk together until the dressing is smooth and the ingredients are well combined. Allow about 1 to 2 tablespoons of dressing for each serving of salad.

2. This dressing separates easily; just whisk the dressing before using each time. The dressing will keep well in a tightly covered, glass container in the refrigerator for several weeks.

To Make the Salad:

1. In a large bowl, combine the romaine and red leaf lettuces and the mustard and turnip greens. Add the salad dressing, 1/4 to 1/2 cup for four people. Toss to completely coat the leaves with the dressing.

2. In medium-sized bowl, combine the white and red cabbages, the carrots, and the tomato, and toss lightly.

3. For this layered salad, begin by arranging the lettuces and greens equally on four individual serving plates. Top the greens with cheese, and place the cabbage mixture on top of the cheese. Top the cabbage mixture with tabbouleh salad. Arrange the eggs, sprouts, and avocado slices around the top of each salad. Drizzle a bit more dressing over the salads, or serve with the dressing on the side. A whole grain muffin or sliced fresh bread would go well with this salad.

Bulgur wheat is a popular Middle Eastern wheat that has been cracked by boiling, and then redried. It's available in natural food stores.

Preparing Fresh Spinach

An essential step in preparing fresh spinach is to wash it thoroughly before you use it. Here are a few guidelines:

1. Trim the stems from the spinach leaves, and discard.

2. Fill a basin with fresh, cool water. Place the spinach leaves in the water, immersing them at first and then letting them float to the surface. Allow the spinach to rest for a few minutes in the water so most of the sand and dirt falls to the bottom of the basin.

3. Gently lift each spinach leaf from the water, rinse it carefully under a cool stream of running water, shake it, and place it in a colander to drain.

ABOUT THE RESTAURANT

The Bluebird Café offers a variety of vegetarian dishes in a casual ambience of Southern hospitality.

2 cups mixed mustard and turnip greens, washed and dried (about 4–6 ounces ; see "Preparing Fresh Spinach" for instructions on washing sandy greens.)

4 cups mixed white and red cabbage, sliced (about $\frac{1}{2}$ head each)

1 cup carrots, sliced matchstick-style (1 medium carrot)

1 Roma (plum) tomato, chopped

2 cups grated white cheddar cheese (about 6 ounces)

2 hard-boiled eggs, cut in quarters, optional

1 cup alfalfa sprouts (about 1 $\frac{1}{2}$ ounces)

2 ripe avocados, sliced

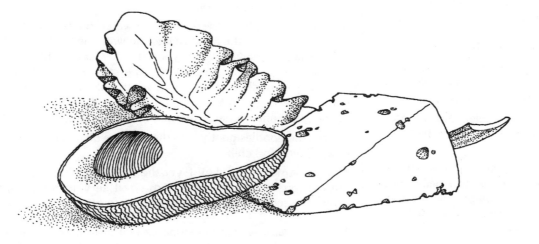

From Natural Café   SANTE FE, NEW MEXICO

Japanese Noodle Salad
with Japanese Noodle Salad Dressing

A lovely array of vegetables and the discreet flavors of the dressing create a distinguished salad.

Yield: 4 servings

Preparation Time: 5 minutes for
the dressing; 1 hour to overnight to soak the mushrooms;
30–40 minutes for the salad

Cooking Time: 10–15 minutes
for the salad

DRESSING

$^1/_2$ cup soy sauce (See "About
Soy Sauce" on page 13.)

$^1/_4$ cup mirin* or other rice wine
vinegar

1 tablespoon ginger juice* or 1
teaspoon freshly ground
gingerroot

1 tablespoon mirin sweet rice
wine

$^1/_8$ teaspoon cayenne pepper,
optional

JAPANESE NOODLE SALAD

1 cup dried shiitake mushrooms
(a 1-ounce package; see "About
Mushrooms" on page 63.)

3 carrots, peeled and cut into
pieces measuring $^1/_8$ by $1^1/_2$
inches

2 cups sugar snap peas, strings
removed, or snow peas, ends
trimmed, diagonally cut into
$^3/_4$-inch pieces (about 6–8
ounces)

1 red bell pepper, cut into $^1/_8$-
by-2-inch strips

To Make the Dressing:

1. In a medium-sized mixing bowl or blender, mix together all of the
ingredients. Use in the salad or reserve until needed. The dressing will
keep for several days stored in a covered container in the refrigerator.

To Make the Salad:

1. Soak the shiitake mushrooms overnight in twice as much water. As
an alternative, place the mushrooms and the water in a saucepan, bring
the water to a boil, and simmer for 10 minutes. Then, turn off the heat,
cover the pan, and let the mushrooms soak for 1 hour.

2. In a large pot or steamer over medium-high heat, steam the carrots,
peas, pepper, and onions until crisp, but tender. Remove the pan from
the heat. Scoop out the vegetables, and put them into a pan of ice water
for 1 minute. Then drain, and place the vegetables in a bowl. Cover and
chill about 30 minutes to 1 hour.

3. Remove the stems from the soaked mushrooms. Discard the stems,
or save them for another use. Slice the mushrooms very thin ($^1/_{16}$- to
$^1/_8$-inch). Put the mirin, soy sauce, and mushrooms in a heavy
saucepan, and bring to a simmer over medium-high heat. Continue to
simmer until the liquid is gone and the mushrooms sizzle, about 5 to 10
minutes. Set aside to cool.

4. In a large pot, bring the 2 quarts of water to a boil over high heat. Add
the salt. Then drop the noodles into the water gently so that they look like
a waterfall cascading from your hand. Cook only 1 to 2 minutes,
watching carefully as the cooking time may vary. Test for doneness by
removing a noodle and cutting it. When only a small white dot remains
in the center of the cut noodle, the noodles are done. Immediately drain
the noodles, and immerse them in ice water. Drain the noodles again.

5. Toss the noodles gently with the sesame oil in a medium-sized mixing
bowl. Cover and chill.

6. To assemble the salad, layer the noodles, steamed vegetables, and
braised mushrooms in a medium-sized serving bowl, topping with a
layer of vegetables. Or you may choose to arrange the ingredients in the

---

* *Mirin* is a Japanese sweet rice wine used for cooking. Used as a seasoning and a
sweetener, it provides a flavor and glaze unique to Japanese cuisine. Mirin can be
found in most grocery stories in the Asian food section. To make *ginger juice*, put
slices of ginger in a garlic press and squeeze the juice into a small bowl.

same way on each individual serving plate. Immediately before serving, drizzle the dressing over the salad and garnish with the black sesame seeds and nasturtium blossoms. This salad must be served the same day it is made, since the noodles will become too soft and the vegetables will lose their color and flavor if stored.

4 scallions (green onions), cut into $\frac{1}{4}$-by-2-inch strips

2 tablespoons mirin sweet rice wine

1 tablespoon soy sauce

2 quarts water for cooking noodles

Pinch of salt

8 ounces somen noodles*

1 teaspoon light sesame oil

GARNISH

1 tablespoon black sesame seeds

4 yellow nasturtium blossoms, optional

Steaming Vegetables

There are a variety of steamers available. You may find a complete set of pot, steamer, and lid, or your may find a small, single steamer basket that fits in your own pot. Either one will work well. Follow this simple basic procedure for steaming:

1. Fill a medium-large saucepan (or the steamer pot) with water, and place over high heat. Put the steamer basket inside the pan.
2. Add the cut vegetables to the steamer, layering the hard vegetables (such as carrots, broccoli, potatoes, and cauliflower) on the bottom of the steamer and the softer vegetables (such as peas, peppers, corn, or green beans) on the top. You may also prefer to steam the hard and soft vegetables separately.
3. Cover the pan with a lid, and allow the vegetables to steam for several minutes. The amount and type of vegetables that you are steaming will determine the length of time required. Green peas and beans may take 3 to 5 minutes while potatoes and broccoli may take 10 to 15 minutes.
4. Test for doneness by piercing the vegetables with a fork. If the vegetables are crisp yet tender, rather than firm and raw, they are done.
5. Turn off the heat, and remove the steamer basket from the pan.
6. Discard the water in the pan. Place the vegetables into a bowl and proceed with the recipe.

ABOUT THE RESTAURANT

Owner-chef Lynn Walters incorporates a wide variety of ethnic cuisines into the restaurant's impressive repertoire of menu selections. Her original recipes may be found in her own cookbook, "Cooking at the Natural Café in Sante Fe" (Freedom, California: Crossing Press of Freedom, 1992).

* *Somen noodles* are thin, light noodles made of sifted wheat flour and salt. They may be found in the Asian food section of grocery stores, in many natural food stores, and in Asian specialty shops.

From Lotsa Pasta   SAN DIEGO, CALIFORNIA

Mama Rita's Broccoli Salad

"The secret to this salad," says John Aldrich, co-owner of Lotsa Pasta, whose mother passed this recipe on to him, "is to let the salad sit overnight so the flavors blend well together."

Yield: 6 servings

Preparation Time: 20 minutes plus overnight to marinate salad

DRESSING

1/2 cup brown sugar

1 cup regular, tofu, or eggless mayonnaise (See "Alternatives to Regular Mayonnaise" on page 8.)

2 tablespoons white wine vinegar

SALAD

2 pounds broccoli florets, cut into bite-size pieces, or a combination of broccoli and cauliflower florets (About 3 pounds of broccoli yields 2 pounds of florets.)

1/3 cups raisins (about 1 ounce)

1/4 cup pine nuts or sunflower seeds (about 1 ounce)

1/2 cup imitation bacon bits (about 1 1/2–2 ounces)

3 scallions (green onions), finely chopped

GARNISH

Red cabbage leaves

1. Prepare the dressing by blending all the ingredients together in a small bowl.

2. Place all the salad ingredients in a large bowl. Add the dressing, and toss until all the vegetables are well coated.

3. Cover the bowl with an airtight lid or with plastic wrap, place in the refrigerator, and allow the salad to marinate overnight.

4. Serve the salad chilled on a bed of red cabbage leaves.

ABOUT THE RESTAURANT

Lotsa Pasta makes its pasta and sauces fresh every day and has over five hundred combinations of pasta dishes. In addition, there is a large selection of wonderful salads, like this broccoli salad, to accompany the pasta entrées.

From Walnut Acres   PENNS CREEK, PENNSYLVANIA

Broccoli Pasta Salad
with Sweet and Sour Poppy Seed Dressing

A broccoli and pasta success story. The Walnut Acres Orange Blossom Honey blends with the tarragon vinegar to make a tangy, sweet and sour, savory dressing.

To Make the Dressing:

1. In a blender, combine all the dressing ingredients. Blend for 1 minute, until well blended. Use with the pasta salad, or store in a covered container in the refrigerator. The dressing keeps well in the refrigerator for two weeks.

To Make the Pasta Salad:

1. In a large pot of salted boiling water, cook the pasta al dente (until it is just done but not soft). Drain, rinse with cold water, drain again, and set aside to cool.

2. In another large pot, bring water to the boil. Blanch the broccoli and carrots by boiling the vegetables for 1 minute, just long enough to brighten their colors. Rinse with cold water, and set aside or put in the refrigerator to cool.

3. Combine the pasta, cooled vegetables, onion, red and green peppers, garlic, celery, salt, and pepper in a large mixing bowl. Add dulse (or imitation bacon bits) to taste. Pour the dressing over the vegetables and pasta, turning gently to mix well. Line a large serving bowl with lettuce leaves. Transfer the salad into the bowl and serve immediately.

4. If you are not serving the salad right away, reserve a small portion of the dressing in a covered container to add to the salad at the time of serving. Cover the salad and refrigerate for up to three days.

ABOUT THE RESTAURANT

In 1947, Paul and Betty Keene made apple butter by simmering down their own fresh-pressed cider and puréed apples in a 30-gallon kettle hung outside over a wood fire. A small article about their apple butter appeared in the "Food Flashes" section of Gourmet Magazine that same year, and from then on, the Keenes have been flooded with orders for the wholesome and natural foods they produce.

Yield: *6–8 servings*

Preparation Time: 5 minutes for the dressing; 30 minutes for the salad

Cooking Time: 10–15 minutes

DRESSING

$1/2$ cup canola oil

$1/3$ cup tarragon vinegar

4 tablespoons Walnut Acres Orange Blossom Honey

1 teaspoon poppy seeds

Pinch of salt

SALAD

1 pound multicolored, spiral pasta

1 head broccoli, cut in small pieces

1 medium carrot, cut into matchstick-sized pieces

1 small onion, finely chopped

1 red bell pepper, chopped

$1/2$ green bell pepper, chopped

2 cloves garlic, minced

1 stalk celery, chopped

1 teaspoon salt

$1/4$ teaspoon black pepper

2–3 tablespoons chopped dulse* or imitation bacon bits, to taste

*Dulse is a seaweed that is reddish purple and has quite a chewy texture. It may be purchased by the package in natural food specialty stores as well as in Asian markets.

From Café For All Seasons   SAN FRANCISCO, CALIFORNIA

Red Potato and Green Bean Salad
with Mushrooms, Purple Onions & Basil Vinaigrette

This scrumptious salad is one that you will want to keep as a part of your regular salad repertoire.

Yield: 8 servings

Preparation Time: 20 minutes; 1 hour for dressing to marinate

Cooking Time: 20 minutes for the potatoes; 5 minutes for the beans

BASIL VINAIGRETTE

1/4 cup white wine vinegar

2 teaspoons salt

2 teaspoons fresh ground pepper

3/4 cup virgin olive oil

1/4 cup chopped fresh basil

SALAD

16–20 baby red potatoes

2 cups fresh green beans, ends trimmed, cut into 1 1/2-inch pieces

1 purple onion, sliced and then cut into 1/4-inch lengths (to make 1 cup)

1 1/2 cups sliced fresh mushrooms, cut 1/3-inch thick

Salt, optional

Black pepper, optional

GARNISH

Sprigs of Italian parsley

16 tiny cherry tomatoes

To Make the Vinaigrette:

1. Place the vinegar, salt, and pepper in a medium-sized bowl, and stir well to dissolve the salt. Stir in the olive oil with a fork. Then add the basil. Allow the dressing to rest for 1 hour before using. Quickly stir the dressing again before tossing with the salad.

To Make the Salad:

1. Place the baby red potatoes in a large pot of salted water, and bring to a boil over high heat. Cover the pot, and reduce the heat to medium. Cook about 20 minutes, until the potatoes are just done. They should be soft, but not mushy, when pierced with a fork. Remove the pot from the heat, drain, and set the potatoes aside to cool.

2. When the potatoes are cool, cut each potato in half.

3. While the potatoes are cooking, place the green beans in a steamer and cook until tender-crisp, about 5 minutes. (See "Steaming Vegetables" on page 31.) Remove the green beans from the steamer, and set aside to cool.

4. Place the cooled potatoes, green beans, onions, and mushrooms together in a large bowl. Add the vinaigrette, and toss gently. Add salt and pepper if necessary.

5. Transfer the salad to a serving bowl, or place on individual serving plates. Garnish with sprigs of parsley and cherry tomatoes.

ABOUT THE RESTAURANT

Donna and Frank Katzl, owners of Café For All Seasons, know their business well. Both of Donna's parents were excellent cooks, and her grandfather raised fruits and vegetables. Sometimes Donna would trek around her hometown of Los Angeles with her father in search of the freshest and most unusual ingredients to make their elaborate family dinners. Frank's heritage in the grocery market business gave him a keen understanding of business as well as of food, and his life with Donna has been a marriage of pure pleasure, blending their business, creativity, and talents together.

Roasted Potato Salad
with Roasted Garlic Vinaigrette

Great for summertime picnics, this versatile salad also makes a cozy, warm entrée on a chilly winter night.

To Make the Vinaigrette:

1. Preheat the oven to 350°F.

2. Place the garlic in a shallow baking dish, drizzle 1 to 2 tablespoons of olive oil over the tops, and cover with foil. Bake for about 1 hour, until soft. Remove the garlic from the oven, and allow it to cool.

3. Squeeze the pulp out of the garlic by placing the flat side of a knife against the stem end of each individual garlic clove. The garlic pulp will have a paste-like texture and will slide easily from the casing.

4. Place the garlic pulp in a blender or mixing bowl. Blend or whisk in the vinegar and then the extra virgin olive oil. The mixture will be somewhat thick. Use immediately in the salad, or place in a covered container and refrigerate for up to one week. Be sure to blend the stored mixture well before using.

To Make the Salad:

1. Preheat the oven to 425°F. Lightly oil two baking sheets.

2. Peel and seed the butternut squash, and peel the yams. Chop the squash into 1-inch cubes, and place in a mixing bowl. In the same way, chop the yams, potatoes, onions, and peppers into 1-inch cubes, and place them in a separate mixing bowl.

3. Toss the vegetables in each bowl with enough olive oil to lightly coat them, about 2 to 3 tablespoons per bowl. Tossing vegetables in separate bowls makes it easier to coat them sufficiently with oil. Season with the salt and pepper.

4. Turn the vegetables onto the baking sheets. Roast in the oven for 30 to 40 minutes, turning them after the first 15 minutes, until they are browned and tender.

5. Remove the vegetables from the oven, and place them in a large mixing bowl. Add the parsley. Lightly toss with about 2 tablespoons of the garlic vinaigrette. Transfer the salad to a large serving platter and serve immediately.

Yield: 8 servings

Preparation Time: 10 minutes for the vinaigrette; 30 minutes for the salad

Cooking Time: 1 hour to roast the garlic; 30–40 minutes for the salad

ROASTED GARLIC VINAIGRETTE

3 unpeeled heads garlic, ¼ inch of the tops cut off

1–2 tablespoons olive oil

½ cup balsamic vinegar

1 cup extra virgin olive oil

SALAD

1 pound butternut squash

4 pounds small yams

4 pounds small red potatoes

2 pounds purple onions

1 pound red bell peppers

4–6 tablespoons olive oil

Salt, to taste

Black pepper, to taste

1 bunch fresh parsley, chopped

ABOUT THE RESTAURANT

With seating for forty people at the downtown location, lunchtime is the busiest time for New Frontiers.

From The Greatest Grains on Earth   DAVENPORT, IOWA

Fresh Corn Salad

In the summer when the corn is fresh and tender, consider making this cool and refreshing salad to accompany your hot Mexican entrées. Use about 5 to 6 pounds of fresh corn, 3 (15-ounce) cans of canned corn, or 4 (10-ounce) boxes of frozen corn.

Yield: 6 servings

Preparation Time: 20 minutes

SALAD

6 cups fresh or canned corn, preferably organic (See "Cooking Fresh Corn" on page 70.)

1 red bell pepper, sliced

1 green bell pepper, sliced

1 medium purple onion, sliced

2 medium tomatoes, sliced

1/3 cup chopped fresh cilantro (coriander)

MARINADE

1/4 cup fresh lime juice (juice of about 3 limes)

2 tablespoons apple cider vinegar

1 tablespoon chili powder

1/8–1/4 cup olive oil

Salt, to taste

Freshly ground black pepper, to taste

GARNISH

Fresh greens

1. In a large mixing bowl place all the salad ingredients, and toss gently.

2. Put the marinade ingredients into a small mixing bowl. Whisk together to blend well.

3. Pour the marinade over the salad ingredients and toss gently. Serve on a bed of fresh greens.

ABOUT THE RESTAURANT

Julie Martins of The Greatest Grains says, "The Greatest Grains on Earth is the area's largest natural foods market and eat-in deli. We are a family-owned business and are proud of the contribution we make to our community by offering the widest selection of natural foods locally available."

Quinoa Tabbouleh

This recipe is a wonderful, fat-free, wheat-free variation on a traditional theme.

1. In a medium-sized saucepan, bring the water to a boil over high heat and add the quinoa. Cover, and lower the heat to medium. Continue to cook until the quinoa is tender, 12 to 15 minutes.

About Quinoa

Quinoa (pronounced "keen-wah"), an herb that originated in the Andes region of South America, grows from 3 to 6 feet in height and produces a bushy head of seeds. These round, usually pale yellow seeds resemble millet. Quinoa is 16 to 20 percent protein and has a high content of essential amino acids. It quadruples in size upon cooking, so you get more per pound than rice or millet.

Cooking quinoa is easy. Rinse the seeds in cool, running water. Put 1 part quinoa to 2 parts water in a pan. Bring to a boil over high heat. Then reduce the heat to medium-low and simmer as you would rice, for 15 to 20 minutes. Quinoa is great with vegetables or added to stews and soups like barley or rice. You may also sprout the seeds and use them fresh in salads and sandwiches.

2. Drain the quinoa, but do not rinse. Allow the quinoa to cool slightly, until warm to the touch. Place the quinoa in a large mixing bowl. While the quinoa is still warm, gently fold the cumin, salt, and orange rind into the quinoa.

3. Allow the quinoa to cool to room temperature. Add the orange juice, lemon juice, tomatoes, scallions, cucumber, parsley, mint, and chickpeas. Season with pepper, and toss gently.

4. Line a bowl with lettuce leaves. Spoon the salad onto the lettuce, and garnish with the radish pieces and the lemon slices.

ABOUT THE RESTAURANT

Located near Brown University, Extra Sensory attracts an international clientele in a city with a flair for music and the arts. Musicians and artists who come to town head for Extra Sensory, one of the only natural foods restaurants in Providence. Some notable visitors are musicians and entertainers Diana Ross, Kenny Loggins, Stanley Jordan, Guess Who, NRBQ, and Bad Company, and various senators and members of Congress.

Yield: 4 servings

Preparation Time: 20 minutes

Cooking Time: 12–15 minutes

5 cups water

1 cup washed and drained quinoa (See "About Quinoa.")

$3/4$ teaspoon ground cumin

1 teaspoon sea salt

$1/4$ teaspoon grated orange rind, orange part only without the bitter white pith

$1^1/2$ tablespoons orange juice

1 tablespoon plus 1 teaspoon freshly squeezed lemon juice

$1/2$ cup diced tomatoes

$1/4$ cup finely sliced scallions (green onions), in rings

$1/4$ cup seeded, chopped cucumber

$1^1/2$ cups chopped fresh parsley

$1/4$ cup chopped fresh mint or 2 tablespoons dried

$1/3$ cup cooked chickpeas (1 can, $8^3/4$ ounces)

Freshly ground black pepper, to taste

GARNISH

Lettuce leaves

Radishes, cut into julienne pieces

Lemon slices

From Beans & Grains & Things   LITTLE ROCK, ARKANSAS

Tofu Salad

With this salad, you can make a sandwich, stuff a tomato, or spread a cracker. It is as versatile as it is good. Variations, such as the one provided in the recipe, are easy. As a variation, omit the soy sauce and use 2 tablespoons chopped fresh dill.

Yield: *4 servings*

Preparation Time: 15 minutes

1 pound firm tofu

3 tablespoons nutritional yeast flakes (less than 1 ounce)

1 tablespoon tamari soy sauce (See "About Soy Sauce" on page 13.)

1 teaspoon garlic granules or 1 teaspoon garlic powder

1 ½ tablespoons mayonnaise (See "Alternatives to Regular Mayonnaise" on page 8.)

1 cup coarsely chopped green, red, or yellow bell pepper (about 1 pepper)

½–1 cup chopped purple onion

1 cup finely chopped celery

Black pepper, to taste

1. Rinse the tofu, and gently squeeze out the excess water. Crumble the tofu into a medium-sized bowl.

2. Add the yeast flakes, soy sauce, garlic, mayonnaise, peppers, onion, and celery. Mix thoroughly. Check the seasonings, and add more soy sauce, more garlic, and black pepper to taste.

3. Serve the salad immediately, or chill in a covered container in the refrigerator for up to three days.

ABOUT THE RESTAURANT

This was the first recipe created by Beans & Grains & Things. People still come from miles around to experience this terrific taste treat!

From The Garden Vegetarian Restaurant   RED BANK, NEW JERSEY

Leek Salad

A delicate blend of flavors combine to make this unique salad.

1. In a small sauté pan, heat the oil over medium heat until your hand placed over the oil feels the warmth of the oil. Add the onion and salt. Sauté until the onions are soft, about 5 minutes.

Cleaning Leeks

Because the bulb and leaves of a leek are filled with sand and dirt, it is important to carefully clean this vegetable.

1. Trim the roots from the bulb end of the leek. Then trim all but about 3 inches from the leafy green end.

2. Cut an X into the bottom of the bulb end with a sharp knife.

3. Place the leek in a small bowl filled with cold water. Add 1 tablespoon of vinegar, and allow the leek to soak for 30 minutes. This procedure helps to remove the sand and dirt that is found in the innermost folds of the leek.

4. Remove the leek from the bowl, and rinse thoroughly in a stream of cool running water. Pat dry and proceed with the recipe.

---

2. Add the leeks and carrots, and sauté an additional 5 minutes, until the vegetables are crisp yet tender.

3. Add the red pepper, and cook another 1 to 2 minutes. Remove the vegetables from the heat, and turn into a medium-sized mixing bowl.

4. Add the brown rice to the vegetables, and mix gently. Season to taste with the tamari soy sauce and lemon juice. Add the parsley and tomatoes, and stir gently to blend. Serve immediately on a bed of garden greens, garnished with lemon slices and sprigs of parsley.

ABOUT THE RESTAURANT

Ty Yolac, owner of The Garden Vegetarian Restaurant, proudly serves vegetarian foods that are unique and original combinations of the finest, freshest ingredients. Japanese-style tempuras, stir-fry dishes, curry specials, steamed veggies, parmigiana dishes, pastas, and jambalayas make up the list of entrées.

Yield: *4 servings*

Preparation Time: 20 minutes

Cooking Time: 10 minutes

1 tablespoon soy oil

1 medium purple onion, finely chopped

$1/2$ teaspoon sea salt

3 leeks, washed carefully and cut diagonally, using some of the green (See "Cleaning Leeks.")

2 medium carrots, peeled and cut diagonally

1 medium red bell pepper, chopped

1 cup cooked brown rice, at room temperature

1–2 tablespoons tamari soy sauce (See "About Soy Sauce" on page 13.)

1–2 teaspoons lemon juice

1 tablespoon chopped fresh parsley

2 medium tomatoes, chopped, optional

GARNISH

Garden greens

Slices of fresh lemon

Sprigs of parsley

From Nan Yang Rockridge   OAKLAND, CALIFORNIA

Burmese Tomato Salad

This simple salad offers a fresh alternative to the typical tomato and lettuce salad combinations. The cilantro, garlic, and lemon juice give it that distinctive Burmese flavor.

Yield: *4 servings*

Preparation Time: 15 minutes

3 medium tomatoes, cut in wedges

$1/2$ iceberg lettuce, shredded

$1/2$ cucumber, peeled and chopped

1 medium yellow onion, shredded and rinsed under cold water

3–4 tablespoons olive oil

2 cloves garlic, chopped

1 tablespoon freshly squeezed lemon juice

1 teaspoon sugar

3 tablespoons chopped cilantro (coriander)

Salt, to taste

Black pepper, to taste

1. Place the tomatoes, lettuce, cucumber, and onion in a large bowl.

2. Put the oil in a small sauté pan, and heat over medium-high heat. When you place your hand over the pan, you should feel the warmth from the oil. Add the garlic, and sauté it until the garlic turns a light brown, stirring gently as the garlic cooks quickly. Put the garlic and oil into a small mixing bowl.

3. Add the remaining ingredients to the garlic and oil, and mix well.

4. Pour the garlic dressing over the salad vegetables, and blend well. Transfer the salad to a serving bowl, and serve immediately.

ABOUT THE RESTAURANT

Nan yang *means "South Seas" in Chinese. All of the menu items at Nan Yang are Burmese. What is Burmese cooking? Owners Philip and Nancy Chu, both of Chinese origin, lived in Burma, which is now known as Myanmar. They say that Burmese cooking is a combination of two great schools of cooking, Chinese and Indian, with the addition of Burma's own natural, rich resources of herbs, vegetables, seafood, and fruits.*

The Chus offer their philosophy on food: "Food is a gift of the earth. The earth is a unique planet in the entire universe because it is blessed with sunshine, rain, and the changing seasons. Father Sun gives the energy and the warmth, and Mother Earth provides it with the fertile soil so that wonderful food is produced. We must celebrate the occasion when food is prepared. We must celebrate by cooking artfully and taking the time to enjoy it. Dining is an art."

Soups

From Dairy Hollow House Country Inn and Restaurant
EUREKA SPRINGS, ARKANSAS

Pumpkin Tomato Bisque

The tomatoes add zest to this brightly colored pumpkin soup. With no cream and very little fat, this soup can be prepared ahead, frozen, and served throughout the fall and holiday season. Try serving it with Spectrum of Summer Salad (see page 22) and a good grain bread. A great feast!

1. Place the oil or butter in a large soup pot, and heat over medium heat. Add the onion, and sauté until soft, about 5 minutes.

2. Add the vegetable stock, and heat thoroughly, bringing the stock to a simmer. Add the pumpkin or squash purée, stirring with a wire whisk to blend completely. Continue to heat over medium heat, stirring frequently.

3. Place the tomatoes in a food processor. Pulse-chop them to a medium-fine consistency, but do not purée.

4. Add the tomatoes and maple syrup to the soup pot, and heat thoroughly, but not to a simmer or boil. Season to taste with salt and pepper. Serve hot with a parsley garnish.

ABOUT THE RESTAURANT

With an entire cookbook devoted to soups and breads—owner Crescent Dragonwagon's "Dairy Hollow House Soup and Bread: A Country Inn Cookbook" (New York, NY: Workman Publishing, 1992)—this unpretentious, luxurious inn, nestled in the Arkansas Ozarks, is known for its inventive potages.

Yield: 8 servings

Preparation Time: 30 minutes

Cooking Time: 20 minutes

3 tablespoons mild vegetable oil or butter

1 large yellow onion, chopped

4 cups vegetable stock

4 cups fresh or canned pumpkin or butternut squash, puréed (about 5 pounds fresh or 2 cans, 16 ounces each)

1 (28-ounce) can whole tomatoes with their juices

1 tablespoon maple syrup

Salt, to taste

Freshly ground black pepper, to taste

GARNISH

Minced parsley

From New Frontiers Natural Foods   SALT LAKE CITY, UTAH

Ginger Carrot Soup

Enchanting and provocative, this soup is elegant as an entrée served with a salad or as a first course for a dinner party any season of the year.

Yield: 6–8 servings

Preparation Time: 30 minutes

Cooking Time: 1 hour

1–2 tablespoons olive oil or butter

1 medium yellow onion, chopped

3 pounds carrots, peeled and coarsely chopped

1 tablespoon chopped fresh garlic

1 (2- to 3-inch) piece of fresh ginger, peeled and grated, or to taste

4 cups vegetable stock or water

1 bay leaf

½–1 cup cream or crème fraîche

GARNISH

Sour cream or crème fraîche

Parsley

1. Place the oil or butter in a large soup pot, and heat over medium-high heat. Add the onion, and sauté until translucent.

2. Add the carrots, and cook for 5 more minutes. Add the garlic and ginger, and continue to cook 2 to 3 minutes.

3. Add the vegetable stock or water and the bay leaf. Bring the soup to a boil, cooking about 10 minutes, until the carrots are soft. Remove the pot from the heat, and discard the bay leaf.

4. Pour small amounts (about 1 cup) of the soup into a blender or food processor. Blend until smooth. Pour the puréed soup back into the soup pot. Stir in the cream or crème fraîche. Heat over low heat until hot, but not boiling.

5. Pour the soup into a soup tureen or individual soup bowls. Garnish with a dollop of sour cream or crème fraîche and a small sprig of parsley, and serve hot.

ABOUT THE RESTAURANT

Chef and deli manager James Calloway created this soup just by combining some of his favorite ingredients.

From Horn of the Moon Café MONTPELIER, VERMONT

Carrot Chowder

Horn of the Moon used the name "carrot soup" for this thick, creamy dish with lots of sweet carrot chunks and bits of onion. When one of the regular customers remarked that this soup was really more of a chowder than a puréed soup, the restaurant changed the name on the spot.

1. Place the oil in a large pot. Heat over medium heat until you can feel the warmth of the oil when you hold your hand over the pan. Add the onions, and both the grated and sliced carrots. Sauté until the onions are translucent, about 5 to 10 minutes.

2. Add the potatoes, salt, honey, and water. Cook over medium-high heat until the potatoes are done, about 20 minutes.

3. In a small pan, melt the butter over medium heat. Add the flour to the melted butter, and stir constantly with a whisk until it bubbles. Let this roux cook for 1 minute more. Then add a little of the hot soup mixture to the roux, stirring to blend well.

4. Pour the roux into the hot soup while stirring to completely blend. Add the cream, paprika, black pepper, and cayenne pepper. If the soup is too thick, add milk a tablespoon at a time until the desired consistency is achieved. Reduce the heat to medium-low to thoroughly heat the soup. Watch carefully to make sure the soup does not boil.

5. Pour the soup into a soup tureen or individual soup bowls, and serve with your favorite bread, muffins, or scones.

ABOUT THE RESTAURANT

The Horn of the Moon Café was first opened in 1977 and named for the beautiful mountainous region outside of Montpelier called "Horn of the Moon." According to a legend, a Native American lost his wife, and after searching for her, he found her in this area, under the horn of the moon.

Yield: 6–8 servings

Preparation Time: 25 minutes

Cooking Time: 30 minutes

1 tablespoon canola oil

4 cups finely chopped onions (about 4 medium onions)

6 cups grated carrots (8–9 medium carrots)

1$^{1}/_{2}$–2 cups half-moon slices of carrots (Cut about 3 medium carrots in half lengthwise and then slice across into half-moon-shaped pieces.)

2 medium potatoes, peeled and chopped into $^{1}/_{4}$-inch cubes

2–3 teaspoons salt

1 tablespoon honey

2$^{1}/_{2}$ cups water

$^{1}/_{4}$ cup butter

$^{1}/_{4}$ cup unbleached white flour

$^{1}/_{2}$–1 cup heavy cream

$^{1}/_{2}$ teaspoon paprika

$^{1}/_{2}$ teaspoon black pepper

$^{1}/_{4}$ teaspoon cayenne pepper, optional

Milk, as needed to thin the soup to desired consistency

From Walnut Acres   PENNS CREEK, PENNSYLVANIA

Sweet Potato Corn Chowder

Savory sweet potatoes and garden-fresh herbs blend to create a slightly sweet, creamy, and delicate chowder.

Yield: *6 servings*

Preparation Time: 25 minutes

Cooking Time: 35 minutes

2 tablespoons vegetable oil

1 small onion, chopped

$1/2$ cup chopped red bell pepper

$1/2$ cup chopped leek, white part only (See "Cleaning Leeks" on page 39.)

1 teaspoon fresh thyme leaves or $1/2$ teaspoon dried

1 teaspoon fresh marjoram or $1/2$ teaspoon dried

$1/2$ teaspoon sea salt

$1/2$ teaspoon black pepper

2 medium sweet potatoes or yams, peeled and cut into $1/2$-inch chunks (about 1 pound)

1 (8-ounce) can corn, drained and liquid reserved (There should be about 1 cup corn and $1/4$ cup liquid.)

1 (16-ounce) can vegetable broth (about 2 cups)

3 cups water

2 teaspoons arrowroot starch

$1/2$ cup heavy cream

Cayenne pepper, optional

1 tablespoon Bakon Yeast (hickory-smoked yeast), optional

GARNISH

Fresh thyme sprigs

1. Place the oil in a 4-quart saucepan. Heat over medium heat until you can feel the warmth of the oil when you place your hand over the pan. Add the onion, red pepper, leek, thyme, marjoram, salt, and pepper. Sauté, stirring occasionally, for about 10 minutes.

2. Add the sweet potatoes, the corn, the reserved liquid from the corn, the vegetable broth, and $2^1/2$ cups of the water. Cover the pan, and cook over medium heat until the sweet potatoes are tender, about 20 minutes.

3. In a small bowl, dissolve the arrowroot starch in the remaining $1/2$ cup of water. Stir the arrowroot into the soup. Increase the heat to medium-high, and bring the soup to the boil, stirring constantly. Cook until the soup is slightly thickened.

4. Reduce the heat to low, and stir in the cream. Heat until bubbles appear at the side of the pan. Be careful not to boil the soup, or the cream will separate. (If the cream does separate, cool the soup and try blending it with a whisk.) Add the optional cayenne pepper and Bakon Yeast to taste. Transfer the soup to a large soup tureen or individual serving bowls. Garnish with fresh thyme sprigs and serve immediately.

ABOUT THE RESTAURANT

Once viewed as radicals for their organic gardening practices, the owners of Walnut Acres are now at the cutting edge of agriculture. Their healthy soils and healthful foods are considered responsible, not radical. Enjoying the fruits of their labor at the Walnut Acres lunch counter is one way to sample their commitment to life. Or you can order their Sweet Potato Corn Chowder and other vegetarian soup selections from the Walnut Acres catalog: 1-800-433-3998.

From Restaurant Keffi   SANTA CRUZ, CALIFORNIA

Vegetable Chowder

This classic chowder offers a nutritionally satisfying entrée.

1. Place the vegetable oil in a large sauté pan, and heat over medium heat. Add the onions, and sauté for 3 to 4 minutes until soft. Add the carrots and celery, and sauté another 3 to 4 minutes.

2. Transfer the onions, celery, and carrots to a large soup pot. Add the water, potato, corn, bay leaf, and oregano. Place the soup pot on medium heat, and cook at a simmer until the vegetables are tender, about 30 minutes.

3. While the vegetables are cooking, make the thickening sauce. Place the canola oil in a medium-sized saucepan. Heat the oil over medium-high heat. Remove the pan from the heat. With a whisk, slowly stir the flour into the oil to make a thick paste. Then slowly stir in the milk or soy milk, blending until the mixture is smooth. Add the salt and black pepper to the sauce, and blend.

4. When the vegetables are cooked, gradually stir the thickening sauce into the vegetable soup base with a wire whisk, and mix well. Add additional salt and pepper to taste.

5. Continue to heat the chowder over low heat, about 15 minutes, until the mixture has thickened. Stir frequently, taking care not to let the chowder boil.

6. Serve the chowder hot, topped with the optional cheddar cheese, accompanied by a big basket of sesame crackers or poppy seed buns.

ABOUT THE RESTAURANT

Keffi—or "having a good time, enjoying yourself"—abounds at Restaurant Keffi!

Yield: 4 servings

Preparation Time: 20 minutes

Cooking Time: 30 minutes

2 tablespoons vegetable oil

1 medium yellow onion, chopped

2 medium carrots, chopped

2 stalks celery, chopped into 1/2-inch pieces

4 cups water

1 large russet potato, peeled and cubed into 1-inch pieces

1 cup corn kernels, fresh or frozen

1 whole bay leaf

1 teaspoon dried oregano

Salt, to taste

Black pepper, to taste

THICKENING SAUCE

4 tablespoons canola oil

4 tablespoons flour

1 1/2 cups milk or soy milk

1 1/2 teaspoons salt

1 teaspoon black pepper

GARNISH

Grated sharp cheddar cheese

From Creative Vegetarian Café   BOULDER, COLORADO

Corn Chowder

A chowder sans dairy really is possible. Umeboshi vinegar (ume plum vinegar) is an essential ingredient for this recipe. You will find it in gourmet and natural food stores.

Yield: 6 servings

Preparation Time: 10 minutes

Cooking Time: 20 minutes

2 tablespoons olive oil

1 medium yellow onion, finely chopped

1 medium head cauliflower, coarsely chopped

1 (10-ounce) box frozen corn or 3 ears fresh corn, kernels removed

1 tablespoon sea salt plus additional to taste

2 cups (about 8 ounces) raw cashew nuts blended with 1–2 tablespoons water

4–6 cups water

2–3 teaspoons umeboshi vinegar,* or to taste

Black pepper, to taste

1. Heat a heavy-bottomed soup pot over medium-high heat. Add a thin layer of olive oil, about 2 tablespoons. Lower the heat to medium, and add the onion. Sauté for 3 to 5 minutes.

2. Add the cauliflower, and sauté for another 3 to 5 minutes. Add the corn. Sprinkle 1 tablespoon of the of the sea salt over the vegetables, reduce the heat to low, and allow the vegetables to simmer for 2 to 3 minutes while you prepare the cashews.

3. Place the cashews in a food processor or blender. Drizzle in the water, 1 tablespoon at a time, blending until the mixture reaches the consistency of heavy cream. Add the cashew mixture to the soup pot. Add 4 to 6 cups of water to the pot, 1 cup at time, stirring to mix thoroughly, until the soup reaches a chowder consistency.

4. Remove one-third of the mixture from the pot, and place the removed portion in a food processor or blender. Purée until smooth. Return this puréed mixture to the soup pot, and stir again to blend.

5. Add the umeboshi vinegar. Add additional salt and pepper. Adjust seasonings to taste. Allow the chowder to simmer until the vegetables are tender-crisp, about 5 to 10 minutes. Add additional water, if necessary, to maintain the desired consistency. Serve hot.

ABOUT THE RESTAURANT

Voted "Best Veggie Restaurant" in Boulder in 1994 by the Colorado Daily People's Choice Awards, the Creative Vegetarian Café brings its customers the finest organic, whole, natural vegetarian and vegan foods, with locally grown and produced ingredients.

* *Umeboshi vinegar* is made from umeboshi, or Japanese pickled plum.

From Hyatt Regency Westshore TAMPA, FLORIDA

Black Bean Soup

This simple recipe yields a rich and flavorful soup that serves well as an entrée with an accompanying salad and tortilla chips.

1. Drain the black beans, and pour them into a large soup pot. Add the vegetable stock, salt, oregano, cumin, pepper, and Maggi's seasoning to the beans. Cover the pot, and place it over medium-high heat. Bring the stock and beans to a boil, reduce the heat to medium-low, and simmer until the beans are tender, about 1 hour.

2. Place the olive oil in a sauté pan, and heat over medium heat. Add the onion, and sauté until translucent. Add the garlic and peppers, and sauté until soft. When the beans are almost tender, add the sautéed vegetables to the soup pot, adding more stock if necessary to reach the desired consistency.

3. Before serving, add the red wine vinegar. Stir well to mix thoroughly. Ladle the bean soup into a soup tureen or individual serving bowls. Serve hot with tortilla chips and a few sprinkles of grated cheese.

ABOUT THE RESTAURANT

Nestled on a private bird sanctuary, the Hyatt Regency Westshore offers a cuisine that is extraordinary in every way: gracious service, lovely presentation, and exquisite gourmet dining.

Yield: 8 servings

Preparation Time: 20 minutes plus overnight to soak the beans

Cooking Time: 1 hour to cook the beans; 15 minutes to heat the soup

3 cups (1½ pounds) black beans, soaked overnight in enough water to cover 3 inches above the beans

8–10 cups vegetable stock, plus additional stock to reach desired consistency

1 teaspoon salt

1 tablespoon dried oregano

1 tablespoon ground cumin

½ teaspoon black pepper

2–4 tablespoons Maggi's seasoning, to taste

1–2 tablespoons olive oil

1 medium red onion, diced

2 cloves garlic, smashed and then diced

1 medium green bell pepper, diced

Scant ¼ cup red wine vinegar

GARNISH

Grated Monterey jack or cheddar cheese

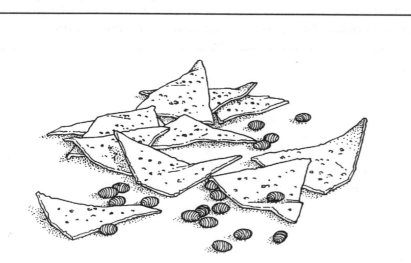

From Beans & Barley Café MILWAUKEE, WISCONSIN

Grandma's Tasty Cold Weather Soup

A deliciously thick soup, this dish is perfect for winter meals. It's quick and easy to prepare and makes a hearty quantity.

Yield: 8–10 servings

Preparation Time: 20 minutes

Cooking Time: 1 hour

2 tablespoons vegetable oil

2 medium yellow onions, chopped

2 cloves garlic, minced

1¾ cups dried split peas

¾ cup dried lentils

¾ cup dried barley

2 medium carrots, chopped

6 ribs celery, chopped

8–10 cups water

1 teaspoon dried thyme

½ teaspoon dried oregano

Pinch of ground cloves

Salt, to taste

Black pepper, to taste

1. Place the oil in a large soup pot, and heat over medium heat. Add the onions and garlic, and sauté for 5 minutes, or until soft.

2. Add the split peas, lentils, barley, carrots, and celery. Add enough water to cover the vegetables, about 8 to 10 cups. Bring to a boil over medium-high heat.

3. Cover the pot, lower the heat to medium-low, and simmer until the peas are cooked, stirring often to keep them from sticking. Watch the water level, and add more water as needed. The soup should be thick, so add just enough water to allow the peas to cook. Allow the soup to simmer about 1 hour.

4. When the vegetables are cooked, add the thyme, oregano, and cloves. Add salt and pepper to taste. Stir well to blend. Serve hot with warm cornbread or fresh baked or toasted rye bread. This soup keeps well in a covered container in the refrigerator for several days and also freezes well in a tightly sealed freezer container for up to three months.

ABOUT THE RESTAURANT

The chefs at Beans & Barley say this is one of their most requested cold weather soups. You can also find other wonderful soups, salads, baked goodies, deli delights, vitamins, and housewares at Beans & Barley.

Vegetarian French Onion Soup

C'est délicieux! The French would be proud to serve this one!

1. Place the butter in a large, heavy soup pot, and melt over medium heat. Add the onions, cooking and stirring until they are golden brown, about 10 to 20 minutes.

2. In a small bowl, place $1/2$ cup of the vegetable stock. Slowly add the flour, whisking with a fork or wire whisk to make a thin paste.

3. Add the flour paste to the onion mixture, whisking to blend well. Add the remainder of the stock. Add the remaining ingredients. Bring to a quick boil, and reduce the heat to low. Cover the pot, and continue to simmer another 30 minutes.

4. Pour into individual serving bowls, garnishing with croutons and cheese. Serve hot with a fresh garden salad and sliced French bread.

ABOUT THE RESTAURANT

The only natural foods restaurant, deli, and bakery in Moab, Honest Ozzie's, owned by Chef Donna Rivette, offers a true oasis for vegetarians, vegans, and anyone else desiring healthy, delicious, and pleasurable dining. Open for breakfast, lunch, and dinner, Honest Ozzie's provides garden seating right in the middle of the desert.

Yield: 6 servings

Preparation Time: 15–20 minutes

Cooking Time: 40–50 minutes

$3/4$ cup butter

5 large yellow onions, sliced

5 cups vegetable stock

3 tablespoons unbleached white flour

1 tablespoon tamari soy sauce (See "About Soy Sauce" on page 13.)

$1/4$ cup dry white wine

$1/2$ teaspoon dry mustard

$1/4$ teaspoon dried thyme

1 bay leaf

$1/2$ teaspoon salt

$1/2$ teaspoon garlic granules or $1/4$–$1/2$ teaspoon powdered garlic

$1/4$ teaspoon white pepper

GARNISH

Croutons

Freshly grated Parmesan or Swiss cheese

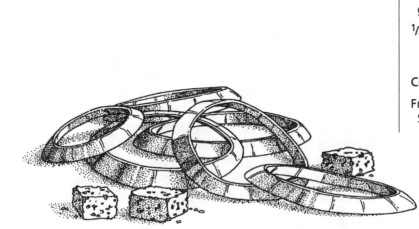

From Rainbow Blossom Natural Foods & Deli   LOUISVILLE, KENTUCKY

Rainbow Veggie Soup

A zillion vegetables grace this tasty soup. The flavors mature when you keep the soup covered in the refrigerator for a day before serving—that is, if you can wait that long!

Yield: 6 servings

Preparation Time: 20–30 minutes

Cooking Time: 30–45 minutes

2 tablespoons olive oil

1 large onion, chopped

1 stalk celery, chopped into 1-inch pieces

1 large head broccoli, chopped into 1-inch pieces

1 small head cauliflower, chopped into 1-inch pieces

3 large potatoes, peeled and chopped into 1-inch pieces

3 large carrots, peeled and chopped into 1-inch pieces

1 medium zucchini, chopped into 1-inch pieces

1 medium yellow squash, chopped into 1-inch pieces

1 (14-ounce) can diced tomatoes or 2 cups diced fresh tomatoes

1 (10-ounce) box frozen baby lima beans

1 (10-ounce) box frozen green beans

1 (10-ounce) box frozen corn

1 (10-ounce) box frozen peas

8 cups water or vegetable stock, approximately

1 (4-ounce) can tomato purée

1. Place the oil in a large (6- to 8-quart) soup pot, and heat over medium-high heat. Add the onion and celery, and sauté until they are translucent.

2. Add the broccoli, cauliflower, potatoes, carrots, zucchini, and yellow squash. Add the tomatoes, lima beans, green beans, corn, and peas. Add the water or vegetable stock.

3. Bring the mixture to a near boil. Add the tomato purée, Spike, garlic flakes, basil, thyme, cumin, chili powder, oregano, and parsley. Add the honey and soy sauce. Stir to blend well.

4. Continue to heat until hot and the veggies are tender-crisp, about 10 to 15 minutes. Serve the soup hot with fresh biscuits, corn muffins, or garlic-cheese French bread.

About Spike

Created in Italy, Spike is a blend of thirty-nine herbs, vegetables, and nonirritating, exotic spices with salt crystals. Some of the ingredients are toasted onion, garlic powder, dill, kelp, Indian curry, orange and lemon peel, summer savory, sweet green and red bell peppers, oregano, basil, and thyme, and celery leaf, mushroom, spinach, parsley, and tomato powders. Spike is sold in most natural food stores.

To Make the Garlic-Cheese French Bread:

1. Preheat the broiler to broil.

2. Slice the French bread in half lengthwise, and place on an ungreased baking sheet. Spread the butter to evenly coat the open face of the bread. Sprinkle the buttered sides with Parmesan cheese and garlic.

3. Place the baking sheet under the broiler for 3 to 5 minutes, watching carefully to make sure the bread does not burn. When the bread turns a golden brown, it is ready.

4. Remove from the oven, and transfer the loaves to a bread board or slice and place in a serving basket. Serve warm.

ABOUT THE RESTAURANT

Healthy and convenient gourmet foods are available for take-out only at Rainbow Blossom Natural Foods & Deli.

¹/₄ cup Spike, or to taste (See "About Spike.")

1 teaspoon garlic flakes

1 teaspoon dried basil

¹/₂ teaspoon dried thyme

1 teaspoon ground cumin

1 teaspoon chili powder

1 teaspoon dried oregano

2 teaspoons dried parsley

2 tablespoons honey

¹/₄ cup tamari soy sauce (See "About Soy Sauce" on page 13.)

GARLIC-CHEESE FRENCH BREAD

1 loaf French bread

2–3 tablespoons butter

¹/₄ cup Parmesan cheese

¹/₄–¹/₂ teaspoon garlic powder, or to taste

From Green Earth Café   BISMARK, NORTH DAKOTA

Poverty-to-Riches Bean Soup

Gary Dire, owner-chef of Green Earth Café, tells this story about the creation of this soup: "This is a recipe that a friend and I created when I went to visit him in Oregon. My friend had bought a big bag of pinto beans because they were cheap—he didn't have much money to spend—and he was wondering what to do with all these beans. So we worked together and created this stew-like soup. It tasted better than I thought it would, and when I returned to the Green Earth Café, I made a pot of this soup and it was a smashing success."

Yield: 8 servings

Preparation Time: 20 minutes, plus 6–8 hours to soak the beans

Cooking Time: 1^1/$_2$ hours to cook the beans; ^{1}/$_2$ hour to heat the soup

1 cup dried pinto beans, washed

^{1}/$_2$ cup dried black-eyed peas or other beans of your choice

1 tablespoon olive oil

6 cloves garlic, minced

1^1/$_2$ cups onions, chopped (about 1^1/$_2$ medium onions)

2 teaspoons dried basil

1 teaspoon dried oregano

1 teaspoon dried thyme

1–2 tablespoons cumin

1 (27-ounce) can chopped tomatoes with liquid

Salt, to taste

Black pepper, to taste

2–3 green bell peppers, chopped

2 cups vegetable stock

4 cups tomato juice, approximately

Tabasco sauce, optional

1. Place the washed pinto beans and black-eyed peas in a medium-sized pan, and fill the pan with water. Allow the beans to soak 6 to 8 hours, or overnight.

2. Drain the beans and peas. Rinse them with fresh water and drain again. Place the beans and peas in a soup pot. Add enough water to bring the water level 1 inch above the beans. Cover the soup pot, and place over medium heat. Cook until tender, about 1^1/$_2$ hours. During this time, stir the beans two or three times, checking to be sure there is about 1 inch of water above the beans. Drain.

3. While the beans and peas are cooking, place the olive oil in a large frying pan. Heat the oil over medium-high heat until your hand placed over the oil feels hot. Add the garlic and onions, reduce the heat to medium, and sauté until the onions are translucent, stirring constantly.

4. Add the basil, oregano, thyme, and cumin to the onion mixture. Sauté for 2 minutes more to blend well. Add the chopped tomatoes with their liquid. Add salt and pepper to taste.

5. Add the green peppers and the onion mixture to the soup pot. Stir well. Add the vegetable stock and enough tomato juice to reach the desired thickness, about 1 quart. If you like, add Tabasco sauce a drop at a time to taste.

6. Allow the soup to simmer for ^{1}/$_2$ hour. Serve hot with your favorite cornbread or biscuits.

ABOUT THE RESTAURANT

Committed to providing wholesome vegetarian foods in Bismarck, North Dakota, Gary Dire invites his customers to relax and enjoy good food in a casual ambience.

From Everybody's Natural Foods LEXINGTON, KENTUCKY

Everybody's Potato Leek Soup

A yummy, nonfat hearty recipe that takes very little time to prepare, this soup is perfect for a lunch or dinner on a chilly day.

1. Put the potatoes, leeks, carrots, and onion in a large soup pot. Add the broth (or water) and pepper. Add salt.

2. Place the pot over high heat, and bring the soup to a boil. Lower the heat to medium, and cover the pot. Cook approximately 1 hour, stirring occasionally, until the potatoes start to fall apart and thicken the soup.

3. Add the chopped spinach, heat for 1 to 2 more minutes, and serve immediately.

ABOUT THE RESTAURANT

A former employee of Everybody's writes, "Customers and cooks have come and gone, but Everybody's hasn't changed that much. If the scarred butcher block counter tops could talk, they'd make us salivate. They've been pounded, chopped, and spilled on for nearly 20 years, and they've seen some great meals emerge, often from sheer chaos. But if the steamy, crowded kitchen with the jars of spices piled haphazardly on the shelves is sometimes chaotic, the front of the deli is always peaceful, where customers tend to linger over lunch."

Yield: 6–8 servings

Preparation Time: 20 minutes

Cooking Time: 1 hour

8–10 washed, unpeeled new potatoes, chopped into bite-sized pieces

3 leeks, chopped, white part only (See "Cleaning Leeks" on page 39.)

2 medium carrots, peeled chopped

1 small onion, chopped

7–8 cups vegetable broth or water

$\frac{1}{2}$ teaspoon black pepper

$1\frac{1}{2}$ teaspoons salt, or to taste if you are using broth

8 ounces fresh spinach, chopped (See "Preparing Fresh Spinach" on page 29.)

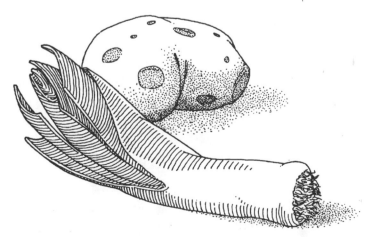

From Golden Temple Natural Foods and Café   BIRMINGHAM, ALABAMA

Potato Cabbage Soup

Sweetly aromatic, this low-fat soup can be made a day ahead to allow the flavors to mature.

Yield: *8 servings*

Preparation Time: 20 minutes

Cooking Time: 30 minutes

4 cups peeled and cubed
potatoes (about 3 large
potatoes)

1 teaspoon sea salt

2 tablespoons vegetable oil

4 cups chopped onion (about 4
medium onions)

4 cups chopped cabbage (about
1 head of cabbage)

2 cloves garlic, chopped

Black pepper, to taste

4 teaspoons dried basil

2–3 tablespoons tamari soy
sauce (See "About Soy Sauce"
on page 13.)

1. Put the potatoes in a large pot of water, add the salt, and cover. Bring to a low boil over medium heat. Cook for 20 to 30 minutes, or until the potatoes are tender when pierced with a fork.

2. While the potatoes are cooking, place the oil in a large sauté pan and heat over medium-high heat. Sauté the onions for 2 to 3 minutes. Add the cabbage, garlic, pepper, and basil. Cook until the cabbage is tender, about 3 minutes.

3. Drain the potatoes, reserving 1 cup of the liquid. Place the potatoes in a blender, and purée, adding a little of the reserved potato liquid if necessary.

4. Return the purée to the pot, and add the sautéed onion mixture. Simmer on low heat to allow the flavors to blend. Add the soy sauce and adjust the other seasonings to taste.

5. Remove from the heat, ladle into serving bowls, and serve hot.

ABOUT THE RESTAURANT

For twenty-one years, owner Hari Nam Khalsa has been serving wonderful, low-fat vegetarian and vegan soups, sandwiches, salads, and daily specials to a steady lunch crowd in Birmingham, Alabama.

From Golden Temple Natural Foods and Café   BIRMINGHAM, ALABAMA

Split Pea Soup

Serve this delicious, simple-to-make soup with your favorite rye or grain bread for a complete, nutritious, and satisfying meal.

1. Place the split peas and water in a large soup pot, and place over medium-high heat. When the split peas reach a gentle boil, add the onion, celery, carrots, bay leaves, basil, dried chilies, pepper, oregano, and sage. Cover the pot, and cook until the peas and vegetables are tender, about another 30 minutes.

2. Add the soy sauce and optional salt to taste, and simmer another 15 minutes. Serve hot.

ABOUT THE RESTAURANT

The owner of Golden Temple Natural Foods and Café reports that Mel Gibson, Danny Glover, Scott Glen, Michael Jackson, and Michael Hedges have all found the restaurant to be a main dining spot in Birmingham.

Yield: 8 servings

Preparation Time: 30 minutes

Cooking Time: 1 hour

2 cups dried split peas

8 cups water

1½ cups chopped yellow onion (about 1½ onions)

1½ cups chopped celery, stalks only (3–5 stalks of celery)

1½ cups grated carrots (2–3 carrots)

2 bay leaves

2 teaspoons dried basil

Pinch of crushed dried chilies

¼ teaspoon black pepper

1 teaspoon dried oregano

Pinch of dried sage

2–4 tablespoons tamari soy sauce or to taste (See "About Soy Sauce" on page 13.)

1–2 teaspoons sea salt or to taste, optional

From Beans & Grains & Things   LITTLE ROCK, ARKANSAS

Jill's Veggie Chili

The list of ingredients looks daunting. However, each ingredient contributes significantly to the rich, hearty flavor of this wonderful chili. This recipe makes so much that you can freeze half to enjoy on another chilly day.

Yield: *8 servings*

Preparation Time: 30 minutes plus 6–8 hours to soak the beans

Cooking Time: 1¹/₂–2 hours

3 cups dried pinto beans

About 8 cups (2 quarts) water to cook the beans plus an addi-tional 4 cups, plus water to soak the beans

1 teaspoon chili powder

3 tablespoons ground plus 1 teaspoon cumin

²/₃ cup safflower oil

5 coarsely chopped white onions

2 bay leaves

5 large cloves garlic, minced

2 large red bell peppers, coarsely chopped

2 large green bell peppers, coarsely chopped

2 large peeled, finely grated carrots

2 tablespoons sea salt

¹/₂ tablespoon black pepper

2 tablespoons dried oregano

1 tablespoon chopped fresh basil

2–4 tablespoons chili powder, according to taste

4 cups Very Veggie Drink, V-8 Juice, or other spicy tomato juice

1. Place the beans in a saucepan, cover with water, and soak 6 to 8 hours or overnight. Drain the beans. Then rinse and drain the beans again. Put them in a large pot, and cover with 8 cups of water. Add the chili powder and 1 teaspoon of the ground cumin. Cover and cook over medium heat for 1¹/₂ to 2 hours or until tender. Drain the beans, and reserve the liquid.

2. Put the oil in a large soup pot, and heat over medium heat. Put the onion, bay leaves, garlic, red and green peppers, carrots, sea salt, black pepper, oregano, basil, chili powder, and the remaining 3 tablespoons of cumin into the pot. Sauté for 2 to 3 minutes.

3. To the onion mixture, add the spicy tomato juice, tomatoes, cilantro (coriander), vinegar, bulgur, Worcestershire sauce, and tomato paste. Add the *chiles de árbol* to taste. Add the remaining 4 cups of water. Stir to mix well.

4. Add the cooked beans to the sauce in the soup pot, and allow to simmer for 1 to 1¹/₂ hours. Serve hot with corn bread and fresh butter. The chili is even better reheated after being refrigerated or frozen.

ABOUT THE RESTAURANT

Right in the heart of Arkansas, you can find ten thousand natural, pure, organic food products, beauty aids, vitamins, and supplements, together with books and a deli, at Beans & Grains & Things.

Bulgur wheat is a popular Middle Eastern Wheat that has been cracked by boiling, and then redried. It's available in natural food stores. *Chiles de árbol* are very hot. Be careful when you are handling chilies because they can burn the skin of your hands, eyes, and mouth. It's best to wear rubber gloves. If the chilies touch your skin, wash carefully with warm (not hot or cold) soapy water to reduce the heat from the chilies.

6 coarsely chopped fresh tomatoes

1 tablespoon dried coriander or 3 tablespoons chopped fresh cilantro (coriander)

2 tablespoons apple cider vinegar

1 cup uncooked bulgur*

$\frac{1}{4}$ cup Worcestershire sauce

6 ounces tomato paste

3 minced *chiles de árbol,** optional

From Natural Café SANTA FE, NEW MEXICO

East Indian Red Lentil Soup

Masoor dal, as these salmon-pink lentils are collectively called in India, is very richly flavored and fast to cook. This soup is a good beginning to an Indian-style meal, or it makes a meal in itself served over basmati rice with yogurt on the side. We love this soup!

Yield: 4 servings

Preparation Time: 20–25 minutes

Cooking Time: 30 minutes

6 cups water

1 cup red lentils,* sorted and washed

1 tablespoon light sesame oil

1 medium yellow or white onion, chopped

1½ teaspoons peeled and grated or minced ginger

¼ teaspoon ground turmeric

½ teaspoon cumin seed

¾ teaspoon salt

1 mild (Anaheim) or hot (jalapeño)* green chili, seeded and finely diced (may be pickled)

2 ripe tomatoes, diced, or 2 cups diced canned tomatoes

2 tablespoons minced cilantro (coriander)

GARNISH

4 tablespoons minced red bell pepper

4 teaspoons fresh cilantro (coriander)

1. Bring the water to a boil in a large saucepan over high heat. Reduce the heat to medium-high, and add the lentils, stirring to prevent clumping or sticking. Bring the water to a boil again, watching to see when it begins to foam. If the foam gets too high in the pan, scoop the foam out gently and discard. Reduce the heat to low, and simmer until the lentils are very soft, about 30 minutes, stirring occasionally.

2. Meanwhile, place the oil in a heavy sauté pan over medium heat. Add the onion, and sauté until translucent. Add the ginger, turmeric, and cumin seed, and ¼ teaspoon of the salt. Cook until the onion is medium brown and very sweet.

3. Add the chili to the onion mixture to taste, and cook until it turns bright green. Stir the tomatoes and ½ teaspoon of the salt into the onion mixture. Cook another 5 minutes.

4. Add the onion mixture to the cooked lentils. Heat gently until the flavors meld. Add the minced cilantro, and taste for salt and spices. Serve immediately garnished with the red bell pepper and cilantro leaves. The leftover soup may be kept covered in the refrigerator for up to two days.

ABOUT THE RESTAURANT

Lynn Walters' Natural Café on Cerrillos Road offers a gourmet experience not to be missed if you are in Sante Fe. If you cannot get to the café, treat yourself to this and other exquisite recipes from her cookbook, "Cooking at the Natural Café in Sante Fe" (Freedom, California: Crossing Press, 1992).

Red lentils are available in natural food stores, gourmet specialty markets, and Indian markets. Be careful when you are handling *chilies* because they can burn the skin of your hands, eyes, and mouth. It's best to wear rubber gloves. If the chilies touch your skin, wash carefully with warm (not hot or cold) soapy water to reduce the heat from the chilies.

Nature Lovers Lentil Soup

What could be easier than tossing these ingredients into a soup pot? Voilà! A savory soup for an autumn or a winter meal!

1. Put all the ingredients in a large soup pot. Place the pot over high heat, and bring to a boil.

2. Cover the pot, and reduce the heat to medium-low. Allow to simmer for 1 hour, until the lentils are soft and the rice is tender.

3. Serve hot with wedges of pita bread, hot brown bread, or a crusty French bread.

ABOUT THE RESTAURANT

Metairie, Louisiana, is located on the Mississippi River in the Delta region near New Orleans. In this quaint corner of the world, where inhabitants and visitors alike relish the natural surroundings, the kitchen at Nature Lovers bustles with the preparation of deli delights, salads, and fresh juices. It's all natural at Nature Lovers!

Yield: 8 servings

Preparation Time: 20 minutes

Cooking Time: 1 hour

4 cups dried lentils, washed

1 cup uncooked brown rice

5 medium carrots, peeled and sliced into rounds

7 bay leaves

2 white onions, chopped

2 green bell peppers, chopped

2 tablespoons chopped fresh parsley

2 stalks celery, including the leaves, chopped

1–2 teaspoons garlic powder, to taste

Spike, to taste (See "About Spike" on page 52.)

16 cups (1 gallon) water

From Chiang-Mai Restaurant   HONOLULU, HAWAII

Tom Yum Pak Soup
(Spicy Sour Vegetable Soup)

This easy-to-make soup is thin and light with colorful, floating veggies.

Yield: *4 servings*

Preparation Time: 10–15 minutes

Cooking Time: 20 minutes

7$\frac{1}{2}$ cups water

4 kaffir lime leaves, washed and patted dry (See "About Thai Ingredients.")

6 2-inch lemongrass pieces

4 slices peeled Thai ginger, $\frac{1}{4}$ inch by 1$\frac{1}{2}$ inches

2 teaspoons chili oil

Salt, to taste

Juice of $\frac{1}{2}$ medium lemon (about 1 tablespoon)

$\frac{1}{4}$ pound firm tofu, cubed

$\frac{1}{2}$ pound steamed mixed vegetables (tomato, broccoli, mushroom, carrots, or others of your choice), cut into small pieces (See "Steaming Vegetables" on page 31.)

1. Put the water in a large soup pot, and add the kaffir leaves, lemongrass, and ginger. Boil for 10 minutes over high heat. Add the chili oil and salt to taste. Stir well, and then add the lemon juice. Stir again to blend completely.

2. Remove from the heat, and pour the liquid through a strainer to remove the lemongrass, ginger, and kaffir leaves. Return the strained liquid to the pot.

3. Add the tofu and the mixed vegetables to the soup. Heat thoroughly over low heat, stirring occasionally, until ready to serve. Serve hot.

About Thai Ingredients

Thai cooking gets its unique flavor from specialty ingredients that can be found in Asian markets and specialty stores.

Bai-ma-grood (kaffir lime leaves) is an herb with a slight lemon-lime flavor.

Kha (galanga) is a root herb similar in appearance to the ginger root. It has a rather mild taste and may be found fresh, frozen, or dried in Thai and Asian markets.

See ew kao (Thai thin soy sauce) is similar to tamari soy sauce, but lighter in color and flavor.

Ta-kai (lemongrass) is a long, thin, green, wood-like herb. It has a thicker stock than common lawn grass and may be purchased fresh, dried, or frozen in Thai and Asian markets. It is more commonly found dried in the spice section of most grocery and natural food stores.

Thai ginger is not substantially different from the fresh ginger found in most grocery stores, and the latter will serve as a fine substitute for Thai ginger, if necessary.

Sen Lek are rice noodles.

ABOUT THE RESTAURANT

Orchids, tropical plants, and lace curtains adorn this sweet, tiny café. Waitresses wearing Thai sarongs serve their exotic northern Thai cuisine with true aloha spirit.

From Tipps Thai Cuisine   VENTURA, CALIFORNIA

Tom Kha Tofu
(Galanga Coconut Soup)

Owner Chang Liampetchakul says, "Galanga soup is very delicious and gives you energy, especially in the wintertime. All the ingredients can be purchased from Thai or Asian specialty markets." If you prefer a spicier soup, you may add roasted dried or fresh chilies. When you add more chilies, add more Thai soy sauce, lemon juice, and sugar in equal parts to balance the flavors. Other mushroom varieties, such as oyster or brown mushrooms, may be substituted, if necessary.

1. Put the water and coconut milk in a large soup pot. Add the galanga, kaffir lime leaves, and lemongrass. Bring to a boil over medium heat.

2. Add the tofu, fresh mushrooms, and straw mushrooms, and stir well. Add the soy sauce and sugar. Simmer on medium heat for 10 minutes.

3. Remove from the heat, and add the lemon juice. Sprinkle with cilantro slices. Serve hot.

Yield: 4 servings

Preparation Time: 20 minutes

Cooking Time: 15 minutes

2 cups water

2 cups canned coconut milk

3–4 sliced dried galanga (See "About Thai Ingredients.")

3 kaffir lime leaves

1 stem lemongrass, cut into 1½-inch lengths

⅓ pound firm tofu, sliced into 1-inch cubes

½ cup sliced fresh white or brown mushrooms

1 can straw mushrooms (See "About Mushrooms.")

2 tablespoons Thai thin soy sauce

¼ teaspoon sugar

2 tablespoons lemon juice

GARNISH

Fresh cilantro (coriander) leaves, snipped into thin slices

About Mushrooms

Common white or brown mushrooms are delicious, but the specialty mushrooms listed below add wonderful textures and tastes to food. You can find them in Asian markets and specialty stores.

Boletus, cepe, or *bolete* are all names for the same type of mushroom that is found in various wooded regions of the United States. It is light colored, with a short, stocky stem and small cap.

Chinese black mushrooms, also called wood ears, are mild-flavored mushrooms that are most commonly found in dried form. They may be black, gray, or speckled.

Chinese straw mushrooms are small, rather stout-looking, and very tasty. They are most commonly available in bottles, although a Chinese market may have them available fresh.

Enoki mushroom is the Japanese term for the mushroom called golden needle by the Chinese. It is flavorful, light colored, and slender stemmed, with a tiny cap.

Shiitake mushrooms are found in both Japan and China. They are brown, with a wide, thin cap and a slender stem. Shiitake mushrooms are most commonly available dried.

ABOUT THE RESTAURANT

With more than twelve years of experience, Chang Liampetchakul has established a solid reputation for serving excellent Thai cuisine.

From Alisan Restaurant   ANAHEIM, CALIFORNIA

Alisan's Hot & Sour Soup

As a variation on this well-balanced soup, add 2 to 3 tablespoons of miso to the broth and omit the red pepper sauce.

Yield: 4 servings

Preparation Time: 20 minutes plus 20–30 minutes to soak the mushrooms

Cooking Time: 10–15 minutes

3 pieces dried Chinese black mushrooms (See "About Mushrooms" on page 63.)

1 part gluten*

8 ounces soft tofu, rinsed and patted dry, optional

2–3 slices fresh or canned bamboo shoots

6¼ cups water

2 tablespoons soy sauce (See "About Soy Sauce" on page 13.)

1 teaspoon sugar

1–2 tablespoons vinegar

1–2 pinches of ground black pepper

Spicy Asian red pepper sauce,* to taste, optional

1 tablespoon cornstarch

1 teaspoon sesame oil

1. Place the mushrooms in a medium-sized bowl, cover with warm water, and soak for 20 to 30 minutes. Remove mushrooms from the water, pat dry with paper towels, and cut into shreds.

2. While the mushrooms are soaking, cut the gluten into shreds. Cut the tofu into small pieces, and cut the bamboo shoots into shreds.

3. Place 6 cups of the water in a large pot, and bring to a boil over high heat. Reduce the heat to medium, and add the gluten, tofu, mushrooms, bamboo shoots, soy sauce, sugar, vinegar, black pepper, and red pepper sauce. Increase the heat to medium-high, and bring the mixture to a boil, stirring frequently.

4. Place the cornstarch and the remaining ¼ cup of water in a small bowl. Stir to mix well. Pour the cornstarch mixture into the boiling pot, stirring continuously. Add the sesame oil, stir well, and bring to a boil. Ladle the soup into individual bowls, and serve hot.

ABOUT THE RESTAURANT

Within walking distance of Disneyland and the Anaheim Convention Center, Alisan Restaurant offers convention-goers and vacationers a soothing respite from work or too much fun!

*See the basic gluten recipe on page 196, or you may use canned gluten, called *moon ch'ai y'a*, found in Asian, gourmet, or natural food stores. You can find a variety of *red pepper sauces* in natural food and Asian specialty stores. Select the one best suited to the degree of hotness you enjoy.

From Beans & Grains & Things   *LITTLE ROCK, ARKANSAS*

Hot and Sour Soup

Sometimes hot and sour soups are thin and watery—not so with this one. The rich broth of this soup provides a nourishing base for the bountiful veggies and tofu.

1. Place the vegetable broth paste or cubes and 8 cups of the water in a large soup pot. Bring to a low boil over medium-high heat.

2. Add the vinegar, soy sauce, tofu, mushrooms, cabbage, onion, bamboo shoots, water chestnuts. Add cayenne pepper to taste. Reduce the heat to low.

3. Place the arrowroot or cornstarch and the remaining cup of water in a small bowl. Whisk until smooth. Stir the arrowroot mixture into the soup. Cook for an additional 20 to 30 minutes, stirring occasionally until the soup is heated thoroughly. Remove from the heat, and serve hot.

ABOUT THE RESTAURANT

Gary Ecklund, owner of Beans & Grains & Things, and his staff are dedicated to "honesty, integrity, friendly service, and being socially and environmentally responsible for our health and the well-being of our planet." Simply put, as the menu states it, the idea is "Healthy soils = healthy plants = healthy foods = healthy people."

Yield: 8 servings

Preparation Time: 30 minutes

Cooking Time: 30 minutes

1/4 cup vegetable broth paste or 4 vegetable broth cubes

9 cups water

1/8 cup cider vinegar

1/4 cup tamari soy sauce (See "About Soy Sauce" on page 13.)

1 pound firm tofu, cut into 1/4-inch cubes

2 cups chopped white mushrooms (about 1/2 pound mushrooms)

2 cups chopped green cabbage (1 small head cabbage)

1 medium yellow onion, chopped

1 (5-ounce) can bamboo shoots

1 (5-ounce) can water chestnuts

Cayenne pepper, optional

3 tablespoons arrowroot or cornstarch

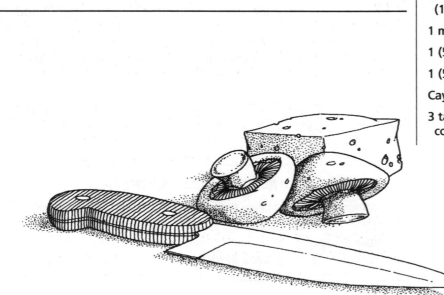

From Cherry Street Chinese Vegetarian   PHILADELPHIA, PENNSYLVANIA

Emerald 3 Mixed Soup

Enoki mushroom is the Japanese name and golden needle is the Chinese name for one of the distinctively flavored mushrooms used in this soup. Here, it blends well with the asparagus for a beautifully presented and exquisite-tasting creation.

Yield: 4–6 servings

Preparation Time: 15 minutes plus 15–30 minutes to soak the mushrooms

Cooking Time: 15 minutes

$1^{1}/_{2}$ pounds plus 4 stems of fresh asparagus

6 dried Chinese black mushrooms (See "About Mushrooms" on page 63.)

3 cups vegetable stock or water

2 ounces enoki mushrooms, gently rinsed

$^{1}/_{2}$ teaspoon sugar, optional

Pinch of black pepper

1 teaspoon sesame oil, optional

$^{1}/_{4}$ cup water

2 tablespoons cornstarch

1. Cut the bottom third off the 4 asparagus stems, and set aside. Diagonally cut the top portion of each of the 4 stems into thin slices, and set aside. Use a juicer to extract about 2 cups of fresh asparagus juice from the asparagus bottoms and the remaining $1^{1}/_{2}$ pounds of asparagus.

2. Place the Chinese black mushrooms in a bowl of cool water, and soak for 30 minutes. You can speed up the process by soaking them for 15 minutes in hot water, but some of the flavor is lost. Drain the mushrooms, and slice into long, thin strips.

3. Place the vegetable stock or 3 cups water in a large soup pot, and bring to a boil over high heat.

4. Add the sliced Chinese mushrooms, the enoki mushrooms, and the asparagus slices, and cook for 1 minute. Then add the optional sugar, the black pepper, and the sesame oil. Stir to dissolve and blend well.

5. Place the cornstarch and 4 tablespoons of water in a small bowl, and stir with a fork or whisk until well blended.

6. Reduce the heat under the soup to medium-high, and add the asparagus juice. Bring the soup just to a boil. Then reduce the heat to low, and immediately add the cornstarch mixture to thicken. Be careful not to boil the mixture too long, or the green color of the asparagus juice will escape from the soup and stick to the side of the pot.

7. Remove the soup from the heat, and pour into a warmed soup tureen or individual bowls and serve. This soup keeps well for 1 to 2 days in the refrigerator, where the flavors develop nicely.

ABOUT THE RESTAURANT

Chef Raymond Fung of Cherry Street Chinese Vegetarian Restaurant creates the bright jade-green broth by juicing fresh asparagus. He loves that particular shade of green and won't compromise the color or the taste of this soup even in wintertime, when fresh asparagus is expensive and rare.

From A Moveable Feast   *HOUSTON, TEXAS*

Cold Avocado & Cucumber Soup

Never tried a cold soup before? You might like it! The creamy smooth avocado is delicately flavored with cucumber and dill to make a luscious soup.

1. Place the avocados, onion, garlic, yogurt, and cucumber in a blender or food processor. Add dill and Spike to taste. Blend until smooth, adding the water a little at a time to achieve the consistency of heavy cream.

2. Pour the soup into a covered container, and chill in the refrigerator for at least 2 hours.

3. Remove the soup from the refrigerator, and pour into individual serving bowls. Float a sprig of parsley in each bowl as a garnish.

ABOUT THE RESTAURANT

Warm hues welcome A Moveable Feast customers to a radiant and fresh ambience.

Yield: *4 servings*

Preparation Time: 10 minutes plus 2 hours for chilling the soup

5 ripe avocados, peeled, pitted, and chopped

1/2 cup chopped purple onion

2 cloves fresh garlic, minced

1 cup nonfat plain yogurt

1 cucumber, peeled and chopped

1–2 tablespoons fresh dill, to taste

1–3 teaspoons Spike, to taste (See "About Spike" on page 52.)

2–3 cups water

GARNISH

Parsley sprigs

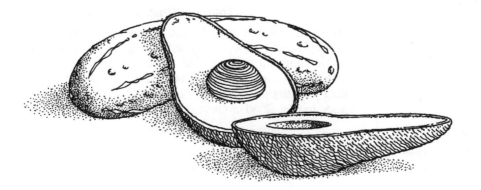

From Benvenuti   INDIANAPOLIS, INDIANA

Chilled Tomato & Vegetable Soup
with Pine Nuts and Purée of Avocado

E elegante! This soup is a delicious summertime treat.

Yield: 4 servings

Preparation Time: 20–30
minutes plus 30 minutes for
chilling the soup

SOUP

5 tomatoes

1 stalk celery, coarsely chopped

1 carrot, chopped

1/2 medium white onion,
quartered

1/2 fennel bulb

2 cups vegetable stock

Dash of champagne vinegar

Dash of Tabasco sauce

Dash of Worcestershire sauce

Salt, to taste

Black pepper, to taste

AVOCADO PURÉE

1 avocado, peeled and pit
removed

1–2 teaspoons lemon juice

Salt, to taste

Black pepper, to taste

GARNISH

1/4 cup toasted pine nuts (See
"Toasting Nuts and Seeds.")

1. Place the tomatoes in a pan of boiling water, and simmer for 1 to 2 minutes. Remove the tomatoes with a slotted spoon, and cool for a few minutes. Under a stream of cool running water, gently remove the skin from each tomato with a paring knife. Slice the tomatoes into wedges, and carefully remove and discard the seeds with their jelly-like pulp.

2. Put the tomato sections, celery, carrot, onion, and fennel in a blender or food processor. Process or blend until finely chopped. For best results, grind with a 3/4-inch-diameter meat grinder.

3. Place the chopped veggies in a large bowl, and add the vegetable stock. Season with the vinegar, Tabasco sauce, and Worcestershire sauce. Add salt and pepper to taste. Chill the soup in the refrigerator for 30 minutes, until well chilled.

To Make the Avocado Purée:

1. Put the avocado in a blender or food processor. Purée, adding lemon juice, salt, and pepper to taste, until the mixture is smooth and thick.

2. Place the avocado mixture in small molds, about 1 1/2 inches in diameter. Flower, geometric, or moon shapes make appropriate molds. Refrigerate until well chilled, about 30 minutes.

Toasting Nuts and Seeds

Preheat the oven to 350°F. Spread the nuts or seeds evenly (so they are not overlapping) on an ungreased baking sheet. Place the baking sheet in the oven, and toast for 3 to 5 minutes. Check periodically to make sure the nuts or seeds do not burn, as they brown quickly. Remove the nuts from the oven when they have turned the desired color, and set aside to cool. Grind or crush if necessary.

To Serve the Soup:

1. To unmold one avocado purée into each individual serving bowl, dip the mold quickly into a basin of hot water. Then, place the inverted bowl over the open end of the mold, and flip the mold and bowl over. The purée will slide out. Ladle about $^3/_4$ cup of the soup around the avocado mold. Sprinkle with a few of the toasted pine nuts. Serve immediately.

ABOUT THE RESTAURANT

J. P. Moraldo also owns a casual restaurant in Indianapolis named Pesto. It's Italian, of course, offering such vegetarian entrees as Vegetable Casserole, Fettucine With Four Cheeses, Creamed Spinach Pasta, pizza, and salads.

From Dairy Hollow House Country Inn and Restaurant
EUREKA SPRINGS, ARKANSAS

Chilled Corn Chowder with Dill

Extraordinarily quick to prepare, this refreshing, uncooked summer soup is scrumptious. With a low-fat buttermilk or yogurt base, it's ideal for today's diet.

Yield: 4 – 6 servings

Preparation Time: 10–15 minutes plus 1–2 hours for chilling the soup

1 bunch scallions (green onions), washed and trimmed

2 cups cooked corn, fresh, frozen, or canned (See "Cooking Fresh Corn.")

Juice of $1/2$ lime or lemon

2 teaspoons fresh dill leaves

$1/2$–1 teaspoon salt

$1/4$–$1/2$ teaspoon freshly ground pepper

4 cups buttermilk or plain, low-fat yogurt

GARNISH

Small sprigs of fresh dill

1. Thinly slice into rounds the white part and 2 inches of the green part of each scallion.

2. Place the corn, scallions, lime or lemon juice, and dill in a food processor. Add salt and pepper to taste. Purée until smooth. Add 1 cup of the buttermilk or yogurt, and purée until well blended.

3. Transfer the mixture to a bowl, and add the remaining buttermilk. Cover and put into the refrigerator to chill for 2 hours. Serve in chilled soup cups, with a sprig of fresh dill for garnish.

Cooking Fresh Corn

Microwave Method: Place the corn kernels in a microwave baking dish, and add 1 to 2 tablespoons of water. Cover the dish, and place in the microwave on high. Cook for 1 to 2 minutes; stir and cook for an additional minute, or until the corn is tender.

Traditional Method: Place the corn in a medium-sized saucepan, and add $1/2$ to 1 cup of water. Cover the pan, and place over medium-high heat. Cook for 5 to 10 minutes, stirring frequently, until the kernels are tender.

ABOUT THE RESTAURANT

Owners Ned Shank and Crescent Dragonwagon offer charming hospitality, cheery smiles, and a gracious ambience at Dairy Hollow House.

From Bagel Works   PORTLAND, MAINE

Chilled Gazpacho Soup

This soup makes a great appetizer or a luncheon entrée.

1. Place all the ingredients in a large bowl. Stir to blend the herbs and spices. Cover the bowl with plastic wrap, place in the refrigerator, and chill deeply, about 1 hour.

2. Remove the soup from the refrigerator, and ladle into individual serving bowls. Garnish with sprigs of cilantro, and serve with a big bowl of tortilla chips, hot nachos, or warm quesadillas.

ABOUT THE RESTAURANT

Bagel Works maintains its socially active commitment to the Portland community by contributing to a variety of local organizations and supplying Trouble Street Soup Kitchen, the Child Abuse Council, and other groups with bagels.

Yield: 4 servings

Preparation Time: 20 minutes

5 large tomatoes, finely chopped

4 cups tomato juice

1 medium onion, finely chopped

2 medium cucumbers, peeled, seeded, and chopped

2 small green bell peppers, seeded and finely chopped

2 medium garlic cloves, minced

$\frac{1}{8}$ cup olive oil

$\frac{1}{8}$ cup wine vinegar

2 tablespoons lemon juice

2 teaspoons chopped fresh parsley

2 teaspoons sea salt

1 teaspoon black pepper

1 teaspoon chopped fresh basil leaves

1 teaspoon dried tarragon

1 teaspoon ground cumin

GARNISH

Sprigs of fresh cilantro (coriander)

Breads

Breads

From Dairy Hollow House Country Inn and Restaurant
EUREKA SPRINGS, ARKANSAS

Skillet-Sizzled Buttermilk Corn Bread

This celebrated corn bread lives up to its outstanding reputation. Vegans can enjoy this bread by omitting the egg, using 2 to 3 tablespoons of oil (enough to cover the bottom of the skillet), omitting the butter, and replacing the buttermilk with soy yogurt. Add 3 extra tablespoons soy yogurt when omitting the egg.

1. Preheat the oven to 375°F.

2. Place the cornmeal, flour, salt, baking soda, and baking powder in a small bowl, and stir to combine.

3. In a medium-sized bowl, place the egg (or egg replacer or yogurt), sugar to taste, oil, and buttermilk, and whisk together until all the ingredients are well blended.

4. Place an 8- or 9-inch cast-iron skillet over medium heat. Put the butter in the skillet, and allow it to melt and begin to bubble.

5. As the butter melts, quickly add the flour mixture to the buttermilk mixture, and stir together using only as many strokes as necessary to combine the ingredients.

6. Scrape the batter into the hot, buttery skillet. The batter should sizzle as it hits the butter. Remove the skillet from the stove, and immediately place it into the oven.

7. Bake about 25 minutes, or until golden brown. Serve warm, cut in wedges like a pie, with fresh butter.

ABOUT THE RESTAURANT

Crescent Dragonwagon has fed her classic corn bread to thousands of people over the years. Among them are a president, Bill Clinton; a princess, Princess Elizabeth of Yugoslavia; a feminist, Betty Friedan; several novelists, Bobbie Ann Mason and Lucian Truscott; a Hollywood biographer, Maurice Zolotow; a Grammy-winning gospel recording artist, Russ Taff; a celebrated singer-songwriter, Judy Collins; and a television personality, Joan Lunden.

Yield: 6 servings

Preparation Time: 15 minutes

Cooking Time: 25 minutes

1 cup stone-ground yellow cornmeal

1 cup unbleached white flour

1/4 teaspoon salt

1/4 teaspoon baking soda

1 tablespoon baking powder

1 egg (See "Alternatives to Eggs" on page 82.)

2–4 tablespoons sugar, to taste

1/4 cup corn or peanut oil

1 1/4 cups cultured buttermilk

1/4 cup butter or soy margarine

From Madison River Inn   THREE FORKS, MONTANA

Buttermilk & Tea Scones

Scones are a great breakfast treat or delightful accompaniment for soups and salads. This easy recipe yields a traditional scone with a rich, moist texture.

Yield: 4 servings

Preparation Time: 10 minutes

Cooking Time: 10–12 minutes for tea scones; 14–16 minutes for buttermilk scones

2 cups unbleached white flour

2 tablespoons sugar

2 teaspoons baking powder

$\frac{1}{2}$ teaspoon salt

$\frac{1}{4}$ cup butter

$\frac{2}{3}$ cup buttermilk for buttermilk scones or $\frac{2}{3}$ cup heavy cream for tea scones

1. Preheat the oven to 425°F.

2. In a large mixing bowl, sift together the flour, sugar, baking powder, and salt.

3. With a pastry cutter or your fingers, cut the butter into the flour mixture until it is in small bits and crumbly.

4. Gently stir in the buttermilk (for buttermilk scones) or the cream (for tea scones).

5. Turn the dough onto a lightly floured surface, and knead 4 or 5 times, until the dough is soft and smooth. Roll or pat the dough into a ½-inch-thick circle, and cut into 4 to 6 wedges.

6. Place the wedges on an ungreased baking sheet. Bake in the oven for 10 to 12 minutes for tea scones and 14 to 16 minutes for buttermilk scones. Serve with fresh butter and homemade preserves.

ABOUT THE RESTAURANT

Taking time for tea and scones is a perfect way to relax and enjoy the beautiful surroundings of the Madison River Inn.

From The Greatest Grains on Earth   DAVENPORT, IOWA

Spinach Scones

Spinach and feta cheese make a great combination in these hearty scones, which make a tasty accompaniment for soups or salads. If you use frozen spinach, thaw, squeeze out the water, and pat dry before chopping.

1. Preheat the oven to 375°F. Lightly butter a round 8-inch pan, and set aside.

2. Place the water and the spinach in a medium-sized saucepan, cover, and place over medium-high heat. Allow the spinach to steam for 2 to 3 minutes, checking to be sure the spinach does not overcook. When the spinach turns a bright, deep green and is tender but not wilted, it is cooked.

3. Drain the water from the pan, and remove the spinach from the pan with a slotted spoon. Pat dry with a paper towel.

4. Place the flour, baking powder, garlic powder, and cayenne pepper in a large bowl. Cut the butter into the flour mixture with a pastry cutter or your fingers until most of the pieces are the size of a pea.

5. In a medium-sized bowl, place the eggs, spinach, and cheese, and whisk together. Add the egg mixture to the dry ingredients, and stir until partially mixed. Turn the dough onto a lightly floured surface, and knead gently until the dough holds together, about 3 to 4 minutes.

6. Pat the dough into the buttered pan. The dough should be 1 1/2 to 2 inches thick. Place the pan on a baking sheet to keep the scones from getting too brown on the bottom. Cut the dough in the pan into 6 or 8 wedge slices.

7. Place the pan on the middle rack of the oven to bake for 20 to 25 minutes, until lightly browned.

8. Remove the scones from the oven. Place the pan on a wire rack, and allow the pan to cool for 1 minute on a wire rack before separating the wedges. Serve the scones warm just as they are or with fresh butter.

Yield: 6 servings

Preparation Time: 20 minutes

Cooking Time: 20–25 minutes

1/4 cup water

1 cup chopped spinach, fresh or frozen (See "Preparing Fresh Spinach" on page 29.)

2 1/2 cups whole wheat pastry or unbleached white flour

2 1/2 teaspoons baking powder

1/4 teaspoon garlic powder

1/8 teaspoon cayenne pepper, optional

1/4 cup cold butter

2 eggs, beaten (See "Alternatives to Eggs" on page 82.)

1/2 pound feta cheese, crumbled

ABOUT THE RESTAURANT

While strolling the aisles of The Greatest Grains food store or sitting in the deli restaurant, you might see Brooke Shields or Tommy Chong, for they both have eaten there. The Greatest Grains Catering Service has come to the rescue of such hungry stars as Melissa Etheridge and Bob Dylan.

From Bluebird Café   ATHENS, GEORGIA

Whole Wheat Buttermilk Biscuits

Mmmmm. A cozy, warm "good-morning-to-you" breakfast treat for the family, these biscuits are also delicious with soups and salads.

Yield: 12–16 biscuits

Preparation Time: 20 minutes

Cooking Time: 20–25 minutes

1^1/$_2$ cups whole wheat flour

1^1/$_2$ cups white flour

1 tablespoon baking powder

1 teaspoon baking soda

1 teaspoon salt

2 tablespoons sugar

1^1/$_2$ sticks (6 ounces) butter, softened

^{3}/$_4$ cup buttermilk

1. Preheat the oven to 350°F. Lightly flour a 13- by 9-inch baking pan or a large baking sheet.

2. In a large mixing bowl, sift together the flours, baking powder, baking soda, salt, and sugar. Using your hands or a pastry cutter, cut the softened butter into the flour mixture until the mixture turns crumbly.

3. Add the buttermilk slowly, stirring as you pour, until the dough reaches the consistency of either crumbled tofu or tunafish salad.

4. Turn the dough onto a lightly floured surface. Knead additional flour into the dough so that you can roll it out easily. Roll dough into a 1^1/$_2$-inch-thick circle.

5. Lightly flour the top surface of the dough, and cut the dough into biscuit shapes with a 2-inch biscuit cutter. (Use a larger cutter for larger biscuits.)

6. Place the biscuits on the floured pan, and bake until lightly browned, 20 to 25 minutes. Remove the biscuits from the pan, and serve hot with fresh butter, honey, or homemade jam.

ABOUT THE RESTAURANT

The Bluebird Café, although small in size, serves its customers generously in a casual, upbeat atmosphere.

Bagel Barn   BOZEMAN, MONTANA

Golden Honey Wheat Bagels

Ahhh . . . a fresh, warm bagel! As a variation, add 1 to 2 cups cut-up, dried cranberries, dried blueberries, or other dried fruit to the dough before you add the flour.

1. Place the water, salt, sugar, honey, and yeast in a large mixing bowl. Stir to blend well.

2. Add the flour, and mix with a large wooden spoon or a bread dough mixer for 12 minutes, until all the dough has been incorporated and the dough pulls away from the side of the bowl. You should be able to work the dough easily with your hands. Turn the dough onto a lightly floured surface, cover with a clean dish towel, and allow it to rest for 15 to 20 minutes.

3. Make the dough into bagel shapes. Roll the dough out flat, about 1 inch thick. Cut the dough into circles the size you want using a biscuit cutter or another suitable cutter. (A glass, cup, or small bowl works fine.) Cut out a hole in the center of each circle of dough to form the center of the bagel. (Again, a small glass or the center of a doughnut cutter works fine.)

4. Sprinkle the countertop with cornmeal. Place the bagels on the counter, cover with a clean dish towel, and set aside to rest for 30 to 45 minutes. The bagels will rise slightly.

5. Preheat the oven to 500°F.

6. To see if the bagel dough has risen sufficiently, place one of the bagels in a pot of cold water. If the bagel floats, the dough is ready.

7. Bring a large pot of water to boil on high heat. Carefully place 5 or 6 bagels, cornmeal side up, in the pot of boiling water. Make sure the water continues to boil. The bagels will float. Allow the bagels to cook for 30 seconds on just the one side. Then remove them from the water with a slotted spoon.

8. Place the bagels on a greased baking sheet, with the cornmeal side up. Place in the oven for 2 minutes. Flip the bagels over, and bake an additional 7 to 8 minutes, until they have reached the desired crispness.

9. Remove the baking sheet from the oven, and place the bagels on a wire rack or basket to cool. Serve with your favorite topping.

*If neither flour is available, start with 4 pounds regular white flour. Remove $3/4$ cup of the white flour, and add $3/4$ cup of gluten flour.

Yield: approximately 3 dozen bagels

Preparation Time: 1 hour; 1 hour resting time

Cooking Time: 10 minutes

1 quart plus scant $1/4$ cup warm water (110–120°F)

1 tablespoon salt

2 tablespoons sugar

$1/2$ cup honey

3 tablespoons fresh, dry yeast

4 pounds high-gluten wheat flour or finely ground whole wheat pastry flour*

ABOUT THE RESTAURANT

A lively spot for an early morning breakfast or lunch, the Bagel Barn in Bozeman serves a delicious variety of fresh bagels and bagel sandwich combinations all day long.

From Creative Vegetarian Café   BOULDER, COLORADO

Multigrain Blueberry Muffins

This hearty muffin makes for a nutritious breakfast on the run or lunch to go.

Yield: 1 dozen muffins

Preparation Time: 20 minutes

Cooking Time: 40 minutes

1 cup whole wheat pastry flour

1 cup unbleached white flour

1 cup wheat bran

1/2 cup uncooked millet

Pinch of sea salt

2 tablespoons baking powder

1/2 cup raw sunflower seeds
   (about 2 1/2 ounces)

1/4 cup sesame seeds (about
   1 1/4 ounces)

2 cups blueberries, frozen or
   fresh (about 8 ounces)

1/3 cup molasses

3/4 cup water

1/4 cup canola oil

1/2 cup maple syrup

4 dates, cut into julienne strips

1. Preheat the oven to 350°F. Lightly oil the muffin tins or line with paper liners. Set aside.

2. Place the flours, bran, millet, salt, baking powder, sunflower seeds, and sesame seeds in a large bowl. If you are using frozen blueberries, add them still frozen to the dry mixture. Use a wire whisk to blend the dry ingredients with the blueberries. Remove about 1 cup of the dry mixture, and set aside.

3. Make a large hole in the center of the bowl of dry ingredients. Add the molasses, water, oil, syrup, and dates. If you are using fresh blueberries, add them with the liquid ingredients.

4. Lightly mix the liquid and dry ingredients together until slightly moist, only 10 to 15 strokes. A light touch is extremely important.

5. Fill each muffin cup to the top with the batter. When they are all filled, top each muffin cup off with an additional 2 tablespoons of the reserved dry mixture. This creates a very tasty top crust.

6. Place the muffin pans on the middle rack of the oven. Bake for 40 minutes, until done and lightly browned. Serve hot from the oven. To store, place in an airtight container or wrap with plastic wrap and refrigerate or keep in a cool place for several days. The muffins freeze well, too.

ABOUT THE RESTAURANT

No refined or processed ingredients line the kitchen shelves of The Creative Vegetarian Café. Nor will you find a microwave on the premises. Ever since the café opened in 1989, originally as a Buddhist work-study project and now privately owned, Mike O'Brian, head chef and manager, and the rest of the staff have made everything from scratch to maintain the highest energetic integrity of the ingredients. Grand kudos for their efforts!

From Horn of the Moon Café MONTPELIER, VERMONT

Molasses Oat Muffins

These wonderful muffins are surprisingly light and ever so flavorful. They are the perfect companion for a fruit and yogurt breakfast or a soup and salad luncheon. If using eggs instead of the yogurt, use 2 eggs and reduce the milk by $1/4$ to $1/2$ cup.

1. Preheat the oven to 400°F. Oil or butter the muffin tins, or use paper liners.

2. Place the flours, oats, baking powder, salt, nutmeg, cinnamon, and ginger in a large mixing bowl, and mix together.

3. Place the oil, honey, molasses, yogurt (or eggs), and milk in a medium-sized bowl, and mix together.

4. Gently fold the flour mixture into the liquid mixture, and mix until just blended. Gently stir in the optional walnuts.

5. Fill the muffin cups two-thirds full, and place in the oven. Bake for 20 minutes, until a toothpick or tester inserted into the center of a muffin comes out clean.

ABOUT THE RESTAURANT

Before Gary Beardsworth started chopping, slicing, dicing, and creating tantalizing dishes at Horn of the Moon Café, he served as finance director for the City of Montpelier. When the café became available for purchase, Gary leaped at the opportunity to mix his business background with his true love for cooking and has never regretted his midlife career change.

Yield: *2 dozen muffins*

Preparation Time: 10 minutes

Cooking Time: 20 minutes

3 cups whole wheat pastry flour

1 cup unbleached white flour

$1/2$ cups rolled oats

4 teaspoons baking powder

1 teaspoon salt

1 teaspoon ground nutmeg

1 teaspoon ground cinnamon

2 teaspoons ground ginger

$3/4$ cup canola oil

$1/2$ cup honey

$1/2$ cup molasses

$1/4$ cup plain yogurt

2 cups milk, dairy or soy

1 cup chopped walnuts, optional

From Pineapples Natural Food Restaurant and Market
MIAMI BEACH, FLORIDA

Apple Bran Muffins

What delicious nutrition! These muffins are moist and flavorful. They make a great breakfast treat or mid-morning snack.

Yield: 2 dozen muffins

Preparation Time: 15 minutes

Cooking Time: 25 minutes

2 cups whole wheat flour

1 1/2 cups wheat bran

1/2 teaspoon salt

1 1/4 teaspoons baking soda

1/2 teaspoon ground cinnamon

2 cups peeled, chopped apples
  (about 2 apples)

1/2 cup raisins

2 tablespoons vegetable oil

1/2 cup orange juice

1 1/2 cups milk, soy or dairy

1/2 cup maple syrup

2 egg whites or egg replacer
  (See "Alternatives to Eggs.")

1. Preheat the oven to 350°F. Lightly grease the muffin pans, or use paper liners.

2. Place the flour, bran, salt, baking soda, and cinnamon in a large bowl, and mix. Stir in the apples and raisins.

3. Place the oil, juice, milk, syrup, and egg in a medium-sized bowl, and mix together.

4. Pour the liquid ingredients into the dry ingredients, and stir gently to blend well.

5. Pour 1/4 to 1/3 cup of the batter into each of the greased or lined muffin cups. Place in the oven to bake for 25 minutes. Remove the muffins from the oven and serve warm. These muffins will keep well for 2 to 3 days when stored in an airtight container.

Alternatives to Eggs

Here are a few suggestions for people who wish to eliminate whole eggs from their diets. Experimenting with these various types of egg replacements will help you to determine the method that suits your culinary preferences.

A variety of egg replacers are now available in most grocery and natural food markets. Some egg replacers are liquid and contain portions of egg white. This type of egg replacer is most commonly found in the dairy refrigerator section of grocery stores. Use these according to package directions as substitutes for eggs.

Another type of egg replacer is a brand name called Ener-G Egg Replacer, from Ener-G Foods of Seattle, Washington. The egg replacer is in powdered form, contains no egg products, and is found most often in natural food stores. I have tasted amazingly good flans and meringues, as well as cookies, cakes, pancakes, and waffles, made with this product.

Another egg substitute method that is effective in recipes is to replace each egg with 1 to 2 tablespoons of plain or vanilla yogurt blended with 1 ounce of tofu. Ground cashews are also known to work well in certain recipes that call for eggs as a thickening agent.

ABOUT THE RESTAURANT

Located on 41st Street in Miami Beach, Pineapples Natural Food Restaurant and Market offers gourmet vegetarian and natural foods.

From Delites of India   MINNEAPOLIS, MINNESOTA

Delites of India Puris

Puris are a deep-fried, organic, whole wheat bread from India and a traditional accompaniment to Indian dinners.

1. Sift the flour with the sea salt into a large mixing bowl.

2. Add 1 teaspoon of the oil, and rub it into the flour with your fingers.

3. Add the water, and mix. Knead the dough in the bowl until you have a moderately stiff ball.

4. Cover the dough with a clean towel, and let it sit for 20 to 30 minutes.

5. Turn the dough onto a lightly floured surface, and knead for 2 to 3 minutes.

6. Divide the dough into 12 small balls. Drizzle a little oil on each ball. Or you can spray a little Pam cooking spray on each ball.

7. With a rolling pin on a greased board, roll out one ball to a 5- or 6-inch circular puri. Roll out the remaining balls in the same way.

8. Pour the remaining 4 cups of oil into a large frying pan. Heat to hot, but not smoking, over medium-high to high heat.

9. Fry the puris one at a time. Place a puri in the hot oil, and fry until it turns almond brown in color. The puri should puff up like a hot air balloon.

10. Remove the bread from the hot oil with a slotted spoon, and place it on several thicknesses of paper towel to drain. Serve hot.

Yield: 4 – 6 servings

Preparation Time: 30 minutes

Cooking Time: 10 minutes

2 cups sifted organic whole wheat flour

1 teaspoon sea salt

4 cups plus 1 teaspoon canola oil

1/2 cup water

ABOUT THE RESTAURANT

The "delites" of Delites have found their way onto the tables of these VIPs: poet Robert Bly, flute master G.S. Sachdeva, Phil Collins, the Beach Boys, Mahesh Yogi Gandharva, and Saint Keshav Das.

From Madison River Inn   BOZEMAN, MONTANA

Homemade French Bread

This handy recipe is great to have in your recipe repertoire as it is easy to prepare, bakes quickly, and lends that delicious homemade taste to any entrée.

Yield: 2 loaves

Preparation Time: 20 minutes plus 1 1/2–2 hours optional rising time

Cooking Time: 30–35 minutes

2 cups warm water

1 1/2 tablespoons dry yeast

1 tablespoon sugar

4–6 cups unbleached white flour

1 tablespoon salt

1–2 tablespoons cornmeal

OPTIONAL EGG WHITE WASH

1 egg white

1 tablespoon water

1. Do *not* preheat the oven. In a large bowl, combine the water, yeast, and sugar, and stir just to blend. Proof the yeast by allowing it to sit for 5 minutes. The yeast should bubble up and rise.

2. Place 3 cups of the flour in a medium-sized bowl. Add the salt, and mix.

3. Add the flour to the yeast mixture, and stir. Add the remaining flour, 1 cup at a time, mixing to make a soft, pliable, and firm dough.

4. Turn the dough onto a lightly floured surface, and knead for 5 to 10 minutes. If you are in a hurry, you may omit the next step and go on to step 6.

5. Place the dough back in the bowl, cover with a towel, and let rise in a warm place for 1 1/2 to 2 hours, or until double in size. With your fist, punch down the risen dough in the middle. Place the dough on a lightly floured surface, and knead gently four or five times.

6. Divide the dough into two portions. Form each portion into a long loaf by rolling the dough with your hands.

7. Sprinkle a baking sheet with the cornmeal, and place the loaves on the baking sheet. Make three short diagonal slashes across the tops of the loaves with a knife.

8. Place the loves in the cold oven. Set the oven temperature to 400°F, and bake for 30 to 35 minutes. Remove the bread from the oven, and place on a wooden board. Slice and serve warm, or allow to cool and serve.

To Make the Optional Egg White Wash:

1. In a small bowl, whisk the egg white with the water until well blended. With a pastry brush, brush the top of each loaf with the mixture.

ABOUT THE RESTAURANT

Perched on the bluffs of the Madison River, the Madison River Inn offers breath-taking Montana-majestic views, gracious accommodations, and gourmet meals.

From The Body Guard   YANKTON, SOUTH DAKOTA

Cinnamon Apple Bran Bread

Soft, moist and flavorful, this bread is a great, "good for you" breakfast bread or a sweet and spicy accompaniment to soup or salad.

1. Preheat the oven to 350°F. Oil a 9- by 5- by 3-inch loaf pan, or if you are using a nonstick loaf pan, lightly oil the bottom of the pan.

2. Place the flour, bran, cinnamon, baking powder, and baking soda in a small mixing bowl. Stir well to blend.

3. Place the apple juice concentrate and sunflower seed oil in a medium-sized bowl, and stir. Add the egg whites, one at a time (or the egg replacer and yogurt), mixing well after each addition. Add the applesauce and apple, and mix well. Add the optional walnuts.

4. Gradually add the dry ingredients to the apple juice mixture, stirring well. Spoon the batter into the prepared loaf pan.

5. Place the pan on the middle rack of the oven. Bake for 45 to 50 minutes, or until a tester or wooden pick inserted near the center comes out clean.

6. Remove the pan from the oven, and place the pan on a wire rack to cool for 10 minutes. Run a knife around the inside edges of the pan to loosen the bread. Invert the loaf on the wire rack to completely cool.

7. Cut the loaf into slices. Serve just as is, or add a cream cheese spread of your choice. This bread keeps well when covered with plastic wrap or aluminum foil and stored in the refrigerator.

ABOUT THE RESTAURANT

The Body Guard offers expanded and complete lines of vitamins, minerals, herbs, and health foods in addition to its natural foods deli and bakery.

Yield: 1 loaf

Preparation Time: 20 minutes

Cooking Time: 45–50 minutes

1 cup whole wheat flour

1 cup unprocessed bran

1 tablespoon ground cinnamon

$1\frac{1}{2}$ teaspoons baking powder

$\frac{1}{4}$ teaspoon baking soda

$\frac{3}{8}$ cup undiluted apple juice concentrate

$\frac{1}{2}$ cup sunflower seed oil

4 egg whites (or equivalent egg replacer plus 4 tablespoons yogurt; for more information, see "Alternatives to Eggs" on page 82)

$\frac{1}{2}$ cup unsweetened applesauce

1 cup peeled, chopped apple (about 1 apple)

$\frac{1}{2}$ cup chopped walnuts

From Madison River Inn   BOZEMAN, MONTANA

Whole Wheat Banana Bread

This recipe is quick and easy to make and produces a beautiful, large loaf of moist, rich bread full of banana flavor. You'll find you'll want to make it over and over again!

Yield: 1 loaf

Preparation Time: 20 minutes

Cooking Time: 1 hour

1/2 cup butter, melted

1 cup sugar

1/4 cup firm tofu

3 tablespoons plain or vanilla yogurt, or cream cheese

3 medium bananas, mashed

1 cup unbleached white flour

1/2 teaspoon salt

1 teaspoon baking soda

1 cup whole wheat flour

1/3 cup hot water

1 cup chopped walnuts, optional

1. Preheat the oven to 325°F. Lightly grease and flour a large bread loaf pan.

2. Place the butter and sugar in a large mixing bowl, and stir. Place the tofu together with the yogurt or cream cheese in a blender or small bowl. Blend to a smooth consistency.

3. Add the tofu mixture to the butter and sugar, and blend well. Add the bananas, and stir.

4. Sift together the white flour, salt, and baking soda into a medium-sized bowl. Stir in the whole wheat flour.

5. Alternately add the dry ingredients and the water to the butter-banana mixture. Stir just enough to blend. Add the optional chopped nuts, and stir in lightly.

6. Pour the batter into the prepared loaf pan. Place the pan in the oven, and bake about 1 hour, or until a tester inserted into the center comes out clean.

7. Remove the pan from the oven, and place the pan on a wire rack to cool for 5 minutes. Run a knife along the inside edges of the pan to loosen the bread. Invert the pan onto the wire rack, and allow the bread to cool slightly before serving warm or cold. This bread is delicious just as it is or served with butter or cream cheese.

ABOUT THE RESTAURANT

An enchanting stay awaits you at the Madison River Inn.

From Madison River Inn   BOZEMAN, MONTANA

Zucchini Bread

Zucchini bread is always a great way to use the extra garden-fresh zucchini you may have at summer's end. This bread is quite moist, and it freezes well for later use through the nippy autumn and winter months. As a variation, try this recipe with 2 cups of cooked and puréed pumpkin in place of the zucchini and 1 cup of softened raisins in place of the chopped walnuts. The pumpkin bread is delicious by itself or served with cream cheese.

1. Preheat the oven to 350°F. Grease and flour two large bread loaf pans.

2. Place the tofu and yogurt (or cream cheese) in a blender or small bowl. Blend until smooth, and place into a large bowl. Add the oil, sugar, and vanilla, and blend together. Add the zucchini, and stir gently to combine.

3. Sift together the flour, salt, baking soda, baking powder, and spices into a medium-sized bowl. Adding small amounts at a time, fold the flour mixture into the zucchini mixture until all the flour is incorporated. Add the optional chopped nuts. Pour the batter into the prepared loaf pans.

4. Place in the oven to bake for 1 hour, or until a tester inserted into the center comes out clean. Remove the loaves from the oven, and place the pans on a wire rack to cool for 5 minutes. Run a knife along the inside edges of each pan to loosen the bread. Invert the loaves onto rack to cool.

5. Slice the bread. Serve warm or cold just as is or with butter or cream cheese. To store, wrap in plastic and refrigerate, or wrap in plastic and then in aluminum foil and freeze for up to three months.

ABOUT THE RESTAURANT

Sunlight shimmers off the water of the Madison River; magnificent deep blue and purple mountains loom in the distance; and sandhill cranes, egrets, American white pelicans, blue herons, and bald and golden eagles fly overhead at the beautiful Madison River Inn.

Yield: 2 large loaves

Preparation Time: 20 minutes

Cooking Time: 1 hour

1/4–1/3 cup firm tofu

3 tablespoons plain or vanilla yogurt, or cream cheese

1/2 cup vegetable oil

1 cup sugar

1 tablespoon vanilla

2 cups grated zucchini (about 2 medium zucchini)

3 cups unbleached white flour (or 1 1/2 cups white and 1 1/2 cups whole wheat flour)

1 teaspoon salt

1 teaspoon baking soda

1/4 teaspoon baking powder

1 teaspoon ground cinnamon

1 teaspoon ground ginger

1 teaspoon ground cloves

1 cup chopped walnuts, optional

From The Body Guard   YANKTON, SOUTH DAKOTA

High-Fiber Onion-Rye Buns

These tasty, toasted buns are a tantalizing combination of subtle onion and rye flavors.

Yield: *18 buns*

Preparation Time: 25 minutes;
$1^{1}/2$ hours rising time

Cooking Time: 12–15 minutes

1 cup skim milk

2 tablespoons undiluted apple
juice concentrate

1 tablespoon safflower oil

1 package active dry yeast

$1/2$ cup lukewarm water

3 cups unbleached white flour

4 tablespoons caraway seeds

1 teaspoon salt, optional

6 tablespoons minced onion

$1/2$ cup wheat germ

1–$1^{1}/4$ cups rye flour

OPTIONAL EGG
WHITE WASH

2 teaspoons water

2 egg whites

ABOUT THE RESTAURANT

The Body Guard makes all of its own soups, sandwiches, salads, and baked goods from scratch and specializes in baking for people with special health needs, including allergies.

1. Scald the milk in a medium-sized saucepan over medium-high heat by bringing it almost to boiling. Pour into a medium-sized mixing bowl, and add the apple juice concentrate and safflower oil. Stir well, and set aside to cool to lukewarm.

2. Dissolve the yeast in the warm water, and add to the milk mixture.

3. Add the white flour, and beat vigorously for 1 minute, or until the batter is very smooth. Add the caraway seeds, optional salt, onion, and wheat germ, and mix. Add enough rye flour to make a dough that is firm enough to knead.

4. Turn the dough onto a floured surface, and knead for 8 minutes. Set the dough aside.

5. Coat a clean mixing bowl with oil. Place the dough in the bowl. Turn the dough around so that it is coated on all sides with the oil. Cover the bowl with a clean towel. Let the dough rise in a warm place for 1 hour, or until it has doubled in size.

6. With your fist, punch down the dough in the middle, and turn onto a lightly floured surface. Roll the dough out with your hands into a long rope about $1^{1}/2$ inches thick. Cut into $1^{1}/2$-inch pieces. Shape the pieces into buns by rolling them into balls. Lightly oil one or two muffin tins, and place the buns in the oiled muffin tins. Cover with a clean towel, and allow to rise until doubled, about 20 to 30 minutes.

7. Turn the oven on and set to 400°F.

8. Place the buns in the oven to bake for 12 to 15 minutes, or until nicely browned. Serve hot from the oven with butter, or allow to cool and store in an airtight container.

To Make the Optional Egg Wash:

1. Combine the water and egg whites in a small bowl, and whisk to blend well. With a pastry brush, brush the tops of the buns with the mixture.

Entrées

Pastas

Veggies

Nut Loaves, Burgers
& Sandwiches

Mexican Dishes

Asian Dishes

Brunch Dishes

Pastas

From Artichoke Café ALBUQUERQUE, NEW MEXICO

Artichoke Hearts Provençal Over Pasta

A subtle mélange of fresh herbs, tomatoes, and artichokes, this dish evokes the feeling of a sunny late summer day in Provence. Quite nice!

1. Place the oil in a deep, large sauté pan, and heat over medium heat. Add the garlic, and sauté until soft. Add the artichoke hearts, capers, olives, and tomatoes. Cook until the tomatoes turn soft.

2. Add the wine, basil, and oregano. Allow the sauce to reduce by one-fourth by simmering over medium-high heat. Season with salt and pepper to taste.

3. Bring a large pot of salted water to the boil. Add the thin spaghetti and cook al dente (until done but not soft). Drain.

4. You may toss the spaghetti with the sauce in the pot, reserving a small amount of the sauce to add as garnish on top, or you may place the cooked spaghetti in a serving bowl and ladle the sauce on top. Serve immediately.

ABOUT THE RESTAURANT

Paintings and sculpture by local artists, light gray walls and classic navy blue furniture—all combine to make this saucy little bistro one of the most cosmopolitan cafés in downtown Albuquerque.

Yield: 4 servings

Preparation Time: 10 minutes

Cooking Time: 20 minutes

2 tablespoons olive oil

2 tablespoons minced garlic

2 (14-ounce) jars quartered artichoke hearts, drained

2 tablespoons capers

1/4 cup niçoise or black olives, chopped

2 cups peeled, seeded, chopped tomatoes (about 3 tomatoes)

1 cup white wine

3 tablespoons chopped fresh basil, or 1 tablespoon dried basil

2 tablespoons chopped fresh oregano, or 2 teaspoons dried oregano

Salt, to taste

Black pepper, to taste

1 1/2 pounds thin spaghetti

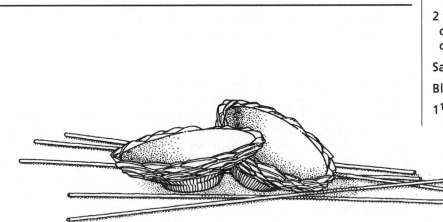

From Benvenuti   INDIANAPOLIS, INDIANA

Linguine with Tomato Pesto

Bravissimo! As this entrée demonstrates, simple ingredients often produce outstanding results.

Yield: 4 servings

Preparation Time: 15 minutes

Cooking Time: 15 minutes

1 pound linguine, fresh or dried

1/4 cup extra virgin olive oil

4 cloves garlic, minced

8 Roma (plum) tomatoes, skinned, seeded, and chopped

8 fresh basil leaves, chopped fine

Salt, to taste

Black pepper, to taste

1 cup toasted pine nuts, crushed (measured before toasting; see "Toasting Nuts and Seeds" on page 68.)

1/4 cup grated Parmesan cheese

GARNISH

Vegetable oil for frying the basil leaves

4 basil leaves

1/4 cup whole toasted pine nuts

ABOUT THE RESTAURANT

Chef Ian Harrison was originally employed as an apprentice at Benvenuti. He spent three months in Italy training at a Michelin Award-winning restaurant.

1. Bring a large pot of salted water to a boil over high heat. If you are using dried linguine, add the linguine, cover, reduce the heat to medium, and cook the pasta al dente (until done but not soft). If you are using fresh linguine, keep the pot of water at a simmer over medium-low heat.

2. Place the oil in a medium-sized sauté pan over medium-high heat. Add the minced garlic, and stir with a wooden spoon until the garlic begins to turn a soft golden color.

3. Add the tomatoes and basil, and season with salt and pepper to taste. Stir gently to blend with the garlic. Allow it to simmer for 2 to 3 minutes.

4. If you are using fresh linguine, bring the pot of salted water back to a boil over high heat and add the fresh linguine. Cook al dente. Drain.

5. Add the crushed pine nuts and Parmesan cheese to the tomato mixture, and stir to blend well. Allow to simmer and heat thoroughly for 2 to 3 minutes to develop the flavors, stirring frequently. Then remove from the heat.

To Make the Basil Leaf Garnish:

1. Place a small sauté pan over medium-high heat, and add enough vegetable oil to make 1 inch of oil in the pan. Heat until an edge of a basil leaf placed in the oil begins to sizzle. Or add enough vegetable oil to fill a deep fryer about 1 inch, and set to 375°F. When the oil is ready, using wooden tongs or a wooden slotted spoon, gently immerse the basil leaves in the hot oil. When they turn crispy, remove them from the oil and place on a paper towel to drain.

To Serve the Linguine:

1. You may serve the linguine in one of two ways. You can add the pasta to the tomato pesto in the sauté pan. Season with salt and pepper to taste, stirring to blend well. Turn the pasta into a serving bowl, garnish with whole pine nuts and the four fried basil leaves, and serve hot. Or you can twirl an individual serving of linguine around a roasting fork and place it in a shallow bowl. Spoon tomato pesto over the top of the linguine, and garnish with whole pine nuts and a fried basil leaf. Repeat for the remaining portions, and serve immediately.

From Sunshine Inn   ST. LOUIS, MISSOURI

Cajun Pasta

Who can resist the playful fusilli pasta? This is a dish your kids will love. The Cajun Spice Mix also adds a zing to veggies and a zip to omelettes.

1. Bring salted water to boil in a medium-sized saucepan. Add the fusilli and cook al dente (until done but not soft).

2. While the pasta is cooking, place the olive oil in a large sauté pan and heat. Add the onion and sauté until translucent. Add the zucchini, squash, mushrooms, and tomatoes. Cook until crisp-tender, about 2 minutes.

3. When the veggies are about done, add the Cajun Spice Mix and the milk. Stir well.

4. Drain the pasta. Add the cooked pasta and the Parmesan cheese to the sauté pan. Stir to mix well. Serve hot.

To Prepare the Cajun Spice Mix:

1. In a small bowl, combine all the ingredients. Whisk or stir with a fork to blend well. Pour into a glass jar, and store in a cool, dry place along with your other spices.

ABOUT THE RESTAURANT

Voted the Best Place to Eat Healthy in the "Riverfront Times" Readers' Poll, the Sunshine Inn on South Euclid Avenue serves tantalizing lunches, dinners, and Sunday brunches. Local artwork and warm, red brick walls with luscious green hanging plants beckon passerby to stop in for a delicious bite to eat. This is a restaurant you can return to again and again—good food, cozy atmosphere, and friendly staff.

Yield: 4 servings

Preparation Time: 15 minutes

Cooking Time: 15 minutes

1 cup tricolor fusilli (or other pasta)

1–2 tablespoons olive oil

$1/4$ medium white onion, sliced

$1/3$ medium zucchini, sliced in rounds (about 1 cup)

$1/3$ medium yellow squash, sliced in rounds (about 1 cup)

$1/3$ cup sliced mushrooms

$1/3$ cup chopped tomatoes

1–2 tablespoons grated Parmesan cheese

1 teaspoon Cajun Spice Mix

$1/2$ cup low-fat (2 percent) milk

CAJUN SPICE MIX

1 tablespoon dried basil

1 tablespoon dried oregano

$1/8$–$1/2$ teaspoon cayenne pepper, to taste

2 tablespoons granulated garlic

2 tablespoons granulated onion

1 teaspoon salt

1 teaspoon white pepper

1 teaspoon black pepper

3 tablespoons Spanish paprika

Tortelloni Verdi al Mascarpone
(Spinach and Cheese Tortelloni with Brown Butter Sauce)

E delizioso! Mangiamo! An absolutely exquisite and authentic Italian dinner! You can prepare the tortelloni ahead of time and freeze them so the final preparations only take a few minutes before serving.

Yield: 6 servings

Preparation Time: 45 minutes

Cooking Time: 10 minutes

SPINACH DOUGH

$3/4$ cup water

12 ounces fresh spinach (See "Preparing Fresh Spinach" on page 29.)

1 egg, optional

Pinch of salt

2 cups unbleached white flour

CHEESE FILLING

8 ounces mascarpone cheese (You may substitute 4 ounces cream cheese and 4 ounces ricotta cheese blended together for the mascarpone.)

2 egg yolks, optional

$1/4$ cup grated Parmesan cheese

$1/4$ cup plain bread crumbs (See "About Bread Crumbs" on page 23.)

Pinch of freshly ground nutmeg

Pinch of salt

Black pepper, to taste

To Make the Tortelloni:

1. Place the water in a large saucepan, and bring to a boil over high heat. Add the spinach, cover, and cook for 6 minutes. Drain the spinach, reserving the liquid. Place the spinach in the refrigerator until cool, about 10 minutes.

2. Place the cooled spinach in a blender or food processor. Purée the spinach for 15 to 30 seconds, until smooth, stopping the machine to add the optional egg, and the salt and flour. Turn the machine on again, and slowly add the reserved spinach liquid 1 tablespoon at a time until a ball forms, about 40 to 90 seconds. This process may also be done by hand by puréeing the spinach in a blender, adding the optional egg plus the salt and flour, mixing with a large wooden spoon, and adding the liquid little by little, stirring to make a dough.

3. Turn the dough into a bowl, cover with plastic wrap, and let rest in a cool place for 15 minutes.

4. While the dough is resting, combine all the filling ingredients together in a medium-sized bowl, adjusting the seasonings to taste. Set aside.

5. Unwrap the dough, and roll out onto a floured surface until the dough is about $1/8$ inch thick. A pasta machine works best for rolling out the dough.

6. Cut the rolled-out dough into 4-inch squares. You should have about two dozen squares.

7. Spoon about 1 teaspoon of filling in the middle of a square. Fold the dough to form a triangle, press with your fingers to seal the edges, and trim. Then overlap the corners and pinch together. (See the diagram.) Repeat for all the squares of dough.

8. Place the tortelloni on a plastic tray, cover with plastic wrap, and freeze until firm, about 20 minutes. (Tortelloni keep well in the freezer for one month.)

(a) *Place filling on dough*

(b) *Fold dough over and pinch edges*

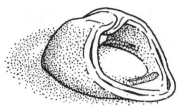
(c) *Overlap corners*

Forming a Tortelloni

9. Place water in a large pot, add salt to taste, and bring to a boil. Remove the tortelloni from the freezer. Drop a few tortelloni at a time into the boiling water. Cook for 10 minutes. Be careful not to cook too many tortelloni at the same time or they will become squashed. If you are cooking for a large party, divide the tortelloni into two or three pots of boiling water.

10. Remove the tortelloni from the boiling water with a slotted spoon. Drain and place on individual serving plates. Sprinkle with Parmesan cheese, and pour Brown Butter Sauce over the top. Serve immediately.

To Make the Brown Butter Sauce:

1. Place the butter, no more than $1/4$ cup at a time, with the sage leaves in a medium-sized sauté pan. Brown over medium-high heat until light brown. Watch carefully so that the butter does not burn.

BROWN BUTTER SAUCE

$1/4$ plus 2 tablespoons butter (*not* margarine)

6 fresh sage leaves

ABOUT THE RESTAURANT

In the early 1980s, when Franca Franchetti left Italy, she carried with her in her recipes a part of her beloved homeland. At Franca's Italian Dining, she offers Northern Italian cuisine, updating and changing her menus so she can continue to share a part of her heart's true love—Italy. Her husband Joseph, an artist whose work is based on western themes, has encouraged Franca and helped to make Franca's Italian Dining a reality.

From Marx Bros. Café   ANCHORAGE, ALASKA

Smoked Pepper Pasta
with Gorgonzola Sauce, Grilled Vegetables, & Bergamot Flowers

Flatter your palate with this exotic entrée. Your local food cooperative or natural food store may assist you in finding edible flowers for a lovely presentation. If making your own pasta is not your specialty, you will find a wide variety of wonderful pastas in the gourmet food sections of most grocery or natural food stores. You may use $1^1/2$ pounds of dried, packaged fettuccine in this recipe.

Yield: *4 servings*

Preparation Time: 15 minutes plus 45 minutes for the fettuccine

Cooking Time: 10 minutes plus 5 minutes for the fettuccine

MARX BROS. SMOKED PEPPER FETTUCCINE

2 red bell peppers

2 large eggs

1 egg yolk

1 tablespoon olive oil

4 cups flour

1 teaspoon sea salt

GORGONZOLA SAUCE

4 tablespoons sweet butter

3 tablespoons flour

$1/4$ cup dry white wine

3 cups heavy cream

$1/2$ cup Gorgonzola cheese

To Make the Fettuccine:

1. Smoke the peppers for 20 to 30 minutes in a smoker, following the manufacturer's directions. Remove the peppers from the smoker.

2. Preheat the broiler. Place the peppers on an ungreased baking sheet, and place under the broiler. Broil until the skin turns black, about 3 to 4 minutes. Rotate the peppers so that all sides broil evenly and blacken. Remove the baking sheet from the oven, and set aside to cool.

3. With a knife, slit an opening in each pepper and remove the seeds and stems. With a spoon, scoop out the soft pulp. Place in a blender or food processor, and purée for 15 to 20 seconds, or until smooth.

4. Add the eggs, egg yolk, and olive oil to the blender or processor, and blend until smooth.

5. Sift the flour and salt together onto a wooden board. Make a well in the center, and pour in the egg mixture.

6. Using a fork, incorporate the egg mixture into the flour and develop into a workable dough. Knead for 10 minutes until the dough is smooth and elastic. Cover with plastic wrap, and refrigerate the dough for 30 minutes to 1 hour.

7. Cut the pasta dough into approximately $3/4$-cup portions. Set the pasta machine to the widest setting, and pass one portion of the dough through the rollers. Fold the dough in half and repeat. Fold the dough in half again and pass through rollers again, making sure that the dough is as wide as the rollers.

8. Proceed in the same manner to roll out the dough through the thinner settings, stopping at the next-to-last setting (or whatever the fettuccine setting is on your machine).

9. Drape the sheet of dough over a pasta drying rack, and allow it to rest for several minutes. Place the dough on a lightly floured board, and with a sharp knife, cut the dough lengthwise into strips about $1/4$ inch in width. Cover the pasta with a clean towel until needed. Or to completely dry the fettuccini, drape the noodles over the drying rack and cover with a towel until they are completely dry. Then remove from the rack and wrap in plastic or place in an airtight container, and store in a cool, dry place.

To Make the Sauce:

1. Place the butter in a heavy saucepan, and melt over low heat. Whisk in the flour, and cook for 5 minutes, stirring constantly. Do not allow the mixture to brown.

2. Slowly add the wine and cream, stirring constantly, and bring to a boil over medium heat. Reduce the heat to low. Allow the sauce to simmer for 10 minutes, or until it thickens slightly.

3. Add the Gorgonzola cheese, and stir until the cheese is melted. Remove the pan from the heat, and set aside in a warm place.

To Make the Vegetables:

1. Heat a grill or broiler. Brush the vegetable slices with olive oil and arrange them on the grill. Brush the side facing up with more olive oil.

2. Grill for 3 or 4 minutes. Then turn the vegetables, and grill on the other side, basting again with olive oil.

To Assemble the Dish:

1. Place water in a large pot, and add salt. Bring to a boil, and add the fettuccine. Cook al dente (until done but not soft). If you are using packaged fettuccine, cook the pasta according to the package directions.

2. Drain and transfer the pasta to a large bowl. Pour the sauce over the pasta, and mix well to coat the noodles.

3. Divide the pasta onto four heated plates. Decoratively arrange the grilled vegetables around the plate and sprinkle with bergamot flowers. Serve immediately.

GRILLED VEGETABLES

2 Japanese eggplants, cut diagonally into $1/4$-inch slices

1 zucchini, cut diagonally into $1/4$-inch slices

1 yellow squash, cut diagonally into $1/4$-inch slices

2–4 portabella mushrooms, sliced

$1/4$ cup olive oil

GARNISH

$1/4$ cup bergamot (bee balm) flowers

ABOUT THE RESTAURANT

Jack Amon, executive chef at the Marx Bros. Café, first began to develop his culinary skills during his teenage years, spending many hours in the kitchen with his Greek grandfather, learning the basics of cooking and seasoning. Today, Chef Amon describes his cooking: "We try to be as creative as possible, but we don't want to startle palates just to be glitzy. I like to update and reinterpret." The cuisine is sophisticated, and the atmosphere is simple elegance. Graced with stained-glass windows and original Alaskan art, the Marx Bros. Café, established in October 1979, occupies one of the oldest houses in Anchorage.

From Jimmy D's   *COEUR D'ALENE, IDAHO*

Fettuccine Casanova

A sensational alternative to traditional fettuccine, this dish is quick and easy to prepare.

Yield: 4 servings

Preparation Time: 5 minutes

Cooking Time: 15 minutes

4 cups heavy cream

1/2 cup of your favorite prepared pesto

2 (14-ounce) jars artichoke hearts, drained and quartered

1/4 cup pine nuts

1 1/2 pounds fettuccine

1 tablespoon olive oil

1. Place the cream, pesto, artichoke hearts, and pine nuts in a medium-sized saucepan, and bring to a gentle boil over medium heat. Reduce the amount of liquid by one half, cooking for about 10 to 15 minutes.

2. While the sauce is cooking, bring a large pot of salted water to a boil over high heat. Add the fettuccine, and cook al dente (until done but not soft). Remove the pot from the heat, and drain the pasta. Return the pasta to the pan, drizzle the olive oil on the pasta, and stir to evenly coat the pasta with the oil. (This helps to keep the pasta from sticking together.) Cover the pot to keep the pasta warm until the sauce is ready.

3. When the cream sauce is reduced, add it to the pot of fettuccini. Stir well to evenly coat the fettuccini. Cook for an additional minute to heat thoroughly. Remove from the heat and serve immediately.

ABOUT THE RESTAURANT

Jimmy D's is located on Sherman Avenue in Coeur D'Alene. Owner Jim Duncan loves to feed a crowd, and he spends a great deal of time helping his staff serve the clientele with the greatest of care.

From A Moveable Feast   *HOUSTON, TEXAS*

Spinach & Basil Pesto Pasta

This dish has to be one of the easiest and tastiest of pasta dishes. It features great nutrition in gourmet fashion and will be especially attractive to vegan vegetarians. For an exciting variation, use this Spinach and Basil Pesto Sauce in a Florentine lasagna.

1. Bring a large pot of salted water to boil. Add the pasta, and cook al dente (until done but not soft) or according to package directions.

2. While the pasta is cooking, put the rest of the ingredients in a food processor, and blend until smooth.

3. Drain the pasta. Rinse in warm or cold water, if you desire.

4. You can combine the pasta and pesto together in a large mixing bowl and then transfer to a serving platter, or you can serve the pasta and pesto in separate serving dishes. Serve hot with your favorite salad and bread sticks.

ABOUT THE RESTAURANT

Owners John and Suzanne Fain began A Moveable Feast in a 900-square-foot space in 1971, selling natural food products, cosmetics, and vitamins. As the community's consciousness grew to a higher understanding of the importance and value of a vegetarian lifestyle, so did the size of the store. Today, the Fains maintain their commitment to provide resources for a healthy lifestyle to their large and loyal clientele in a 7,500-square-foot store.

Miso is a thick brown paste made by fermenting soybeans, rice, or barley under pressure. It may be light or dark. The lighter the color, the more delicate the flavor. Miso is found in most natural food stores.

Yield: *6 servings*

Preparation Time: 10 minutes

Cooking Time: 10 minutes

2 pounds of your favorite pasta

4 cups fresh spinach, firmly packed (See "Preparing Fresh Spinach" on page 29.)

2 cups fresh basil, firmly packed

1 pound firm tofu, rinsed and squeezed dry

1 cup pine nuts

1 cup olive oil

1 tablespoon miso*

2 cloves garlic, minced

California Pizza

This gourmet pizza is an absolutely heavenly pizza experience! The blend of ingredients is amazingly good, and the presentation is well suited to a special party. Six ounces of prepared pizza dough may be used if you don't want to make your own crust.

Yield: 6–8 servings per 16-inch pizza

Preparation Time: 1 hour 45 minutes

Cooking Time: 6–8 minutes

THE PIZZA KITCHEN DeBURGO BUTTER

³/₄ cup soft margarine

³/₄ tablespoon minced garlic

10 fresh, large basil leaves, chopped, or ³/₄ tablespoon dried basil

¹/₄ cup fresh chopped parsley

PIZZA CRUST

1 cup water at 115°F (slightly warmer than lukewarm to the touch)

³/₄ tablespoon yeast

1¹/₂ tablespoons sugar

3 cups unbleached white flour

1¹/₂ tablespoons vegetable oil

1 teaspoon salt

PIZZA TOPPINGS

¹/₄ cup DeBurgo butter

To Make the DeBurgo Butter:

1. Place all the ingredients in a food processor, and process until well mixed. Use right away for the pizza, or place in a covered container and store in the refrigerator for later use.

To Make the Crust:

1. With a wire whisk, mix the water and yeast in a large mixing bowl. Add the sugar and 1 cup of the flour. Stir to mix well. Allow to rise for 15 to 20 minutes.

2. Add the oil and salt, and stir well to blend. Then add the remaining 2 cups of flour, a cup at a time, stirring until the dough reaches a soft consistency. The dough should not be sticky, and it should not stick to the sides of the pan.

3. Return the dough to the mixing bowl, cover with a light, clean towel, and allow the dough to rise in a warm place for another 15 to 20 minutes.

4. Roll the dough out with a rolling pin on a lightly floured surface, or shape it with your hands. Then toss it up, as in a pizzeria, twirling it in the air to stretch it, or roll out the dough with a rolling pin to stretch the pizza to the size of the pizza pan. The dough shoud be about 16 inches in diameter.

To Assemble and Bake the Pizza:

1. Preheat the oven to 550°F. Lightly oil a 16-inch pizza pan and set aside. If you are using a stone oven, lightly flour the bottom of the pizza dough so it will slide easily into the oven. If you are using a pizza stone, lightly sprinkle cornmeal on the stone.

2. Place the rolled-out pizza dough on the pizza pan. If you have too much dough, form a large rim around the edge of the pizza—it's a great-tasting baked crust!

3. Spread the DeBurgo butter evenly over the surface to within ¹/₄ inch of the edge of the dough.

4. Sprinkle the toppings over the butter in the following order: sundried tomatoes, black olives, Gouda cheese, mozzarella cheese, provolone cheese, and walnuts.

5. Place the pizza on the middle rack of the oven, and bake for 6 to 8 minutes. The cheeses should brown slightly, and the crust should turn a golden brown. Remove the pizza from the oven. Slice into wedges and serve immediately.

1 cup sundried tomatoes*

1/2 cup sliced black olives

1 cup grated smoked Gouda cheese

2 cups grated mozzarella cheese

2 cups grated provolone cheese

1/2 cup chopped walnuts

ABOUT THE RESTAURANT

Located near Iowa State University, The Pizza Kitchen serves unique and tasty gourmet pizzas and pasta dishes.

*If the sundried tomatoes are not packed in oil, you will need to soften them by placing them in a medium-sized bowl of hot water and soaking for about 30 minutes. You can speed up this process by placing the tomatoes in a small saucepan, covering them with water, and bringing the water to a low boil over medium heat. Simmer for 15 minutes, or until the tomatoes are soft.

From Slice of Life Restaurant   *NASHVILLE, TENNESSEE*

Slice of Life Lasagna

This interesting dish is a wonderful blend of seasonings, veggies, and cheeses. It freezes well.

Yield: 8 servings

Preparation Time: 30–40 minutes

Cooking Time: 30–45 minutes

12 lasagna noodles

1 tablespoon vegetable oil

TOMATO SAUCE

2–3 tablespoons olive oil

1 medium onion, chopped

1 tablespoon minced garlic

1 green bell pepper, chopped

1 cup burgundy wine

1/4 cup tamari soy sauce (See "About Soy Sauce" on page 13.)

1/4 cup water

1 (15-ounce) can whole tomatoes

1 (15-ounce) can tomato sauce

1 (3-ounce) can tomato paste

1 teaspoon dried basil

1 teaspoon coarsely ground black pepper

2 teaspoons dried oregano

1 teaspoon dried thyme

SPINACH-TOFU FILLING

1 pound fresh or frozen spinach, well drained and chopped (See "Preparing Fresh Spinach" on page 29.)

To Cook the Lasagna:

1. Bring a large pot of salted water to boil over high heat. Add the lasagna noodles and the oil, and cook al dente (until done but not soft) or according to package directions. Remove the pot from the heat, and drain the noodles. Set aside and allow the noodles to cool slightly.

To Make the Sauce:

1. Place the oil in a heavy-bottomed pot over medium heat. Add the onion and garlic, and sauté until the onion is translucent, about 5 minutes.

2. Add the green pepper, wine, soy sauce, and water. Cover and let simmer, stirring occasionally, for 10 minutes. Remove the pan from the heat, and set aside to cool.

3. In a large mixing bowl, place the whole tomatoes, tomato sauce, tomato paste, basil, black pepper, oregano, and thyme. Stir to combine. Add the onion mixture to the tomato mixture, and blend well.

To Make the Spinach-Tofu Filling:

1. Place all the filling ingredients in a large mixing bowl, and stir well to blend all the seasonings and achieve a coarse consistency.

To Make the Cheese Mixture:

1. Place the cottage cheese and Parmesan cheese in a medium-sized mixing bowl. Add Spike to taste. Blend well.

To Assemble and Bake the Lasagna:

1. Preheat the oven to 350°F.

2. Place about 1/2 cup of tomato sauce in a 13- by 9-inch, deep-dish lasagna pan. Spread evenly to cover the bottom of the pan. Place one layer of cooked lasagna noodles on top of the tomato sauce. Follow it with another layer of tomato sauce. Then spread with a layer of the spinach-tofu filling. Finally, end with a layer of cheese mixture.

3. Repeat the layers of noodles, sauce, spinach-tofu, and cheese two or three times. Finish the lasagna with a layer of tomato sauce on top of the noodles. Top with the grated mozzarella cheese. (Unbaked lasagna can be frozen at this point; thaw before cooking.)

4. Place in the oven, uncovered, and bake for 30 to 45 minutes, until the lasagna is heated thoroughly, the sauce is bubbly, and the cheese is golden brown on top.

5. Remove the pan from the oven, and allow the lasagna to rest for 10 minutes before serving.

ABOUT THE RESTAURANT

One of Nashville's most highly respected natural foods restaurants, Slice of Life caters weekly to over three thousand musicians, producers, and health-conscious diners who return week after week to enjoy really great food. The light, sun-filled dining room reflects the hues and tints of stained glass displayed by local artists. You experience a slice of the good life with the polished wood floors, the fresh flowers, and the high energy put into preparing and serving the food. Sunday brunch is an event not to be missed at the Slice of Life Restaurant.

*Packaged and labeled this way in most grocery stores, *Italian seasoning* includes marjoram, thyme, rosemary, savory, sage, basil, and oregano as its main ingredients.

1 pound firm tofu, drained, squeezed, and mashed

1 teaspoon ground oregano

1 teaspoon dried thyme

1 teaspoon Italian seasoning*

1 teaspoon ground fennel

1/2 teaspoon celery seed

1/2 teaspoon ground cumin

1 teaspoon dried basil

1/2 teaspoon black pepper

1 tablespoon tamari soy sauce

1–2 cloves garlic, minced

CHEESE MIXTURE

2 cups cottage cheese

1/2 cup grated Parmesan cheese

1/2–1 tablespoon Spike, or to taste (See "About Spike" on page 52.)

TOPPING

2 cups grated mozzarella cheese

Everybody's Vegetable & Tofu Lasagna

This dairy-free lasagna blends tofu with herbs and spices to create a tantalizing pasta dish.

Yield: *8 servings, including 5 cups of sauce*

Preparation Time: 20 minutes for the sauce; 45 minutes to assemble

Cooking Time: 1 1/2 hours for the sauce; 45 minutes to bake

ITALIAN TOMATO SAUCE

2–3 tablespoons olive oil

2 cups chopped onion (2 onions)

3 cloves garlic, minced

6 cups crushed tomatoes (2 cans, 1 pound 12 ounces each)

1 bay leaf

2 teaspoons dried basil

2 teaspoons dried oregano

1 teaspoon salt

1 tablespoon honey

1/2 teaspoon black pepper

1 teaspoon dried thyme

TOFU FILLING

2 pounds firm tofu, rinsed and squeezed dry

1/3 cup lemon juice (juice of about 1 1/2 medium-large lemons)

1 teaspoon granulated garlic

2 teaspoons dried oregano

2 teaspoons dried basil

To Make the Sauce:

1. Place the oil in a large sauté pan, and heat over medium-high heat. Add the onion and garlic. Sauté until the onion is translucent, stirring often.

2. Add the crushed tomatoes, bay leaf, basil, oregano, salt, honey, black pepper, and thyme. Simmer uncovered about 1 1/2 hours, stirring occasionally, adding water if the sauce begins to thicken too much. Taste the sauce after 1 hour to adjust the seasonings.

3. Remove the pan from the heat. Use immediately, or allow to cool and then store in a covered container in the refrigerator for up to three days.

To Make the Tofu Filling:

1. In a food processor or blender, place all of the ingredients, and blend until smooth and creamy.

To Assemble and Bake the Lasagna:

1. Preheat the oven to 350°F.

2. Cook the lasagna noodles al dente (until done but not soft) or according to the package directions. Drain.

3. While the noodles are cooking, place the broccoli and spinach together in a large steamer. Steam over medium-high heat until crisp-tender. Remove from the heat.

4. Place about 1 cup of the sauce in a 9- by 13-inch baking pan, and spread to cover the bottom of the pan sparingly. Cover the sauce with a layer of the lasagna noodles. Spread one-third of the tofu filling on the noodles, and add a thin layer of sauce on top of the tofu filling layer. Spread one-half of the chopped vegetables on top of the sauce.

5. Repeat with another layer of noodles, tofu filling, sauce, and vegetables. Add a layer of noodles, tofu filling, and sauce, and top it off with a final layer of noodles and sauce. Top the sauce with the grated mozzarella or soy cheese.

6. Bake, uncovered, for 45 minutes, or until the lasagna is heated thoroughly and the cheese is bubbly and golden. It may be necessary to place the lasagna under the broiler for a minute or two to slightly brown the cheese. Serve hot with your favorite loaf of French bread and a green salad.

ABOUT THE RESTAURANT

"Hetty is a big part of what makes Everybody's so nice. She does things like making workers and customers step out onto the back patio on summer evenings to watch the miracle of fragrant moonflowers popping open. She gives good advice but never preaches. She's a great dart player, and she's fun to work for. On top of all that, Hetty might just be the best cook in town. She can make a burrito sing." Jenny Williams, former employee at Everybody's, talks about Hetty Carriero, owner of Everybody's.

2 teaspoons salt

2 tablespoons honey

LASAGNA ASSEMBLY

12 lasagna noodles, white or whole wheat

1 pound fresh broccoli, finely chopped

$\frac{1}{2}$ pound fresh spinach, finely chopped (See "Preparing Fresh Spinach" on page 29.)

5 cups Everybody's Italian Tomato Sauce

2 cups grated mozzarella or soy cheese

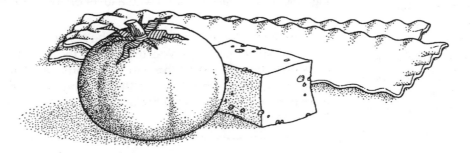

From El Sombrero   DOVER, DELAWARE

Vegetarian Lasagna

To add a bit of variety and spice to your lasagna life, try this rich and creamy recipe.

Yield: 8 servings

Preparation Time: 1 hour

Cooking Time: 1 hour

12–18 lasagna noodles, white
   or whole wheat

TOMATO SAUCE
1 (8-ounce) can tomato paste
1 (28-ounce) can tomato purée
1 teaspoon salt
2 teaspoons minced garlic
2 teaspoons dried oregano
1 teaspoon sugar
2 teaspoons dried basil
1 teaspoon dried thyme

VEGETABLES
1/4 cup margarine
1 cup peeled, shredded carrots
1 cup chopped broccoli
1 cup chopped zucchini
1 cup chopped fresh spinach

CHEESE MIXTURE
3 beaten eggs, optional
1 cup cottage cheese
1 cup ricotta cheese
1 cup grated mozzarella cheese
1/4 cup grated Parmesan cheese
1 tablespoon dried parsley or
   1/4 cup chopped fresh parsley

TOPPING
1 cup shredded Monterey jack
   cheese
1 cup shredded mozzarella
   cheese

To Make the Tomato Sauce:

1. Place all the ingredients in a medium-sized saucepan, mix, and simmer on low heat for 20 minutes.

To Prepare the Vegetables:

1. Place the margarine in a large sauté pan, and melt over medium heat. Add the vegetables. Sauté until crisp-tender, about 5 to 10 minutes. Remove the pan from the heat, and set aside.

To Make the Cheese Mixture:

1. Place the optional beaten eggs, all the cheeses, and the parsley in a bowl. Stir to blend well. Set aside.

To Assemble the Lasagna:

1. Preheat the oven to 350°F.

2. Bring salted water to a boil in a large pot, and cook the lasagna noodles al dente (until done but not soft). Rinse.

3. Spread about 1 cup of the tomato sauce on the bottom of a large lasagna pan or a 13- by 9- by 2-inch pan. Place one layer of noodles on top of the sauce, and spread a little tomato sauce on top of the noodles. Follow with a layer of the cheese mixture and then a layer of vegetables.

4. Repeat this layering of noodles, tomato sauce, cheese, and vegetables one or two more times, depending on the amount of ingredients you have left. End with a layer of noodles and tomato sauce on top.

5. To make the topping, mix together the Monterey jack and mozzarella cheeses. Generously sprinkle the top of the tomato sauce with the shredded cheeses. Cover the pan with aluminum foil, and bake for 1 hour. After 30 minutes, remove the foil and allow the top bake to a golden brown. Remove from the oven, and allow to rest for 10 minutes before serving.

ABOUT THE RESTAURANT

For a restaurant named El Sombrero, this place has a variety of international cuisines. Owner Kamlesh Sheth's menu includes many excellent, eclectic entrées.

Veggies

Sundried Tomato Polenta

Sundried tomatoes and polenta, a northern Italian cornmeal staple, come together as an extraordinarily good blend in this recipe.

1. Lightly oil two 9-inch pie pans.

2. Place the oil in a large sauté pan, and heat over medium heat. Add the onion and green pepper. Sauté until the onion is translucent, about 5 minutes.

3. While the onion is cooking, in a separate bowl, place the polenta and 3 cups of the water. Soak for 10 minutes.

4. Add the remaining 6 cups of water to the cooking onions and green peppers. Add the sundried tomatoes, garlic, and salt, and bring to a boil. Add the softened polenta or cornmeal, and cook over medium heat until creamy, stirring constantly and watching carefully as it may splatter. Continue to cook until thick, about 15 to 30 minutes.

5. Pour the polenta into the prepared pie pans. Cool for at least 2 hours to allow the polenta to become firm.

6. To serve, reheat the polenta for 10 minutes in a 350°F oven. Then slice and serve. The polenta is excellent served warm and is especially delicious served cold on warm summer days with a fresh green salad.

Yield: 8 servings

Preparation Time: 25 minutes

Cooking Time: 15–20 minutes

2 tablespoons olive oil

1 large yellow onion, finely chopped

$\frac{1}{2}$ green bell pepper, finely chopped

3 cups polenta or yellow cornmeal

9 cups water

$\frac{1}{2}$ cup chopped sundried tomatoes (packed in oil)

1 tablespoon chopped garlic

1 tablespoon salt

ABOUT THE RESTAURANT

Coeur d'Alene is a lovely summer and winter vacation destination, and a dining experience at Jimmy D's would put the finishing touch on your days of play!

From Extra Sensory   PROVIDENCE, RHODE ISLAND

Vegetarian Shepherd's Pie

A very hearty and satisfying one-dish meal, this recipe makes a large quantity and is excellent reheated the next day. I recommend serving this dish with Golden Gravy (page 143).

Yield: 8 servings

Preparation Time: 45 minutes

Cooking Time: 30–40 minutes

2 tablespoons extra virgin olive oil

2 cups finely chopped leeks, white parts only (See "Cleaning Leeks" on page 39.)

2 tablespoons minced fresh garlic

2 tablespoons fresh thyme or 2 teaspoons dried thyme

3 cups gluten (see page 196)

$4^1/4$ cups water

$^3/4$ cup bulgur*

Soy sauce to taste

Freshly ground black pepper

$1^1/2$ cups small broccoli florets

$1^1/2$ cups small cauliflower florets

1 cup peeled, chopped carrot

12 ounces soft tofu, drained and rinsed

1 tablespoon lemon juice

1 cup fresh corn or frozen corn, thawed

1 cup fresh peas or frozen peas, thawed

3 cups potatoes, peeled and cut into small cubes (about $1^1/2$ pounds)

To Make the Bottom Layer:

1. Place the oil in a large sauté pan, and heat over medium-high heat. Add the leeks, and sauté for 5 minutes. Add the garlic and thyme, and sauté for 1 minute more. Set aside.

2. Place the gluten in a food processor, and grind until very fine. Or chop with a knife until very fine. Set aside.

3. Place $1^1/2$ cups of the water in a pan, and bring to a boil. Put the bulgur into the boiling water, remove from the heat, and allow the bulgur to absorb the water, about 15 minutes.

4. In a large mixing bowl, place the leek mixture, gluten, and bulgur. Season with soy sauce and pepper to taste, and combine ingredients. Stir to blend well.

To Make the Middle Layer:

1. Bring water to a boil in a large pot. Cook the broccoli, cauliflower, and carrots until crisp-tender by immersing them in the boiling water for 3 to 5 minutes. Pierce with a fork to check for doneness. Drain and set aside.

2. In a blender or food processor, blend the tofu, $1^1/2$ cups of the water, and the lemon juice for 45 seconds. Set aside.

To Make the Top Layer:

1. Place the potatoes in a pot, and cover with water. Cook over medium-high heat until tender, about 20 minutes. Drain.

2. In a medium-sized saucepan, place the millet and the remaining $1^1/4$ cups of water. Bring to a boil over medium-high heat. Reduce the heat to low, and allow the mixture to simmer for 20 minutes, until done. The millet will be soft and fluffy.

3. Add the millet to the potatoes. Coarsely mash, adding dairy or soy milk to moisten. Season with salt and pepper, and add the optional butter for additional flavor.

**Bulgur wheat* is a popular Middle Eastern wheat that has been cracked by boiling, and then redried. It's available in natural food stores.

To Assemble the Pie:

1. Preheat the oven to 350°F. Lightly oil a 3- or 4-quart casserole pan.

2. Place the bottom layer of seitan, leeks, and bulgur in the pan, and spread to make an even layer. Create the middle layer by adding the vegetables, spreading them evenly, and pouring in the tofu mixture. Top with the final layer of mashed potatoes.

3. Sprinkle with the paprika, and cover with aluminum foil. Place the covered casserole in the oven for 20 to 30 minutes to warm thoroughly. Then remove the foil and bake until the top is lightly browned, about 10 minutes. Remove the casserole from the oven, and serve hot with additional soy sauce, your favorite gravy, or just as it is.

$^1/_2$ cup millet

$^3/_4$ cup dairy or soy milk

Salt, to taste

Butter, optional

Sprinkle of paprika

ABOUT THE RESTAURANT

The warmth from a wood-burning oven, the aroma of fresh-baked goods, and a display of local artwork greet you in the casual atmosphere of Extra Sensory.

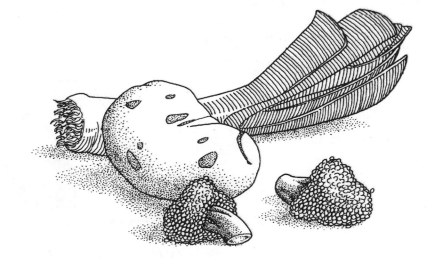

From Green Earth Café   BISMARCK, NORTH DAKOTA

Veggie Crescent

A yum-fun Saturday night dinner! The whole family will enjoy making and eating it together. If you want a softer dough, use only white flour. If you want a tougher but more flavorful dough, go with the white and whole wheat flour mixture. And the Mock Hollandaise Sauce has a much lower fat content then most hollandaise sauces. What a bonus!

Yield: 2–4 servings, including 1 1/2–2 cups of sauce

Preparation Time: 1 hour to prepare the dough and let rise; 20 minutes to prepare the veggie filling; 5–10 minutes for the sauce

Cooking Time: 30 minutes; 3–5 minutes for the sauce

CRESCENT

1/2 cup warm water

1 tablespoon yeast

1 tablespoon salt

1 1/2 cups unbleached white flour or 3/4 cup whole wheat and 3/4 cup white flour

2 tablespoons olive oil

3/4 cup chopped onion

To Make the Crescent:

1. Place the water in a medium-sized bowl. Add the yeast and allow it dissolve in the water. Add the salt, and add the flour a little at a time to form a soft dough.

2. Turn the dough onto a floured surface, and knead for 10 minutes. Return the dough to the bowl, cover with a clean towel, and allow to rise for 1 hour.

3. Preheat the oven to 350°F. Lightly brush a baking sheet with oil.

4. While the dough is rising, place the olive oil in a large sauté pan over medium-high heat. Add the onion and garlic, and sauté until the onion is translucent.

5. Add the chopped veggies, basil, oregano, and thyme or tarragon to the pan. Season with salt and pepper to taste. Sauté until crisp-tender, about 10 minutes. Turn the veggies into a colander to drain. Set aside.

6. With your fist, punch down the dough in the middle. Roll into a rectangle about 1/2 inch thick.

7. Sprinkle the cheese on the lower half of the dough, along the long side of the rectangle. Top the cheese with the sautéed veggies,

Forming the Crescent

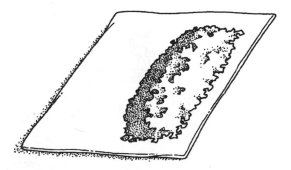

(a) Place filling on dough

spreading to about 1 inch from the edge of the dough. Fold the top half of the dough over the veggies, and press the edges together to seal the dough (see the diagram). Slice the top of the dough in the center diagonally to make four openings. Curve the ends of the dough inward to make a crescent shape.

8. Place the crescent carefully on the baking sheet, and bake for 30 minutes, or until golden brown.

To Make the Sauce:

1. In a medium-sized sauté pan, combine the mayonnaise and butter, stirring to melt together gently over medium heat.

2. Add lemon juice to taste.

3. Remove from the heat as soon as the sauce is warm and well blended, taking care that it does not become too hot. (The sauce will separate if it becomes too hot.)

To Serve the Crescent:

1. Slice the crescent into $1/2$-inch slices. Ladle some sauce over each serving, top with a sprig of parsley, and serve warm.

ABOUT THE RESTAURANT

The Green Earth Café was started as part of the One World Coffee House—a meeting place for the North Dakota Peace Coalition. "The simple things in life, like good food, friendship, music, and peace, are the important issues. We also believe, and act upon, the idea that businesses have social responsibility, a social contract with the community and the world. Most of all, we are a bunch of people who love good food and have fun providing this service to others," states owner Gary Dire.

3 or 4 large cloves garlic, minced

4–5 cups assorted veggies, such as broccoli, cauliflower, carrots, mushrooms, bell green peppers, finely chopped

1 teaspoon dried basil

1 teaspoon dried oregano

1 teaspoon dried thyme or dried tarragon

Salt, to taste

Black pepper, to taste

$3/4$ cup grated cheddar cheese

MOCK HOLLANDAISE SAUCE
(From the Madison River Inn)

1 cup mayonnaise, regular, tofu, or eggless (See "Alternatives to Regular Mayonnaise" on page 8.)

1 cup butter

Lemon juice, starting with 1 tablespoon

GARNISH

Parsley sprigs

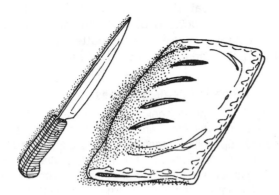

(b) Fold dough, pinch edges, make cuts with knife

(c) Form crescent

From Cornucopia Restaurant   LAWRENCE, KANSAS

Spinach Crêpes

These spinach crêpes are simply wonderful. If you have any extra batter, make additional crêpes and fill them with jam and butter, cinnamon sugar, or honey for a dessert that your kids will love! (To prepare this recipe without eggs, see "Preparing Eggless Crêpes.") If only frozen spinach is available, be sure to thaw, squeeze firmly to remove all excess water, and pat dry before use.

Yield: 6 servings (12–16 crêpes)

Preparation Time: 20 minutes for filling; 10 minutes for crêpes

Cooking Time: 12–16 minutes

FILLING

$1/2$ cup margarine

$1/2$ pound white mushrooms, sliced

1 large yellow onion, finely chopped

$1^1/2$ pounds chopped fresh spinach (See "Preparing Fresh Spinach" on page 29.)

2 fresh cloves garlic, pressed, or 1 tablespoon garlic powder

1 teaspoon salt

1 teaspoon white pepper

2 tablespoons lemon juice

1 tablespoon ground nutmeg

12 ounces cream cheese, cut into 6 pieces

CRÊPES

2 eggs

$2^1/2$ cups milk

$2^1/2$ cups flour

$1/4$ cup melted butter

To Prepare the Filling:

1. Melt the margarine in a large skillet over medium-high heat. Add the mushrooms and onion, and sauté until the onions are translucent.

2. Add the spinach, garlic, salt, and pepper. Cook until the spinach is partially cooked—wilted and deep green in color—about 5 minutes.

3. Remove the mixture from the heat, and drain well in a colander. Return the mixture to the pan over medium heat. Add the lemon juice, nutmeg, and cream cheese. Stir well until all the ingredients are well blended. Remove the pan from the stove.

To Prepare the Crêpes:

1. Preheat the oven to Warm.

2. Place the eggs and milk in a large mixing bowl. Beat with an electric beater until well blended. Add the flour in small amounts while continuing to beat. The batter will be rather thin, the consistency of cream.

3. Brush the bottom of a 9-inch frying pan with melted butter. Place the pan over medium-high heat. Pour a 1-ounce ladleful or $1/8$ to $1/4$ cup of crêpe batter into the bottom of the pan, and immediately rotate the pan over the heat to make sure the batter covers the entire bottom surface of the pan. The crêpe should be as thin as possible.

Preparing Eggless Crêpes

If you do not eat eggs, you can still enjoy delicious crêpes. This recipe makes 6 servings and takes the same preparation and cooking time as regular crêpes. Place 2 cups milk, $1/4$ teaspoon salt, 2 cups flour, and $1/4$ cup melted butter in a blender. Blend for 1 minute. Scrape down the sides with a rubber spatula, and blend for another 15 seconds, or until smooth. Refrigerate the batter for 1 hour. Alternatively, make the batter the night before and refrigerate overnight. Cook and fill as you would regular crêpes.

4. Cook until the edges of the crêpe begin to separate from the pan. Turn the crêpe with a spatula, and lightly brown on the other side.

5. Remove the crêpe from the pan to a serving platter, and cover with a soft, clean towel. Place the crêpes in the oven to keep warm until you are ready to fill them while you continue to make as many crêpes as you need.

6. Remove the plate of crêpes from the oven. Fill the center of each crêpe with about $1/4$ cup of the filling. Roll the crêpe lengthwise to make a rather flat, long roll. Alternatively, fold the four "sides" of the crêpe into the middle, with edges overlapping to make a square shape.

7. Place two crêpes, with folded edges down, on the serving plate, sprinkle with nutmeg, and serve hot. Or drizzle the crêpes with a light white sauce, sprinkle with nutmeg, and serve hot.

GARNISH

2 cups light white sauce, optional (See "Preparing a Light White Sauce.")

Ground nutmeg, to taste

Preparing a Light White Sauce

This recipe, which yields about 2 cups of white sauce, uses less flour than a traditional recipe. Place $1/4$ cup of butter in a saucepan, and melt over medium heat. Add $1^1/2$ to 2 tablespoons of flour, stirring with a whisk or wooden spoon to make a thick roux. Slowly add 2 cups of milk, stirring constantly to blend well. Add salt and pepper to taste, and continue to cook until the sauce thickens, about 10 to 15 minutes. Remove from the heat, and use according to recipe directions. For additional flavor, you can add a dash of nutmeg; 2 tablespoons fresh or 2 teaspoons dried chives, dill, or parsley; or 1 cup grated Parmesan or shredded cheddar cheese.

ABOUT THE RESTAURANT

The owners of Cornucopia, Glen and Terri Sohl, have served these crêpes to their customers for years.

From Marx Bros. Café   ANCHORAGE, ALASKA

Wild Mushroom Tart

Smooth and creamy chèvre cheese, succulent mushrooms, and golden onions make an irresistible combination in this excellent tart. Real Men and Real Women will love this "quiche-like" dish in small servings as an appetizer or in larger slices with a crisp green salad as a luncheon or dinner entrée. White or brown mushrooms will serve as a fine substitute for the boletus mushrooms.

Yield: 6–8 servings

Preparation Time: 45 minutes

Cooking Time: 25–30 minutes

TART SHELL

$2^1/_4$ cups flour

1 teaspoon salt

$^1/_2$ teaspoon sugar

$^3/_4$ cup chilled sweet butter

1 egg

$^1/_2$ cup sour cream

WILD MUSHROOM TART FILLING

$^1/_4$ cup unsalted butter

$^1/_2$ pound fresh Alaska boletus mushrooms, sliced (See "About Mushrooms" on page 63.)

2 large onions, sliced

2 tablespoons sugar

2 tablespoons cider vinegar

5 large eggs

1 cup cream

$^1/_2$ cup milk

$^1/_4$ teaspoon salt

$^1/_4$ teaspoon white pepper

$^1/_2$ teaspoon ground nutmeg

To Make the Tart Shell:

1. Preheat the oven to 350°F.

2. Place the flour, salt, and sugar in a bowl, and mix together. Cut in the butter, a tablespoon at a time, with a pastry cutter until the mixture resembles cornmeal.

3. Mix the egg and sour cream together in a separate bowl. Add to the flour mixture, working quickly until the pastry is well blended and holds together.

4. Press into a ball, cover with plastic wrap, and refrigerate for 1 hour.

5. Roll the dough out to $^1/_4$-inch thickness, and fit it into a 10-inch tart pan with a removable bottom. Fill the pie with weights—dry beans work well as weights for the pie crust—and bake for 10 minutes, or until the bottom is set. Remove the weights, and bake for an additional 5 to 10 minutes, or until the crust is lightly browned. Remove from the oven, and set aside to cool while you prepare the filling. Do not turn off the oven.

To Make the Filling:

1. In a large sauté, pan melt 2 tablespoons of the butter over medium heat. Add the mushrooms, and lightly sauté the mushrooms until just tender. Remove the pan from the heat, place the mushrooms in a dish, and set aside.

2. In the same sauté pan, melt the remaining 2 tablespoons of butter. Add the sliced onions, and cook over low heat until the onions begin to brown. Add the sugar and cider vinegar, and cook to a light caramel color, stirring frequently. Remove the pan from the heat, and set aside.

3. To make the custard mixture, place the eggs, cream, and milk in a large mixing bowl, and beat together. Add the salt, white pepper, and nutmeg, and stir again to blend well.

To Assemble and Bake the Tart:

1. Spread the caramelized onions on the baked tart shell. Pour the egg custard mixture over the top. Sprinkle the custard with the chopped thyme. Then arrange the mushroom slices on top. Cover with the crumbled chèvre cheese.

2. Bake for 25 to 30 minutes, or until the custard is set and the top is golden brown. A knife inserted in the center should come out clean. Allow to cool to room temperature. Cut into six to eight slices, and serve on a bed of garden greens.

TOPPING

2 tablespoons chopped fresh thyme with flowers

1 cup crumbled chèvre cheese

ABOUT THE RESTAURANT

With a degree in the field of hotel and restaurant management and thirty years' experience in the restaurant business, Van Hale joined Jack Amon and Ken Brown in creating a weekly gourmet dinner at the Jade Room Lounge in Alaska. Known as the Wednesday Night Gourmet and Volleyball Club, it became so successful that the three decided to open the Marx Bros. Café. Since the opening of the café, Van Hale, the maitre d', has become known throughout the Pacific Northwest as a regional wine expert. He is also charged with overseeing the Marx Bros.'s catering operation. Jack Amon is the café chef, and Ken Brown is the business manager.

From John Bozeman's Bistro   BOZEMAN, MONTANA

Fried Green Tomato Tailgater's Tart

This dish is ideal for picnics, potlucks, or tailgate parties!

Yield: 6 – 8 servings

Preparation Time: 30 minutes

Cooking Time: 30 minutes

$1/2$ cup plus 1 tablespoon olive oil

2 eggs

1 tablespoon milk

$3/4$ cup plus 2 tablespoons grated Parmesan cheese

$1/2$ cup cornmeal

$1/4$ cup flour

3 green tomatoes, sliced into $1/4$-inch rounds

8 sheets phyllo pastry,* thawed

$3/4$ cup prepared marinara sauce

$1 1/2$ cups grated provolone cheese

3 ripe red tomatoes, sliced into $1/4$-inch rounds

2 medium zucchini, sliced into $1/4$-inch rounds

Salt, to taste

Black pepper, to taste

Fresh thyme sprigs

1. In a small bowl, place the eggs, milk, and 2 tablespoons of the Parmesan cheese, and whisk together. Set aside.

2. Place $1/4$ cup of the olive oil in a large sauté pan, and heat over medium-high heat. As the oil is heating, combine the cornmeal and flour in a shallow bowl.

3. Dip the green tomato slices first into the egg mixture and then into the cornmeal and flour mixture. Place each slice into the hot oil. Cook until the tomatoes are light brown on both sides. Remove them from the pan, and drain on paper towels.

4. To assemble the phyllo tart crust, use a sharp knife to cut the stack of 8 phyllo sheets into 11-inch diameter rounds. Transfer 1 phyllo round to the oiled tart pan, pressing the round into place and allowing the sides to extend above the rim of the tart pan. Lightly brush the phyllo with olive oil, and sprinkle with 1 teaspoon of the remaining Parmesan cheese. Place another phyllo round on top of the first one, brush with olive oil, and sprinkle with 1 teaspoon of Parmesan cheese. Repeat this process with the remaining rounds.

5. Preheat the oven to 450°F. Brush a 9-inch tart or pie pan with 1 tablespoon of the olive oil.

6. Place overlapping layers of the fried green tomato slices on the bottom of the phyllo shell. Spread the marinara sauce over the fried green tomatoes. Cover the sauce evenly with the Provolone cheese.

7. Overlap alternating slices of red tomato and zucchini on top of the cheese in concentric circles, starting with the outermost circle. Drizzle the remaining $1/4$ cup of olive oil over the top, and season with salt and pepper. Sprinkle with the remaining Parmesan cheese and fresh thyme.

8. Place the tart in the oven. Bake until the zucchini is tender and the crust is golden, about 30 minutes. Remove the tart from the oven and slice into pie wedges. Serve each slice with a dollop of mustard.

ABOUT THE RESTAURANT

People in hiking boots and high heels all dance through the door of John Bozeman's Bistro for a lively and absolutely delectable dining experience.

Phyllo dough is a flaky pastry dough most commonly found packaged in the grocery frozen food section. Phyllo must be handled carefully, as it tends to break apart easily.

From Café For All Seasons   SAN FRANCISCO, CALIFORNIA

Spinach Polenta

Polenta is enjoying renewed interest. A coarse cornmeal grain that has long been considered a mealtime staple by northern Italians, this simple food sets the stage for a variety of combinations. This delicious recipe, with spinach and Asiago cheese, is a wonderful, cozy-comfy dish that works well as a side dish or as an entrée with a scrumptious green salad on the side.

1. Place the polenta (or cornmeal) and 1 cup of the water in the top part of a double boiler, and stir to mix well.

2. Place the remaining $3^1/2$ cups of water in a medium-sized saucepan, and bring to a boil. Stir the boiling water into the polenta. Place the top part of the double boiler directly over very low heat, and cook, stirring constantly until the polenta comes to a boil. Add the salt.

3. Put enough water in the bottom of the double boiler to come to just below the top part of the double boiler, and bring to a simmer over medium heat.

4. Cover the polenta mixture and place it in the double boiler of simmering water. Steam the polenta for 30 minutes. (If you use fine cornmeal, it will take 15 to 20 minutes to cook.)

5. While the polenta is cooking, prepare the spinach mixture. Place the olive oil in a large sauté pan, and heat over medium heat. Add the garlic, and sauté for 1 to 2 minutes. Then, add the spinach, lemon juice, and salt to taste, stirring well to completely blend. Heat the spinach thoroughly, about 5 minutes.

6. After the polenta has steamed, stir in the butter, cheese, and spinach mixture. Blend well.

7. Serve hot in a serving bowl, like mashed potatoes. Alternatively, pour into a buttered baking pan and allow to cool; then cover and refrigerate for up to two days. To reheat, cut the polenta into serving portions, place on a baking sheet, cover with aluminum foil. Heat in a preheated 300°F oven for 25 minutes, and serve hot.

Yield: 6 servings

Preparation Time: 25 minutes

Cooking Time: 15–20 minutes for finely ground cornmeal; 30 minutes for polenta

$1^1/2$ cups polenta or traditional, finely ground cornmeal

$4^1/2$ cups cold water

1 teaspoon sea salt for polenta plus salt to taste

2 tablespoons virgin olive oil

1 teaspoons chopped garlic

1 pound finely chopped, fresh spinach, cooked, drained, and squeezed dry (See "Preparing Fresh Spinach" on page 29.)

Juice of $1/2$ lemon

$1/4$ cup unsalted butter

$3/4$ cup grated Asiago cheese

ABOUT THE RESTAURANT

Café For All Seasons first opened in the West Portal neighborhood of San Francisco in 1983. The café, with a wholesome menu consisting of both vegetarian and traditional foods, has prospered. "Our menu has a lot of variety, yet everything is simple and familiar. We want people to come in for dinner two or three nights a week and to also bring their special out-of-town guests," relates Donna Katzl, executive chef and co-owner with her husband, Frank Katzl.

From Blue Heron Natural Foods Restaurant   RENO, NEVADA

Spinach Pie

Making spinach pie is one way to fix spinach so that your kids will love it! The pie crust, made with dried rosemary, is particularly flavorful, and the filling is a savory blend of cheeses and spinach.

Yield: 4 servings

Preparation Time: 45 minutes

Cooking Time: 25 minutes

PIE DOUGH

2 cups warm water

1 tablespoon honey

1 tablespoon dry yeast

$1/4$ cup olive oil

1 teaspoon dried rosemary

1 cup whole wheat flour

1 cup unbleached white flour

$1/2$ teaspoon salt

SPINACH FILLING

16 ounces fresh spinach, finely chopped (See "Preparing Fresh Spinach" on page 29.)

4 cloves garlic, minced

$1/8$ teaspoon ground nutmeg

2 cups grated mozzarella cheese (about 6 ounces)

$1/2$ cup grated fresh Parmesan cheese

3 teaspoons olive oil

Salt, to taste

Black pepper, to taste

TOPPING

2 cups marinara sauce

$1/4$–$1/2$ cup pesto sauce

To Make the Dough:

1. Place the water and honey in a large bowl, and stir to mix well. Add the yeast, and allow the mixture to proof for 5 minutes.

2. When the yeast is ready, stir the yeast mixture and add the olive oil, rosemary, wheat flour, white flour, and salt. Stir the dough well, cover with a clean towel, and let rise for 20 to 30 minutes.

To Make the Filling:

1. Place the spinach, garlic, nutmeg, mozzarella cheese, Parmesan cheese, and oil in a large bowl. Add salt and pepper to taste. Stir to blend.

To Prepare the Pie:

1. Preheat the oven to 400°F. Lightly oil a baking sheet.

2. On a lightly floured surface, roll the dough into a large circle, $1/4$ inch thick.

3. Place the spinach mixture in the center of the dough, fold over the dough, and pinch the sides to seal.

4. Place the pie on the baking sheet, and put in the oven to bake for 25 minutes.

5. Remove from the oven to a serving platter. Top each serving with $1/2$ cup of marinara sauce and then 1 to 2 tablespoons of pesto sauce. Serve hot and listen to the rave reviews!

ABOUT THE RESTAURANT

The Blue Heron crew believes that using fruits, grains, and vegetables grown by sustainable agricultural methods—which maintain the productivity of the soil without the use of chemicals and pesticides—will benefit all of us and our families now and for years to come. They live their philosophy by using organic food whenever possible. Their wide selection of ethnic and international vegetarian meals ranges from lacto-vegetarian and vegan to macrobiotic. "All of our efforts at the Blue Heron strive to improve both our personal and our common environments. We sincerely hope our service assists you in your healthful and wholesome endeavors," states owner Steve Flack.

Jimmy D's COEUR D'ALENE, IDAHO

Vegetable Tortino

Rich in cream, eggs, and cheese, this entrée is heartier than a quiche and will be a hit for brunch, lunch, or dinner.

1. Preheat the oven to 400°F. Lightly oil a 2-quart baking dish, and set aside.

2. Heat the olive oil in a large sauté pan over medium heat. Add the onions and celery, and cook until they are slightly translucent. Add the zucchini and eggplant, and continue to cook until the eggplant is tender but firm. Remove the veggies from the heat, and set aside.

3. In a medium-sized mixing bowl, place $1/2$ cup of the Parmesan cheese. Add the eggs, vinegar, cream, salt, and pepper. Stir well to blend. Then add the veggies, and mix thoroughly. Pour into the oiled baking dish.

4. Bake for 30 to 35 minutes, until lightly golden brown on top. Remove from the oven, and top with the remaining $1/2$ cup of Parmesan cheese. Return the tortino to the oven to brown for an additional 6 to 8 minutes. Then serve with your favorite bread and a crisp green salad.

ABOUT THE RESTAURANT

The atmosphere at Jimmy D's is relaxed, casual, and upbeat—a setting conducive to good food and good company. As a favorite night spot in Coeur d'Alene, the restaurant offers traditional as well as vegetarian cuisine.

Yield: 6 servings

Preparation Time: 25–30 minutes

Cooking Time: 40–45 minutes

2 tablespoons olive oil

1 medium yellow onion, chopped

1 cup chopped celery

1 medium zucchini, chopped

1 small eggplant, peeled and chopped

1 cup grated Parmesan cheese (about 4 ounces)

5 eggs, beaten

$1/4$ cup balsamic vinegar

1 cup heavy cream

1 teaspoon salt

1 teaspoon black pepper

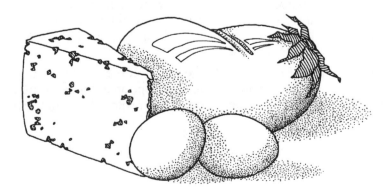

From John Bozeman's Bistro   BOZEMAN, MONTANA

Beet Soufflé

Chef Tyler Hill reveals the secret of making something from nothing: "I designed this recipe one evening at home for dinner from the contents of my nearly empty refrigerator. I just let my imagination go wild. The Beet Soufflé can be used as a main entrée or a side dish. It is very flavorful, versatile, and colorful. It is not a classical soufflé, and it is much more than beets the eye!"

Yield: 8 servings

Preparation Time: 1 hour
Cooking Time: 45–60 minutes

1 cup wild rice

2 cups water

3–4 large fresh beets, washed and stemmed, or 3 cups cubed canned beets (reserve the juice)

2 cups chopped fresh red Swiss chard or fresh spinach

1 tablespoon olive oil

1 cup chopped yellow zucchini

1/2 cup chopped scallions

1/2 cup chopped yellow bell pepper

1 1/2 cups toasted bread crumbs (See "About Bread Crumbs" on page 23.)

1/2 cup dried parsley

2/3 cup shredded sharp cheddar cheese

2/3 cup shredded Monterey jack cheese

2/3 cup shredded Kasseri or Asiago cheese

1/2 cup grated Parmesan cheese

6 eggs, beaten

1. Preheat the oven to 350°F. Lightly oil a 9- by 13-inch baking pan.

2. Place the rice and water in a medium-sized saucepan over high heat. When the water comes to a boil, cover the pan, and reduce the heat to low. Simmer until the rice is cooked, about 30 minutes.

3. While the rice is cooking, you may either boil or bake the beets. To boil, place the whole beets in a large pot of water, cover, place over medium-high heat, and boil until tender, about 45 minutes. To bake, wrap the beets in foil and place in the oven for 45 minutes, until tender. Remove the beets from the water or the oven. Reserve the cooking liquid. Peel the skin from each beet. Chop the beets into small cubes and set aside.

4. While the beets are cooking, place the chard or spinach in a steamer. Steam with a small amount of water over high heat until tender, about 10 minutes.

5. In a medium-sized sauté pan, place the 1 tablespoon olive oil and heat over medium-high heat. Add the zucchini and sauté until crisp-tender, about 2 to 3 minutes. Remove from the heat and set aside.

6. In a large mixing bowl, place the rice, beets, and zucchini. Add the remaining ingredients. Mix well with your hands.

7. Place the mixture in the oiled baking pan. The mixture should be about 1 inch deep. Cover the pan with aluminum foil, and place in the oven to bake for 30 minutes. Then uncover the pan, and bake an additional 15 to 30 minutes. The soufflé is done when a toothpick inserted into the dish comes out clean. Remove the pan from the oven, and allow to rest for 10 minutes on a wire rack. Cut into squares.

8. To prepare the topping, combine the sour cream and optional beet juice in a small bowl. Spoon a dollop of the sour cream topping on each square, and garnish with a fresh dill sprig.

ABOUT THE RESTAURANT

John Bozeman's Bistro, most often referred to as The Bistro, offers a creative cuisine featuring local produce, meats, and fish. The restaurant encourages diners to experiment with a variety of new foods, flavors, and wines. The staff is happy to guide you through a pleasurable dining experience, from appetizers to desserts.

1 tablespoon Dijon mustard

1 teaspoon black pepper

1 teaspoon fresh dill

2 teaspoons Spike (See "About Spike" on page 52.)

TOPPING

1 cup sour cream

2 teaspoons beet juice, optional

Fresh dill sprigs

From Parma Pierogies   CLEVELAND, OHIO

Pierogies

These tasty little pockets are Eastern Europe's version of the familiar Italian ravioli. They are easy to make, and it is fun to experiment with various fillings—for example, a combination of grated Parmesan and ricotta cheeses would be delicious. Another kid-pleaser!

Yield: 2¹/₂–3 dozen pierogies

Preparation Time: 5 minutes for the dough

Cooking Time: 5–6 minutes; 30 minutes for the filling

POTATO CHEESE FILLING

3 cups hot mashed potatoes (about 6 large boiled potatoes)

1 cup shredded cheddar cheese

2 tablespoons melted butter

Salt, to taste

Black pepper, to taste

SAUERKRAUT FILLING

4 tablespoons margarine

2 medium onions, finely chopped

1 (24-ounce) jar sauerkraut, squeezed dry and finely chopped

Salt, to taste

Black pepper, to taste

2 tablespoons bread crumbs

¹/₂ cup mashed potatoes (about 1 large boiled potato)

To Make the Potato Cheese Filling:

1. Place the potatoes, cheese, and butter in a medium-sized bowl. Season with salt and pepper to taste. Stir to blend well. If you are not going to make the pierogi dough right away, allow the filling to cool, place in an airtight container, and refrigerate for later use. The filling will keep in the refrigerator for one to two days.

To Make the Sauerkraut Filling:

1. Melt the margarine in a medium sauté pan. Add the onions, and sauté until tender. Add the sauerkraut, and season to taste with salt and pepper. Cook for 5 minutes. The onion and sauerkraut will be soft.

2. Add the bread crumbs and mashed potatoes to the sauerkraut mixture, and mix well. Remove from the heat and use as the filling for the pierogi dough. To store for later use, allow the mixture to cool, place in an airtight container, and refrigerate for one to two days.

To Make the Dough:

1. Place the flour and salt in a small bowl, and combine.

2. In a 1-cup measure, place the optional egg, the oil, and equal parts of milk and water to reach the "1 cup" line. Add the contents of the cup all at once to the dry ingredients. Mix the dough until it forms a ball.

3. Turn the dough onto a floured surface, and knead the dough until it is no longer sticky. The dough should be smooth. Cover with a clean towel, and let rest for 15 minutes.

To Prepare and Cook the Pierogies:

1. Roll out the dough about ¹/₈ inch thick. Cut the dough into 2¹/₂-inch to 3-inch circles with a biscuit cutter.

2. Put 1 tablespoon of the filling on half of each circle of dough. Make sure no filling touches the sides of the dough, or it will cause them to open. Fold the dough in half to resemble half circles, and pinch the edges together to seal the sides. You may also crimp the edges with a fork.

3. Bring a large pot of water to a boil. Place about twelve pierogies in the water. After the water has resumed boiling, cook for about 5 minutes. Cover the pot for the first and last minute of cooking. Remove the pierogies from the boiling water with a slotted spoon, and allow to drain on a dry cloth towel.

4. Serve warm with melted butter and onion or with sour cream. Or you may sauté the pierogies as follows: Melt 1 tablespoon of butter in a large sauté pan. Add the pierogies, and sauté until golden brown. Then transfer to a serving dish and top with melted butter, butter and onion, or sour cream, and serve.

PIEROGI DOUGH

2 cups flour

1 teaspoon salt

1 egg, optional

1 tablespoon oil

Equal parts milk and water to measure about 1 cup

ABOUT THE RESTAURANT

The first fast-food pierogi restaurant in the country, Parma Pierogies attracted the Clintons and the Gores, who stopped by on their famous bus tour campaign in 1992. Impressed with the great food and good people, the soon-to-be president extended an invitation to the owners of Parma Pierogies to the White House for five days of Inaugural festivities. And during his presidency, Mr. Clinton made a second stop at Parma Pierogies!

From Artichoke Café   ALBUQUERQUE, NEW MEXICO

Sweet Potato Gratin

This gratin makes a delicious, innovative autumn dish served with the Artichoke Café's Mixed Greens, Oranges, and Fennel Salad With Orange-Balsamic Vinaigrette (see page 24).

Yield: 6 servings

Preparation Time: 30 minutes

Cooking Time: 45 minutes to roast the garlic; 30 minutes to bake the gratin

1 head garlic

1 pound sweet potatoes, peeled and sliced into $1/16$-inch rounds

$1^1/2$ pounds baking potatoes, peeled and sliced into $1/16$-inch rounds

$1/2$ pound baking apples, peeled and sliced into $1/16$-inch rounds

1 teaspoon salt

$1/2$ teaspoon black pepper

$1/4$ cup butter

1 cup heavy cream

1. Place the oven rack in the middle of the oven, and preheat the oven to 425°F. Lightly oil an 8-inch baking dish.

2. Wrap the garlic in foil, and roast in the oven for 45 minutes. Remove the garlic from the oven, unwrap from the foil, and cool.

3. Slice off the top of the head of garlic, and squeeze out the softened garlic cloves.

4. In the baking dish, layer the sweet potatoes and baking potatoes with the apples, baked garlic, and butter as follows. First, put an overlapping layer of sweet potatoes on the bottom of the pan. Next, cover the sweet potatoes with a layer of overlapping apple slices. Then cover the apples with an overlapping layer of baking potato slices. Dot the baking potatoes with the garlic and butter. Repeat the layers until you reach within 1 inch of the top of the pan. Season each layer with salt and pepper.

5. Pour the cream over the entire dish—the cream should be halfway up in the pan—and cover with foil.

6. Place the baking dish on the middle rack of the oven, and bake for 20 minutes. Remove the foil from the pan, and bake 10 minutes longer.

7. When the potatoes are tender, remove the gratin from the oven and serve immediately.

ABOUT THE RESTAURANT

At the heart of creative cuisine at the Artichoke Café is the ability to combine ordinary ingredients and have them yield a sensational entrée or side dish.

From The Garden Vegetarian Restaurant   *RED BANK, NEW JERSEY*

Vegetarian Jambalaya

Just the right touch of cayenne pepper sets this jambalaya apart from other stir-fry entrées.

1. Place the oil in a large sauté pan, and heat over medium-high heat. Add the onion, and sauté until translucent, about 5 minutes. Add the bell pepper, mushrooms, and scallions. Sauté an additional 5 minutes.

2. Add the carrots, cauliflower, and broccoli, and sauté for another 3 to 4 minutes. Add the zucchini, snow peas, tofu (or tempeh), soy sauce, thyme, basil, and cayenne pepper. Sauté an additional 5 to 10 minutes.

3. Add the chopped tomato, and sauté until heated thoroughly.

4. Remove the pan from the heat, transfer the jambalaya to a serving bowl, and serve with brown rice on the side. Or combine the jambalaya with the brown rice before transferring to the serving bowl. Serve hot.

ABOUT THE RESTAURANT

"The Garden Vegetarian Restaurant, where food is made with love" greets you when you open the menu, and "Thank you for not eating animals. God Bless You" are the closing remarks.

* *Tempeh* is a delicious, high-protein food made from soybeans.

Yield: *6 servings*

Preparation Time: 30 minutes

Cooking Time: 20 minutes

1 tablespoon vegetable oil

1 medium purple onion, chopped

1 medium green bell pepper, chopped

1 pound white mushrooms, sliced

3 tablespoons chopped scallions (green onions), including 1/2-inch of the green

2 carrots, peeled and chopped

1 cup chopped cauliflower

1 cup chopped broccoli

1 zucchini, sliced

1/2 pound snow peas, stem ends removed

1 pound firm tofu or tempeh*, cubed

1/4 cup tamari soy sauce, or to taste (See "About Soy Sauce" on page 13.)

1 teaspoon dried thyme

1 teaspoon dried basil

Pinch of cayenne pepper, or to taste

1 fresh tomato, chopped

From John Bozeman's Bistro   BOZEMAN, MONTANA

Jamaican White Beans & Squash

A savory dish, this exotic combination of beans and squash tickles the palate with a soft, smooth texture and richly spiced beans. For a complete meal, add a side dish of rice or couscous, or serve it with a sesame bun and a tossed green salad sprinkled with sunflower seeds.

Yield: 6 servings

Preparation Time: 1 hour plus overnight to soak the beans

Cooking Time: 2 hours

1 pound white beans

$1^1/_2$ quarts vegetable stock

1 teaspoon dried basil

1 teaspoon dried thyme

1 teaspoon dried oregano

1 tablespoon ground allspice

2 teaspoons ground ginger

2 teaspoons ground coriander

2 medium squash, either acorn or butternut

$^1/_4$–$^1/_2$ cup olive oil

1 carrot, peeled and coarsely chopped

1 stalk celery, coarsely chopped

1 medium yellow onion, coarsely chopped

1 green bell pepper, seeded and coarsely chopped

2 jalapeño peppers*, seeded, optional

1 unpeeled potato, coarsely chopped

4 cloves garlic, peeled

4 shallots, peeled and coarsely chopped

1 bunch fresh parsley, chopped

1 bunch fresh cilantro (coriander), chopped

Salt, to taste

Freshly ground pepper, to taste

Chili sauce, to taste, optional

1. Place the beans in a large bowl. Add water to cover. Soak overnight.

2. Drain the beans, and place into a large soup pot. Add the vegetable stock, basil, thyme, oregano, allspice, ginger, and ground coriander. Cover the soup pot, and cook the beans over medium-low heat until tender, about $1^1/_2$ to 2 hours, adding more water, if necessary. Drain, reserving the liquid. Set aside.

3. Preheat the oven to 375°F.

4. While the beans are cooking, cut the squashes in half, remove the seeds, and place, cut side down, on a baking sheet or roasting pan. Bake the squash until very soft, about 45 to 60 minutes. Or you may microwave the squash by placing the halves, cut side down, on a microwave plate, and cooking for about 15 minutes, until very soft. Remove the squash pulp from the skin, and set aside.

5. While the squash is baking, place the olive oil in a roasting pan. Place the pan in the oven until the oil is hot. Add the carrot, celery, onion, green pepper, optional jalapeño pepper, potato, garlic, shallots, parsley, and fresh coriander (cilantro). Stir well to coat them with the hot oil. Roast the vegetables in the oven until very tender, about 30 to 40 minutes.

6. Remove the vegetables from the oven, allow them to cool, and place them in a food processor or blender. Add the squash pulp. Purée the roasted vegetables and the squash, adding just enough reserved bean liquid to reach a thick, smooth consistency.

7. Place the puréed squash and veggies in a large bowl, and add the beans. Adjust the seasoning with salt, freshly ground black pepper, and optional chili sauce. Serve hot in a large serving bowl, or scoop single portions onto individual serving plates.

ABOUT THE RESTAURANT

The chefs at the Bistro are artists at work, continually evolving their menu selections.

Jalapeño peppers are hot! Be careful when you are handling chilies because they can burn the skin of your hands, eyes, and mouth. It's best to wear rubber gloves. If the chilies touch your skin, wash carefully with warm (not hot or cold) soapy water to reduce the heat from the chilies.

From Angel Fish   CHARLESTON, SOUTH CAROLINA

Vegetable Paella

This lovely array of vegetables, discreetly spiced with fresh ginger and a hint of red chili pepper, is combined with AngelFish Saffron Rice to make a tasty vegetable paella.

To Prepare the Rice:

1. Place the oil in a large saucepan, and heat over medium heat. Add the onion, and sauté for 2 to 3 minutes. Then add the garlic, saffron, pepper, turmeric, salt, and water.

2. Bring to a boil over high heat, and add the rice. Return to a boil, cover, and reduce the heat to low.

3. Simmer for 30 minutes, or until cooked. Remove the rice from the heat, and fluff with a fork.

To Prepare the Paella:

1. Place the oil in a large sauté pan, and heat over medium heat. Add the onion, and sauté for 2 to 3 minutes, until onion is translucent and soft. Add the red, yellow, and green peppers, the artichoke hearts, the snow peas, and the green peas. Sauté for 2 to 3 minutes.

2. Add the ginger and red chili peppers, to taste. Stir to blend well. Remove from the heat.

3. At this point you can add the Saffron Rice to the veggies and return to the heat to stir-fry just long enough to blend and heat them well together. Or you can mound the rice on a serving platter, or on the individual serving plates, and spoon the veggies on top of the rice. Garnish with fresh parsley and serve.

ABOUT THE RESTAURANT

Tucked away in the Merchant Village Center of Charleston, Angel Fish offers innovative cuisine, made with the very freshest of ingredients, in its daily specials and regular menu items.

Yield: 4–6 servings

Preparation Time: 20–30 minutes for vegetables; 10–15 minutes for rice

Cooking Time: 5–10 minutes for vegetables; 30 minutes for rice

SAFFRON RICE

1/4 cup olive oil

1/2 large yellow onion, chopped

1 tablespoon minced garlic

3/4 teaspoon saffron threads

1/2 teaspoon white pepper

1/2 teaspoon turmeric

1/2 teaspoon sea salt

4 cups water

2 cups uncooked long-grain white rice

PAELLA

2 tablespoons vegetable oil

1 medium yellow onion, sliced

1 medium red bell pepper, sliced

1 medium yellow bell pepper, sliced

1 medium green bell pepper, sliced

1 cup artichoke hearts, drained and sliced

1 cup fresh or frozen snow peas, stem ends removed

1 cup fresh or frozen green peas

1 tablespoon grated fresh ginger, or to taste

1/2 teaspoon crushed red chili peppers, or to taste

GARNISH

Chopped fresh parsley

From Beans & Barley Café   MILWAUKEE, WISCONSIN

Sautéed Winter Vegetables

A food processor comes in handy for all the diced vegetables in this recipe. Except for the peeling and dicing, there's not much preparation.

Yield: 4 servings

Preparation Time: 20 minutes

Cooking Time: 20–25 minutes

3–4 tablespoons olive oil

1 medium red potato, peeled and diced into 1/2-inch pieces

1 medium sweet potato, peeled and diced into 1/2-inch pieces

2 large carrots, cut into julienne strips

1 small rutabaga, peeled and diced into 1/2-inch pieces

1 medium parsnip, peeled and diced into 1/2-inch pieces

1/2 cup vegetable broth

1 medium yellow onion, cut into strips

2 cloves garlic, chopped

1/4 cup chopped fresh parsley

Salt, to taste

Black pepper, to taste

1. Heat a 12-inch nonstick sauté pan over medium heat. Add the olive oil, and immediately add the red potato, sweet potato, carrots, rutabaga, and parsnip. Cook the vegetables over medium heat, stirring and tossing frequently to prevent sticking. Sauté for 5 to 10 minutes. Then add the vegetable broth. (If you use a pan that does not have a nonstick surface, take care to constantly stir the vegetables or they will stick and burn.)

2. Add the onion and garlic to the pan, and cook for 3 to 5 minutes, until the onions are soft. Add the parsley, and season with salt and pepper to taste.

3. Cover, and allow the vegetables to steam, stirring frequently until the vegetables are completely cooked. Test for doneness by piercing the vegetables with a fork. The vegetables should be soft in the center. If necessary, cook longer, continuing to stir and toss.

4. Remove the vegetables from the heat, and serve immediately accompanied by sour cream and chives, freshly grated Parmesan cheese, or soy or cottage cheese.

ABOUT THE RESTAURANT

After twenty years of business, Beans & Barley Café was leveled by a fire. The owners—Lynn Sbonik, Peg Silvestrini, Pat Sturgis, and Patty Garrigan—seized the opportunity for a renaissance of the café. They immediately redesigned and rebuilt the restaurant to offer even more of their great food to their clientele.

From Doe Bay Café   OLGA, WASHINGTON

The Green Earth

Doe Bay Café serves The Green Earth anytime of the day. It makes a hearty breakfast, a warm, cozy lunch, or a satisfying supper.

1. Place the potatoes in a medium-sized saucepan, fill with enough water to completely cover the potatoes, and add salt. Cover the pan with a lid, and bring to a boil over medium-high heat. Boil the potatoes until tender, about 15 to 20 minutes. Drain, and set aside to cool.

2. Place 1 tablespoon of the oil in a large sauté pan. Heat over medium heat. Add the potatoes, and cook until they are brown.

3. In another large sauté pan, place the remaining tablespoon of oil. Heat over medium-high heat, and add the onion. Sauté the onion until translucent. Then add the mushrooms, broccoli, basil, and tarragon to the onions.

4. When the onion mixture begins to sizzle, add $1/4$ to $1/2$ cup of water. Cover and steam the vegetables until the broccoli turns bright green.

5. To the onion and vegetable mixture, add the sautéed potatoes and the sunflower seeds, and mix well with the vegetables. Add the optional cheese. Cover the pan, and continue to cook over low heat until heated thoroughly and the cheese melts.

6. Divide into wedges. Place wedges on individual plates, and top with the fresh sprouts. Serve hot with slices of fresh fruit on the side.

ABOUT THE RESTAURANT

Probably one of the best views available on Orcas Island is from the Doe Bay Café, where "the green earth" blends with the deep blue sea. Nurture your soul, mind, and body with a healthful meal served by a caring staff.

Yield: 4 servings

Preparation Time: 20 minutes

Cooking Time: 30 minutes

1 pound unpeeled red potatoes, cut into $1/2$-inch cubes

2 tablespoons vegetable oil

$3/4$ cup chopped yellow onion

2 cups sliced white mushrooms (about 6 ounces)

2 cups broccoli florets

1 teaspoon dried basil

1 teaspoon dried tarragon

$1/4$–$1/2$ cup water

$1/4$ cup toasted sunflower seeds (See "Toasting Nuts and Seeds" on page 68.)

2 cups grated cheddar cheese, optional

$1/4$ cup fresh alfalfa or mung bean sprouts

From The Mediterranean Bakery *ALEXANDRIA, VIRGINIA*

Mdardra (Modardara)

Lentils and rice make a perfect protein combination, and offer a deliciously satisfying meal. As a variation, you may want to try fried onions instead of sautéed onions as the topping to this tasty dish.

Yield: 6 servings

Preparation Time: 20 minutes

Cooking Time: 40–45 minutes

1½ cups uncooked lentils

6 cups water

3 tablespoons olive oil

3 large yellow onions, thinly sliced

1½ cups white basmati rice*

1 teaspoon salt

1. Rinse the lentils under cool running water, removing any grit or debris.

2. Place the lentils in a large pot, add the water, cover, and cook over medium heat for 15 minutes.

3. While the lentils are cooking, pour the oil into a large sauté pan and heat over medium-high heat for 10 seconds. Add the sliced onions, and sauté until the onions are translucent and begin to turn golden, about 10 minutes. When the onions are done, remove them from the heat, and set aside.

4. When the lentils have cooked for 15 minutes, add the rice and salt. Cover the pan again, and allow the lentils and rice to cook until done about another 20 to 25 minutes, until all the water is absorbed. (If you are using a long-grain rice, you may need to adjust the cooking time.)

5. Place the lentils and rice in a serving bowl or on individual serving plates, and top with the sautéed onions. Serve warm with pita bread or another hearty bread. The Mdardra also may be refrigerated and served cold.

ABOUT THE RESTAURANT

Sleiman A. Kysia, owner of The Mediterranean Bakery, has been serving his loyal customers for seventeen years. Other delicious entrées you can find at the restaurant include Lubyi Bi-zayt, a green bean and tomato dish; Mjadra, a lentil dish; and Mousaka.

*Basmati rice, from India, is a particularly aromatic long-grained rice. Be sure to rinse it according to the package directions.

From Fasika's Ethiopian Restaurant   *WASHINGTON, D.C.*

Ye'atakit Alich'a (Vegetable Stew)

This is a savory stew that you really must try. This dish is exotic, yet familiar. As a variation, try substituting cauliflower or broccoli for the cabbage and potatoes.

1. Place the oil in a large sauté pan, and heat over medium-high heat. Add the onion, and sauté until soft.

2. Add the tomato paste, and mix well. Add the potatoes, carrots, cabbage, bell peppers, garlic powder, salt, black pepper, turmeric, and ginger to the onions. Continue to cook for another 30 to 45 minutes, until the vegetables are tender.

3. Remove the pan from the heat, and add the optional sliced green chilies. This stew may be served either hot or cold, and goes well with Yekik We't (Red Lentil Sauce), page 132.

ABOUT THE RESTAURANT

Fasika T. Mariam, owner of Fasika's Ethiopian Restaurant, has offered a lovely dining experience to his Washington, D.C. clientele for more than ten years.

*Anaheim chilies are hot! Be careful when you are handling chilies because they can burn the skin of your hands, eyes, and mouth. It's best to wear rubber gloves. If the chilies touch your skin, wash carefully with warm (not hot or cold) soapy water to reduce the heat from the chilies.

Yield: 6 servings

Preparation Time: 25 minutes

Cooking Time: 30–45 minutes

3 tablespoons olive oil

1 1/2 cups chopped purple onions (about 1 1/2 onions)

1 (6-ounce) can tomato paste

6 medium potatoes, peeled and chopped

5 medium carrots, peeled and chopped

1 small green cabbage, chopped

2 green bell peppers, chopped

1/4 teaspoon garlic powder

Salt

1/4 teaspoon black pepper

1/2 teaspoon turmeric

2 tablespoons freshly grated ginger or to taste

6 medium green Anaheim chilies,* sliced, optional

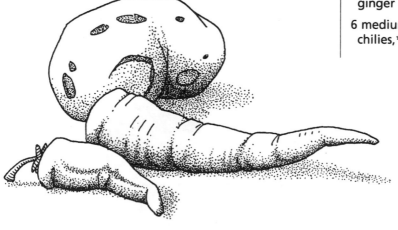

From Fasika's Ethiopian Restaurant   WASHINGTON, D.C.

Yekik We't (Red Lentil Sauce)

This delicious sauce may be served over rice, with pita bread, or as an accompaniment to Fasika's Ye'atakit Alich'a (Vegetable Stew) on page 131.

Yield: 6 servings

Preparation Time: 15–20 minutes

Cooking Time: 35–45 minutes

2 cups red lentils,* washed

6 cups water plus extra as needed

2 tablespoons olive oil

2 cups chopped red onions (about 2 onions)

1/4 teaspoon ground fenugreek*

Salt, to taste

1 cup chopped red bell pepper

1/2 cup red wine (nonalcoholic wine works well, too)

1 teaspoon ground ginger

1. Put the lentils in a medium-sized pot with the water. Cover and boil over medium heat until soft, about 20 minutes. Drain the lentils, reserving the liquid. There should be about 4 cups of reserved liquid.

2. Place the oil in a large sauté pan, and heat over medium heat. Add the onion and the fenugreek. Cook until the onion is soft, adding 1 to 3 tablespoons of water if necessary to prevent the onion from burning.

3. Add 1½ cups of the reserved lentil water to the onions. Season with salt to taste, and stir well. Add the cooked lentils, bell pepper, and wine. Sprinkle in the ginger.

4. Add the remaining reserved lentil water, and cook for 15 minutes to allow the spices to blend well. Remove from the heat. The lentil sauce may be served hot or cold.

ABOUT THE RESTAURANT

Other wonderful entrées at Fasika's Ethiopian Restaurant include falafel, hummus, baba ghanouj, stuffed grape leaves, and various salads, spinach pies, and casseroles.

Red lentils are available in natural food stores, gourmet specialty markets, and Indian markets. *Fenugreek* is a spicy, rather bitter herb popular in Indian and Middle Eastern cooking.

From Everybody's Natural Foods   LEXINGTON, KENTUCKY

Baked Eggplant Parmesan

Why not vary from the norm and try this delightfully different version of eggplant Parmesan? This lighter version of the standard recipe uses baked rather than sautéed eggplant, as well as less cheese than usual.

1. Peel the eggplants, and slice into $1/2$-inch slices. Place in a large bowl, cover with water, and add the sea salt. Soak for 45 minutes.

2. Preheat the oven to 350°F. Lightly oil a baking sheet, and set aside.

3. While the eggplant is soaking, place the bread crumbs, flour, oregano, garlic, pepper, and salt in a medium, shallow bowl. Mix together, and set aside.

4. Pour the milk into a small, shallow bowl, and set aside.

5. Drain the eggplant, rinse with fresh water, and pat dry with a paper towel. Dip each eggplant slice into the milk, and then dredge each slice in the bread crumb mixture. Place the slices on the oiled baking sheet.

6. Bake in the oven for about 20 minutes on each side, or until golden brown.

7. While the eggplant is baking, place the tomato sauce in a medium-sized saucepan. Heat over medium heat until hot, but not boiling.

8. Remove the baking sheet from the oven, and ladle a small amount of sauce over each eggplant slice. Top each slice with the grated mozzarella or soy cheese, and bake an additional 10 minutes, or until the cheese is melted.

9. While the eggplant is baking, cook the spaghetti according to the directions. Drain and place the hot spaghetti on individual plates. Scoop servings of the eggplant on top of the spaghetti. Top each serving with a ladle of tomato sauce and freshly grated Parmesan cheese. Serve immediately.

Yield: 8 servings

Preparation Time: 50 minutes

Cooking Time: 1 hour

2 medium eggplants

1 tablespoon sea salt

$3/4$ cup bread crumbs

$3/4$ cup unbleached white flour

1 teaspoon dried oregano

1 teaspoon granulated garlic

$1/4$ teaspoon black pepper

$1/2$ teaspoon salt

$1/2$ cup soy or dairy milk

Everybody's Italian Tomato Sauce (See page 104.)

$1/2$ pound mozzarella or soy cheese, grated

$1/4$ pound freshly grated Parmesan cheese

2 pounds spaghetti

ABOUT THE RESTAURANT

"Everybody's is tucked away in a sunny storefront near the University of Kentucky campus in Chevy Chase, a small, diverse, sort of funky neighborhood—students rub shoulders with lawyers. It's pretty hard to walk by Everybody's without wanting to go in. Calico curtains frame the big plate glass windows, and tempting smells drift from the screen door. Inside, shelves loaded with natural foods and health care products line the walls. It's clean and bright, and people sit at small tables eating and talking while music comes from a boom box in the corner," comments Jenny Williams, a former employee of Everybody's.

From Bloodroot   BRIDGEPORT, CONNECTICUT

Stuffed Baby Eggplant

Tasty! Tasty! Tasty! This delicious dish is a snap to prepare, and the Spicy Tomato Sauce drizzled on top makes this an elegant, yet simple, entrée. If baby eggplants are not available, two to three medium-sized regular eggplants may be substituted.

Yield: *6–8 servings, including 2¹/₂ cups of sauce*

Preparation Time: 25 minutes plus 15 minutes for the sauce

Cooking Time: 1 hour plus 10 minutes for the sauce

EGGPLANTS

1 cup tightly packed sundried tomatoes

¹/₂ cup fresh Italian parsley, if available

6 cloves garlic, peeled

2–3 tablespoons olive oil

1 large yellow onion, coarsely chopped

1 cup water

¹/₂ cup bulgur*

1¹/₂ teaspoons salt

12–16 baby eggplants, each 4 to 5 inches long

SPICY TOMATO SAUCE

2 tablespoons olive oil

1 small yellow onion, chopped

2 cloves garlic, crushed

2 teaspoons dried oregano

1 teaspoon dried basil

To Prepare the Eggplants:

1. Preheat the oven to 400°F. Lightly oil a 13- by 9-inch baking pan.

2. If you are using sundried tomatoes that are not packed in oil, you will need to soften them. Soak the tomatoes in a medium-sized bowl of hot water for about 30 minutes. To speed up this process, place the tomatoes in a small saucepan, cover with water, bring to a low boil over medium heat, and simmer for 15 minutes or until the tomatoes are soft.

3. For the stuffing, coarsely cut up the sundried tomatoes. Place the parsley, sundried tomatoes, and garlic in the food processor, and set aside.

4. Place 1 tablespoon of the oil in a small sauté pan, and heat over medium high heat. Add the onion, and sauté, stirring constantly, until the onion is soft. Remove from the heat, and spoon the onion into the food processor.

5. Turn on the food processor, and process until the mixture becomes a thick paste. Set aside.

6. Put the water into a small saucepan, and bring to a boil over high heat. Add the bulgur. Remove the pan from the heat and allow the bulgur to soften, about 10 minutes. Add the bulgur and the salt to the food processor, and process briefly to mix.

7. Cut off the stem ends of the eggplants, and make a long slit, about ¹/₂-inch deep, along the length of each eggplant. Using your fingers, stuff each eggplant with the tomato-bulgur mixture. You may have more stuffing than you can use.

8. Lay the eggplants in the baking pan, slit side up, and drizzle the remaining 1 to 2 tablespoons of olive oil over the eggplants. You may fill in the space in the baking pan with the extra stuffing. Cover the pan tightly with foil. Place the pan in the oven, and bake for 1 hour.

Bulgur wheat is a popular Middle Eastern wheat that has been cracked by boiling, and then redried. It's available in natural food stores.

To Prepare the Sauce:

1. Place the olive oil in a medium-sized sauté pan, and heat over medium-high heat. Add the onion, garlic, oregano, and basil. Sauté until the onion is golden brown.

2. Add the tomato sauce. Rinse the tomato sauce can with the red wine, and add the wine to the sauce.

3. Add the optional jalapeño chilies to the simmering sauce, and continue to simmer over low heat for 10 minutes. Taste for seasonings, and add salt or pepper, if necessary. Remove from the stove.

To Serve the Eggplants:

1. Remove the eggplant pan from the oven, and transfer the eggplants to a large serving platter or individual serving plates. Drizzle with Spicy Tomato Sauce. Serve hot with rice pilaf, plain rice, or pasta.

1 (15-ounce) can tomato sauce

¼ cup red wine

1 tablespoon minced jalapeño chilies,* optional

ABOUT THE RESTAURANT

"Bloodroot has made a name for itself with its innovative, all-vegetarian menus that change every three weeks," reports the "Vegetarian Times." Founded in 1977 by a group of three women—Selma Miriam, Betsy Beaven, and Noel Furie—Bloodroot offers a casual and homey atmosphere. In addition to this recipe, many other Bloodroot recipes are available in the "Perennial Political Palate," by the Bloodroot Collective (Bridgeport, Connecticut: Sanguinaria Publishing, 1993).

---

*These *chilies* are very hot. Be careful when you are handling chilies because they can burn the skin of your hands, eyes, and mouth. It's best to wear rubber gloves. If the chilies touch your skin, wash carefully with warm (not hot or cold) soapy water to reduce the heat from the chilies.

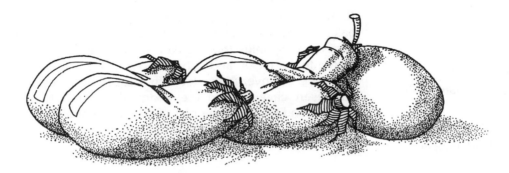

From John Bozeman's Bistro   BOZEMAN, MONTANA

Eggplant Garden Parmesan

This dish is an exceptionally delicious variation of eggplant Parmesan. The richly spiced breading combines with the eggplant, zucchini, and spinach to create a tantalizing success. If you omit the eggs in the dip, use either an additional 1 cup cream or 1 cup milk. Also see "Alternatives to Eggs" on page 82.

Yield: 6 servings

Preparation Time: 30–45 minutes

Cooking Time: 30 minutes

1–3 tablespoons olive oil

2 cups chopped leeks (3–4 large leeks; see "Cleaning Leeks" on page 39.)

3 medium zucchini, sliced into $1/2$-inch rounds

3 cloves garlic, minced

1 large, firm eggplant, peeled and sliced into $1/4$-inch slices

6 cups prepared marinara sauce

1 pound mozzarella cheese, sliced $1/4$-inch thick

$1/2$ cup grated sharp Romano cheese

$1/2$ cup grated Parmesan cheese

2 cups chopped fresh spinach (See "Preparing Fresh Spinach" on page 29.)

DIP

3 eggs, optional

$1/3$ cup heavy cream

1 tablespoon prepared Italian salad dressing

$1/2$ cup grated Parmesan cheese

1 teaspoon black pepper

1. Preheat the oven to 425°F. Lightly oil a 13- by 9-inch baking pan.

2. Place 1 tablespoon of the oil in a large sauté pan, and heat over medium heat. Add the leeks, and sauté for 2 to 3 minutes, until soft. Remove them from the oil using a slotted spoon, and set aside.

3. Into the same sauté pan, put an additional 1 tablespoon of olive oil, if necessary. Add the zucchini, and sauté until tender-crisp, about 2 minutes. Remove the zucchini slices with a slotted spoon, and place on a towel to drain.

4. To make the dip, place the eggs, cream, salad dressing, Parmesan, and black pepper in a medium-sized bowl. Whisk together to blend well. If you omit the eggs, add the extra cream or the milk and whisk into the dip.

5. To make the breading, place the bread, parsley, Parmesan cheese, flour, cornmeal, and seasoning salt in a food processor or blender. Process until thoroughly mixed. Pour the breading mixture into a shallow dish, and set aside.

6. Check the oil in the sauté pan, and add 1 tablespoon olive oil if needed. Add the garlic, and sauté for 1 minute.

7. Place each eggplant slice into the dip and then into the breading mixture. Add the eggplant slices to the oil, as many as will fit at one time in the sauté pan. Slowly sauté the eggplant slices until they are golden brown on both sides. Remove the slices from the pan, and drain on several thicknesses of paper towel.

8. Spread a light layer of marinara sauce on the bottom of the baking pan. Then layer half of the eggplant slices, overlapping if necessary. Sprinkle the eggplant with some of the Romano cheese, then add the leeks, and dabble more of the marinara sauce on top of the leeks. Cover the sauce with mozzarella slices and some of the Parmesan cheese. Add the chopped spinach to the top of the cheese, and then add the rest of the eggplant slices.

9. Generously cover the entire dish with more marinara sauce, and top with the sautéed zucchini rounds. Sprinkle with the remaining Romano and Parmesan cheese, and bake, uncovered, for 30 minutes. The eggplant should be soft when pierced with a fork.

10. Remove the pan from the oven, and place on a wire rack to rest for 10 minutes before serving. Serve with a fresh garden salad.

ABOUT THE RESTAURANT

Tyler Hill and Pius Ruby opened The Bistro in 1982, and it has grown in popularity and size since then. Today, The Bistro maintains its reputation as a trendy, upscale restaurant serving provocative and palate-pleasing cuisine.

BREADING

3 slices assorted toasted bread (white, whole wheat, rye, etc.)

$1/4$ cup chopped fresh parsley

$1/4$ cup grated Parmesan cheese

$1/2$ cup unbleached white flour

$1/4$ cup cornmeal

$1/2$ teaspoon seasoning salt, such as Vege-Sal

From Restaurant Keffi   SANTA CRUZ, CALIFORNIA

Eggplant Moussaka

This is a most delectable eggplant entrée. Working moms and dads might want to consider making the moussaka in several stages to reduce the preparation and cooking time: Prepare the eggplant and vegetables the day before, and do the béchamel sauce and the final baking stage when you serve the dish.

Yield: 6–8 servings

Preparation Time: 30 minutes

Cooking Time: 1 hour for the eggplant slices; 1 hour for the casserole

EGGPLANT SLICES

2 medium eggplants

1 tablespoon plus 1 teaspoon salt

1 cup dairy or soy milk

1/3 cup whole wheat flour

1/3 cup cornmeal

1/2 tablespoon dried oregano

1/2 teaspoon black pepper

VEGETABLE MIXTURE

1 tablespoon olive oil

1 large yellow onion, chopped

6 cloves garlic, minced

2 medium zucchini, sliced into rounds

2 medium carrots, sliced into rounds

2 medium tomatoes, coarsely chopped

2 tablespoons chopped fresh parsley

1/2 teaspoon ground cinnamon

1/2 teaspoon salt

1/2 teaspoon black pepper

To Prepare the Eggplant Slices:

1. Cut off and discard the stem ends of the eggplants. Slice the eggplants into 1 inch-thick rounds. Place in a large bowl, and cover with water. Add 1 tablespoon of the salt, and soak for 45 minutes. Drain, and rinse the eggplant slices with fresh water. Allow to dry on paper towels.

2. Preheat the oven to 350°F. Lightly oil a large baking sheet.

3. Pour the milk into a medium-sized bowl, and set aside.

4. In another medium-sized bowl, put the flour, cornmeal, oregano, black pepper, and the remaining teaspoon of salt, and mix with a fork.

5. Dip each eggplant slice in the milk, and then dredge in the flour mixture. Place the slices on the lightly oiled baking sheet. Bake until the eggplant is tender, when a fork easily pierces the eggplant, or about 45 minutes. Set aside.

To Prepare the Vegetable Mixture:

1. Heat a large sauté pan over medium heat for 30 seconds. Add the oil. Then add the onion, and sauté until the onion is translucent.

2. Add the garlic, zucchini, carrots, tomatoes, parsley, cinnamon, salt, and black pepper. Sauté for 5 minutes longer. Set aside.

To Prepare the Béchamel Sauce:

1. Place the oil in a medium-sized saucepan, and heat over medium heat. When the oil is hot, remove the pan from the heat and stir in the flour with a whisk to make a thick paste.

2. Slowly stir in the milk. Place the pan over low heat, and heat this mixture, stirring frequently until thickened. Add the salt and pepper to taste. Set aside.

To Prepare and Bake the Moussaka:

1. Preheat the oven to 350°F, if you have not already done so. Lightly oil a 2-quart or 13- by 9-inch baking pan.

2. Place half the eggplant slices in a single layer in the baking pan. Add the vegetable mixture, and spread evenly. Top with the remaining eggplant slices.

3. Pour the béchamel sauce over the entire pan, place the pan in the oven, and bake for 30 minutes. Remove the moussaka from the oven, and allow to rest for 5 minutes before serving. Serve with a fresh garden salad.

BÉCHAMEL SAUCE

$1/2$ cup canola oil
$1/2$ cup whole wheat or
   unbleached white flour
2 cups dairy or soy milk
Salt, to taste
Black pepper, to taste

ABOUT THE RESTAURANT

Chef-owner Judith De La Rosa lived in Greece for several years, and she came to appreciate the enjoyment and satisfaction good food can provide. Having a good time and enjoying yourself is called "keffi" in Greek. States Judith, "We believe that delicious vegetarian food with its healthy properties helps generate that 'good-time, keffi feeling' in each of us."

From Restaurant Keffi   SANTA CRUZ, CALIFORNIA

Eggplant Imam

The cinnamon and basil take this celebrated vegetable to new dimensions of flavor. According to the legend, the original Turkish version of this eggplant dish was named after the priest who fainted in delight after tasting the dish. Swoon you might, with this easy-to-make, easy-to-eat dinner treat.

Yield: 6 servings

Preparation Time: 45 minutes

Cooking Time: 45 minutes–1 hour

3 medium eggplants

1 tablespoon plus 1 teaspoon salt

¼ cup olive oil

2 tablespoons canola oil

1 cup sliced yellow onion

5 medium-sized ripe tomatoes, chopped

6 cloves garlic, minced

¼ cup chopped fresh parsley

1 tablespoon dried basil

½ teaspoon ground cinnamon

1. Slice the eggplants into 1 inch-thick rounds, discarding the stem ends. Place the slices in a large bowl, and cover with water. Add 1 tablespoon of the salt, and soak for 45 minutes.

2. Preheat the oven to 350°F. Lightly oil a 13- by 9-inch baking dish.

3. Drain the salted water from the bowl, rinse the eggplant slices with fresh water, and drain them on paper toweling.

4. Place 2 tablespoons of the olive oil and all the canola oil in a wok or large sauté pan, and heat over medium heat. Add the eggplant slices, and sauté until soft, stirring and turning frequently.

5. Remove the eggplant slices from the sauté pan, and place on several thicknesses of paper toweling to drain. Layer the eggplant slices in the baking dish.

6. While the eggplant is being sautéed, put the remaining 2 tablespoons of olive oil in a medium-sized saucepan over medium heat. Add the onions, and sauté for about 5 minutes, until soft. Then add the tomatoes, garlic, parsley, basil, and cinnamon, and the remaining teaspoon of salt. Mix well. Cover, and stew the tomato mixture over low heat until the tomatoes are very soft, about 10 minutes.

7. Pour the tomato mixture over the eggplant slices in the baking dish, and bake for 45 minutes to 1 hour, or until the eggplant slices are soft when pierced with a fork. Serve immediately with rice or couscous.

ABOUT THE RESTAURANT

At Restaurant Keffi in Santa Cruz, owner Judith De La Rosa offers wonderful gourmet vegetarian foods.

Nut Loaves, Burgers, & Sandwiches

From High Noon Café *JACKSON, MISSISSIPPI*

Mixed Nut Roast

Serve this protein-rich loaf as a hot entrée, and slice the leftovers for hot or cold sandwiches the next day.

1. Preheat the oven to 350°F. Lightly oil a $3^1/_2$- by $9^1/_2$- by $5^1/_2$-inch loaf pan, or use a nonstick pan.

2. Place the nuts, rice, onion, sage, salt, cornstarch, and Grape Nuts in a large bowl, and combine together.

3. In a separate, small bowl, place the tomato juice (or sauce), the soy sauce, and the optional liquid smoke together, and mix. Pour over the dry ingredients. Mix the ingredients together with your hands or a wooden spoon as briefly as possible, just enough to moisten the mixture.

4. Press the mixture firmly into the loaf pan. Place in the oven, and bake for 45 minutes.

5. Remove the roast from the oven, and loosen the edges of the loaf from the sides of the pan with a knife. Invert the nut roast onto a serving platter to slice. Serve the roast with mashed potatoes and your favorite brown or golden gravy.

ABOUT THE RESTAURANT

High Noon Café features homemade breads and desserts along with its vegan cuisine, and much of the produce for the café is organically grown at Harvestime Farm by the chef, Regina Glass. This recipe for Mixed Nut Roast is adapted from Regina Glass's cookbook, "The Basics of Vegetarian Cooking" (1993), available from Harvestime Farm, P.O. Box 39, Puckett, MS 39151.

Yield: 6 servings

Preparation Time: 25 minutes

Cooking Time: 45 minutes

$1/_2$ cup chopped mixed raw nuts

1 cup cooked and cooled white or brown rice

2 tablespoons dried onion or $1/_4$ cup fresh chopped onion

1 teaspoon dried sage

$1/_2$ teaspoon garlic salt

2 tablespoons cornstarch

2 cups Post Grape Nuts

$1^3/_4$ cups tomato juice or thinned tomato sauce

1 tablespoon soy sauce (See about Soy Sauce" on page 13.)

$1/_4$–$1/_2$ teaspoon liquid smoke, optional

Vegetarian Stuffed Roast
with Herbed Whole Wheat Stuffing and Golden Gravy

The soy and orange bastes make a beautiful, light golden glaze on the roast, adding a crispy texture to the outside of the soft tofu interior. The roast is the perfect entrée for holiday or special occasion dinners, and the gravy is by far one of the best-tasting vegetarian gravies.

Yield: *10–12 servings, including 2³⁄₄ cups of gravy*

Preparation Time: 1 hour for the roast; 5 minutes for the gravy

Cooking Time: 1¹⁄₂ hours for the roast; 15 minutes for the gravy

5 pounds firm tofu, drained and squeezed dry

1 cup nutritional yeast flakes

2 teaspoons sea salt

HERBED WHOLE WHEAT STUFFING

2 tablespoons sesame oil

2 large cloves garlic, minced

1 cup finely chopped yellow onion

1 cup finely chopped mushrooms

1 cup diced celery

1 tablespoon poultry seasoning

¹⁄₄ teaspoon sea salt

¹⁄₄ cup tamari soy sauce (See "About Soy Sauce" on page 13.)

4 cups dried whole wheat bread cubes

¹⁄₄ cup chopped fresh parsley

1 cup peeled, diced Granny Smith apple, optional

To Prepare the Tofu:

1. Place the tofu in a large bowl, and mash well.

2. Line an 11-inch colander with a single layer of moistened cheesecloth. Transfer the mashed tofu to the colander, and press it down to flatten it against the edges. Fold the edges of the cheesecloth over the tofu to cover it.

3. Place a heavy object—about 10 pounds—on top of the tofu for 1 hour to press out the liquid. If you want a very dry tofu, spin the tofu in a salad spinner before or after pressing it.

To Prepare the Herbed Stuffing:

1. In a large sauté pan, place the sesame oil and heat over medium-high heat. Add the garlic, onion, mushrooms, and celery, and sauté until soft.

2. Sprinkle the poultry seasoning over the vegetables. Dissolve the salt in the soy sauce, and add to the sauté pan.

3. Stir the mixture, cover the pan with a lid, and continue to cook until the vegetables are done, or about 5 minutes.

4. Transfer the veggies to a large mixing bowl, and add the bread cubes, parsley, and optional apple. Stir to mix well, adding tablespoons of melted butter, vegetable broth, or water to moisten if too dry.

To Stuff and Bake the Roast:

1. Preheat the oven to 375°F. Lightly oil a baking sheet with a rim or a small jelly roll pan.

2. Remove the tofu from the cheesecloth, and place in a large bowl. Add the nutritional yeast and salt, and gently blend into the tofu.

3. Place the cheesecloth either back into the colander or into a similar-sized bowl, and place about 4 pounds of the tofu mixture in the cheesecloth.

4. Make a well or pocket in the tofu mixture to within 1 inch of the rim of the bowl. Pack in the stuffing, and cover with the remaining tofu. Pat the tofu down carefully so the surface is firm.

5. Invert the bowl or colander over the baking sheet. Slip the filled tofu onto the baking sheet so the flat surface faces down. Remove the cheesecloth.

6. To prepare the soy baste, combine the sesame oil and the soy sauce in a small bowl, and stir with a whisk or fork to blend.

7. Brush the tofu loaf with the soy baste, and place the baking sheet in the oven to bake for 30 minutes. Brush the loaf again with the soy baste, and bake 30 minutes more.

8. To prepare the orange baste, combine the orange juice concentrate and the honey in a small bowl, and mix with a whisk or fork to blend.

9. After the second baking, brush the roast with the orange baste. Garnish the roast with overlapping slices of grilled or broiled pineapple slices around the base of the roast, and bake the roast another 20 minutes.

To Make the Gravy:

1. In a medium-sized saucepan, place the nutritional yeast and flour, and toast over medium heat, stirring frequently, until you smell the ingredients starting to brown.

2. Add the oil, stirring with a whisk while the mixture bubbles and turns to a golden brown paste.

3. Add the water or broth, still stirring with a whisk, until the mixture changes to gravy consistency.

4. Stir in the soy sauce, salt, and black pepper. Reduce the heat to low and cook a few more minutes.

To Serve the Roast:

1. Again, baste the roast with the orange baste, and bake another 10 minutes, or until golden brown. Transfer the tofu roast to a serving platter and garnish with pomegranate seeds and sprigs of fresh rosemary. Serve with mashed potatoes, gravy, and all the holiday trimmings!

Melted butter, vegetable broth, or water to moisten

SOY BASTE
1/2 cup sesame oil

1/4 cup tamari soy sauce

ORANGE BASTE
1/4 cup frozen orange juice concentrate

4 tablespoons honey

GOLDEN GRAVY
1/2 cup nutritional yeast flakes

1/4 cup unbleached white flour

1/4 cup vegetable oil

2 cups water or vegetable broth

2–3 tablespoons reduced-sodium or tamari soy sauce

1/4–3/4 teaspoon sea salt, optional

1/8 teaspoon black pepper

GARNISH
Fresh sliced pineapple, grilled or broiled

Pomegranate seeds

Fresh rosemary sprigs

From The Higher Taste, Ltd. PORTLAND, OREGON

Cheddar Walnut Loaf

This scrumptious loaf is easy to make and leaves you with that "Mmmm, good" feeling on a cold, wintry day. If you want an eggless dish, you may substitute 2^1/$_2$ teaspoons Ener G brand egg replacer mixed with 4 tablespoons water for the eggs. (See "Alternatives to Eggs" on page 82.)

Yield: 6 servings

Preparation Time: 15 minutes

Cooking Time: 30–40 minutes

^{1}/$_2$ cup wheat germ

1 cup chopped walnuts (about 4 ounces)

^{1}/$_2$ cup cooked brown rice (about 3 tablespoons raw)

^{1}/$_2$ cup chopped onion

2 cups grated cheddar cheese (about 6 ounces)

^{1}/$_2$ teaspoon garlic powder

^{1}/$_2$ teaspoon sea salt

Dash of cayenne pepper

2 eggs, beaten

Parsley, optional

2^3/$_4$ cups Golden Gravy (see page 143)

1. Preheat the oven to 350°F. Lightly oil an 8- by 4-inch loaf pan, and set aside.

2. Sprinkle the wheat germ on an unoiled baking sheet. Place the baking sheet in the oven for 3 to 5 minutes, watching carefully so the wheat germ does not burn. Remove from the oven, and set aside to cool.

3. In a large bowl, place the walnuts, rice, wheat germ, onion, cheese, garlic powder, sea salt, cayenne pepper, and eggs (or egg replacer). Mix together.

4. Pour the mixture into the loaf pan, and place on the middle rack of the oven. Bake for 30 to 40 minutes.

5. Remove the pan from the oven, and allow the loaf to cool in the pan for 5 minutes. Then, loosen the edges of the loaf with a knife, and invert it onto a serving platter or a cutting board, where you can slice it into individual servings. Garnish the serving platter or individual plates with the optional parsley, and serve with mashed potatoes or rice and Golden Gravy.

ABOUT THE RESTAURANT

Hans and Rhonda Wrobel, owners of The Higher Taste, Ltd., consider their cooking a service. Rhonda reports in the Oregonian, *"Food that is made with a commitment of love can nourish the spirit, too." With four children, their active life takes them into the garden or out on hikes, where they like to hunt for chanterelle mushrooms.*

The Wrobels believe that experimentation is the key element in the success of their Portland business. They love to be creative with their seasonings and to continually improve and evolve their recipes. Moreover, they want to reach working people with good vegetarian fast food. With over a dozen items in their product line, they supply over thirty stores with their prepared foods.

From Joy Meadow   REDWOOD CITY, CALIFORNIA

Nepal Loaf

The tofu and rice in this dish are nutritionally balanced to provide a protein-rich meal.

To Prepare the Loaf or Patties Mixture:

1. Place 1 tablespoon of the olive oil in a medium-sized saucepan, and heat over medium heat. Add the garlic, onions, carrots, and celery, and sauté until the onion is translucent.

2. Add the brown rice, tofu, water chestnuts, sage, thyme, salt, pepper, and parsley. Stir well. Add the red wine and soy sauce, and mix well.

3. Add the gluten flour to bind the ingredients, and stir to mix. Remove the pan from the heat, and let cool.

To Prepare the Gravy:

1. In a medium-sized saucepan over medium heat, place the soy sauce, white pepper, and mushrooms. Cook over medium heat until the mushrooms are soft and have released some of their juices.

2. Combine the cornstarch with the water in a small bowl, and mix until smooth. Add the cornstarch mixture to the soy sauce, stirring constantly until the sauce thickens and is heated thoroughly. Serve immediately.

To Cook and Serve as a Loaf:

1. Mold the mixture into a loaf pan, packing firmly with your fingers.

2. Place the loaf pan in the oven to bake for 20 to 30 minutes.

3. Remove the pan from the oven, and allow to cool on a wire rack for 5 minutes. Invert the loaf onto a serving platter, and serve with the gravy.

To Cook and Serve as Patties:

1. Pour the bread crumbs into a shallow dish.

2. When the mixture is cool enough to handle with your hands, form into patties.

3. Dip each patty in the bread crumbs, coating both sides.

4. Place the remaining 1 tablespoon of olive oil in a frying pan, and heat over medium-high heat.

5. Brown both sides of the patties in the oil. Remove the patties from the pan to a serving plate, and serve with the gravy.

ABOUT THE RESTAURANT

Valencia Chan of Joy Meadow creates a variety of vegetarian entrées with fascinating names: Nepal Loaf, Golden Chalice, and Enchanted Forest.

Yield: 6 servings

Preparation Time: 20 minutes for the loaf; 5 for the gravy

Cooking Time: 20–30 minutes for the loaf; 10 minutes for the gravy

LOAF OR PATTIES MIXTURE

2 tablespoons olive oil (1 tablespoon for the loaf)

1 teaspoon crushed garlic

2 medium yellow onions, chopped

2 medium carrots, chopped

1 stalk celery, chopped

2 cups cooked brown rice (about 1 cup raw rice)

7 ounces firm tofu, drained and squeezed dry

$1/4$ cup finely chopped water chestnuts

$1/2$ teaspoon dried sage

$1/2$ teaspoon dried thyme

1 teaspoon salt

$1/2$ teaspoon white pepper

1 tablespoon dried parsley

1 tablespoon red wine

1 tablespoon soy sauce

1 tablespoon gluten flour

1 cup bread crumbs

MUSHROOM GRAVY

$1/2$ cup dark soy sauce

2 teaspoons white pepper

4 cups sliced mushrooms

1 tablespoon cornstarch

$1/2$ cup water

From Chicago Diner   CHICAGO, ILLINOIS

Lentil Loaf

The Lentil Loaf contains a savory blend of herbs and is chock full of protein-rich nuts, grains, and beans. The loaf freezes nicely, and it's great to have an extra loaf in the freezer ready to pull out for those quick dinners or for sandwich fixings.

Yield: 8–10 servings

Preparation Time: 30 minutes

Cooking Time: 45 minutes

$6^{1}/_{2}$ cups water plus additional water as needed

2 cups dried lentils, washed

1 cup bulgur*

$^{3}/_{4}$ cup sesame seeds, toasted (See "Toasting Nuts and Seeds" on page 68.)

$^{3}/_{4}$ cup sunflower seeds, toasted

$^{3}/_{4}$ cup chopped walnuts, toasted

2 tablespoons soy oil

6 medium carrots, finely chopped (about 3 cups)

1 large onion, finely chopped

6 stalks celery, finely chopped (about 2 cups)

1 tablespoon plus $^{1}/_{2}$ teaspoon ground sage

1 tablespoon plus $^{1}/_{2}$ teaspoon dried thyme

$^{1}/_{2}$ teaspoon salt

$^{1}/_{4}$ teaspoon black pepper

$^{1}/_{4}$ cup dried parsley

$^{1}/_{4}$ cup tamari soy sauce (See "About Soy Sauce" on page 13.)

$5^{1}/_{2}$ cups rolled oats

1. Preheat the oven to 350°F. Lightly oil three 3- by $9^{1}/_{2}$- by $5^{1}/_{2}$-inch bread loaf pans.

2. In a medium-sized saucepan, place the lentils and 5 cups of the water. Cover with a lid, place over medium-high heat, and bring to a boil. Reduce the heat to medium-low, and simmer for 35 to 45 minutes, or until the lentils are soft. Remove from the heat, but do not drain. Set aside.

3. In a small pan, place the remaining $1^{1}/_{2}$ cups of water, and bring to the boil over high heat. Add the bulgur, stir to blend well, and remove the pan from the heat. Set aside.

4. Place the oil in a large sauté pan, and heat over medium heat. Add the carrots, onions, and celery. Add the sage, thyme, salt, and black pepper, and sauté until the vegetables are soft.

5. Stir the parsley, soy sauce, toasted nuts and seeds, lentils, and bulgur into the onion mixture. Mix well. Stir in the oats, adding more water if necessary to moisten. Remove from heat.

6. Press the mixture firmly into the loaf pans, and bake uncovered for about 45 minutes. Remove the pans from the oven, and turn out the loaves onto a serving platter. Serve warm with the Artichoke Cafe's delicious Sweet Potato Gratin (page 124).

ABOUT THE RESTAURANT

Mickey Hornick, owner of the Chicago Diner, brings his excitement and enthusiasm for vegetarian food everywhere he goes. As organizer and president of Chicago's North Halsted annual Market Days Fair, Mickey almost convinced the Market Days Fair Board that a vegetarian fair would contribute to a kinder, gentler weekend fair. Even if the board wasn't convinced, Mickey says, "At least I got them talking. . . . I accomplished what I wanted to."

*Bulgur wheat is a popular Middle Eastern wheat that has been cracked by boiling, and then redried. It's available in natural food stores.

From The Community Food Co-op   BOZEMAN, MONTANA

Bean Burgers

The Community Food Co-op delivers the best bean burgers I've ever tasted. The beans, grains, and spices are perfectly combined to yield a smooth, rich flavor in every bite.

1. Preheat the oven to 350°F. Lightly oil a baking sheet.

2. Place the soybeans in a food processor or blender, and process until ground medium fine. Turn the ground soybeans into a large mixing bowl, and set aside.

3. Place the sunflower seeds, peanuts, and oatmeal in the food processor or blender. Process until ground medium fine. Add to the soybeans.

4. Add the remaining ingredients to the mixing bowl, and stir well to blend.

5. With your hands, form the mixture into patties or burgers, making them about 1/2-inch thick. Place each burger on the oiled baking sheet. Place the baking sheet in the oven, and bake for 1 hour. If you make the burgers thinner in size, they won't need to bake as long, but the thicker burgers are tastier and have a fuller flavor.

6. Remove the burgers from the oven, and serve on a bun with your favorite burger condiments.

7. Cooked burgers may be individually wrapped in plastic wrap or sandwich bags and frozen for up to three months. To reheat, simply allow the frozen burgers to thaw at room temperature; then place them on a lightly oiled baking sheet and reheat for 10 to 20 minutes at 350°F. Or thaw and reheat the burgers in a microwave oven for 3 to 4 minutes.

ABOUT THE RESTAURANT

From a one-bedroom house, which served as the store and office for a buying club of thirty-five members, to the present store of 7,200 square feet and six thousand members, The Community Food Co-op has experienced many changes since it first opened in 1978. "Every time I look at our vegetable bin, I am reminded of one of the most significant changes I have seen," remarks Meylahn Sai, one of the original members. "In the early days we used to have fresh produce about twenty percent of the time. Now it's fully stocked all the time. And we like to use as many organic Montana growers as possible."

Yield: 12 burgers

Preparation Time: 30 minutes

Cooking Time: 1 hour

4 cups cooked soybeans (about 2 cups raw soybeans)

1 1/2 cups unsalted sunflower seeds

1 1/2 cups unsalted peanuts

1 cup oatmeal

3 medium yellow onions, finely chopped

5 medium carrots, grated

2 stalks celery, minced

1/4 cup minced garlic

1 cup tamari soy sauce (See "About Soy Sauce" on page 13.)

1 tablespoon black pepper

2 teaspoons dried oregano

1 tablespoon dried basil

2 teaspoons dried thyme

2 cups bread crumbs (See "About Bread Crumbs" on page 23.)

1/3 cup Worcestershire sauce

From Madison River Inn   THREE FORKS, MONTANA

Tofu Burgers

This burger recipe was provided by Margaret Hower. We have loved it for years. Thanks, Margaret!

Yield: 12 burgers

Preparation Time: 30 minutes

Cooking Time: 3–5 minutes per side

2 cups water

1 1/2 teaspoons salt

1 cup bulgur*

1 pound firm tofu, drained, rinsed, and mashed

1 tablespoon cumin

4 tablespoons nutritional yeast flakes

1 1/2 cups whole wheat flour

1/2 tablespoon dried basil

1/2 tablespoon dried oregano

2 tablespoons dried parsley

Black pepper, to taste

1/2 teaspoon garlic powder or to taste

1 medium onion, finely chopped

1 tablespoon vegetable oil (if frying)

Slices of cheddar or Swiss cheese, optional

1. If you plan to broil the patties, preheat the broiler and lightly oil a baking sheet or broiler pan.

2. Place the water and salt in a medium-sized saucepan, and bring to the boil over high heat. Add the bulgur, stir, lower the heat to low, and simmer for 10 minutes. When the water is absorbed, the bulgur is done.

3. In a large mixing bowl, mash the tofu and add the bulgur, cumin, yeast flakes, flour, basil, oregano, and parsley. Add black pepper and garlic powder to taste. Stir to blend well. Add the onion, and gently mix.

4. Form the tofu mixture into patties. If you don't plan to cook all the burgers right away, place the burgers you want to freeze into separate plastic bags. If using frozen burgers, thaw in the microwave or at room temperature before cooking.

5. Heat a large sauté pan over medium heat, and add the 1 tablespoon of oil. When the oil is hot, add the patties. Fry for 3 to 5 minutes per side, until golden brown. Or place the patties on the baking sheet, and put under the broiler for 3 to 5 minutes, until golden brown on each side.

6. With either cooking method, when the patties are cooked, top them each with a slice of cheese and cover the pan or allow the cheese to melt under the broiler. Transfer the patties from the pan or baking sheet to your favorite whole grain bun, and top with lettuce, tomato, and all the fixings.

ABOUT THE RESTAURANT

The sounds of the wind whispering through the trees, the gentle lapping of the water, and the chirping of crickets in the grass greet you at the Madison River Inn. A tranquil setting that provides nourishment for the spirit and comfort to the soul. The lovely accommodations and meals complete this heavenly scenario.

---

* *Bulgur wheat* is a popular Middle Eastern wheat that has been cracked by boiling, and then redried. It's available in natural food stores.

From Paradise Café   LAWRENCE, KANSAS

Garden Burgers

Everybody loves a burger. These burgers combine veggies, spices, beans, and cheese to make a protein powerhouse!

1. Place the oil in a large sauté pan, heat over medium heat, and add the onions. Sauté until translucent. Add the celery, carrots, and walnuts. Continue to sauté until the carrots are crisp-tender.

2. Add the bread crumbs, Italian seasoning, salt, pepper, and garlic powder. Stir to mix well. Remove the pan from the heat, and turn the mixture into a large bowl.

3. Add the optional eggs or egg replacer and puréed beans, and mix well. Chill the mixture covered in the refrigerator for 1 hour.

4. Preheat the broiler. Lightly oil the broiler pan.

5. When the mixture is firm, remove from the refrigerator. Portion into patties, about 4 ounces each. If you don't plan to broil all the burgers, place the patties in individual sandwich bags and store in the freezer for up to three months. Thaw at room temperature or in the microwave before broiling.

6. To broil, place the patties on the broiler pan. Broil for 3 to 5 minutes per side. As a variation, add a slice of cheddar, Swiss, or Monterey jack cheese to each burger, return to the broiler, and broil until the cheese melts. Remove the pan from the oven, and serve the burgers hot on a fresh whole grain bun with your favorite condiments.

ABOUT THE RESTAURANT

"We serve good real food" is the motto of the Paradise Café. Forest greens and sun-drenched reds permeate the casual, homey atmosphere of the Paradise Café interior. The demand for their "good real food" has enabled the owners, Fran Zillner and Steve McCoy, to expand the café, opened in 1983, to three storefronts on the main street of Lawrence.

Yield: 10 burgers

Preparation Time: 25 minutes plus 1 hour chilling time

Cooking Time: 5 minutes

3 tablespoons sesame oil

$1\frac{1}{4}$ cups finely chopped yellow onions

$1\frac{1}{4}$ cups finely chopped celery

$1\frac{1}{4}$ cups grated carrots

$1\frac{1}{4}$ cups finely chopped walnuts

$1\frac{1}{4}$ cups dry bread crumbs (See "About Bread Crumbs" on page 23.)

1 scant tablespoon Italian seasoning

1 teaspoon salt

1 teaspoon white pepper

$\frac{1}{4}$ teaspoon garlic powder

5 eggs (See "Alternatives to Eggs" on page 82.)

1 cup puréed pinto beans or canned, nonfat refried pinto beans

10 ($\frac{3}{4}$-ounce) slices of cheddar, Swiss, or Monterey jack cheese ($7\frac{1}{2}$ ounces total), optional

From John Bozeman's Bistro   BOZEMAN, MONTANA

Fantastic Unburgers

These burgers live up to their name—Fantastic! Tyler Hill, the chef and one of the owners of The Bistro, says, "There have been oodles of veggie burgers, most tasting like cardboard and resembling a shingle. This ingredient-intensive, yet simple-to-make, recipe is tried and proven to be absolutely delicious." If you wish to omit the eggs, see "Alternatives to Eggs" on page 82.

Yield: 8 burgers

Preparation Time: 30 minutes

Cooking Time: 10 minutes per burger

VEGGIE MIXTURE

4 cups finely chopped fresh spinach (See "Preparing Fresh Spinach" on page 29.)

$1/2$ cup lentil, bean, or other hard sprouts

$1/3$ cup finely chopped celery

$1/3$ cup finely chopped scallions (green onions)

$1/3$ cup finely chopped red bell pepper

$1/3$ cup fresh parsley, basil, and cilantro (coriander), combined

1 cup shredded Monterey jack or cheddar cheese (or a combination)

$1/3$ cup grated Parmesan cheese

1 cup finely chopped cold baked potato

1 teaspoon minced garlic

1 cup finely chopped nuts and seeds (pecans, sunflower seeds, walnuts, sesames, or a combination)

$1/2$ cup bread crumbs (See "About Bread Crumbs" on page 23.)

1. Place all the ingredients for the veggie mixture in a large mixing bowl. Mix well with your hands to blend thoroughly.

2. Place all the ingredients for the wet mixture in a food processor. Pulse just until all the ingredients are mixed together.

3. Add the wet mixture to the veggie mixture. Work intensely with your hands, squeezing the ingredients through your fingers until the preparation is completely mixed.

4. Place the cornmeal in a shallow bowl. Portion the mixture into 4 balls about $2^1/2$ inches in diameter. Flatten and shape into burger forms. Clean and dry your hands, and coat each burger by dredging it in the cornmeal.

5. Place the canola oil in a large sauté pan, and heat over medium heat. Fry the burgers in the oil, allowing about 5 minutes per side.

6. To garnish, top each burger with a slice of Swiss cheese and sautéed onions. Cover the pan with a lid to melt the cheese.

7. Remove the burgers to individual serving plates, and serve on an open-faced, multigrain toasted bun with humus, sliced tomatoes, and cucumbers on the side.

ABOUT THE RESTAURANT

Nestled on Main Street in downtown Bozeman, The Bistro maintains a wonderful tradition of providing a fine dining experience. The Fantastic Unburger is the most sought-after Bistro recipe.

1 teaspoon garlic salt

Pinch of fresh dill

Pinch of freshly ground black pepper

Pinch of ground cumin

Pinch of dried coriander

Pinch of dried oregano

WET MIXTURE

2 eggs or egg replacer

1 cup tahini (sesame seed paste)

1 tablespoon tamari soy sauce (See "About Soy Sauce" on page 13.)

2 teaspoons roasted sesame oil

Juice of $\frac{1}{2}$ lemon

3 dashes of Tabasco sauce, or to taste

BREADING AND FRYING

2 cups cornmeal

1 tablespoon canola oil

GARNISH

Sautéed onions, about 1 cup

Slices of Swiss cheese

Humus

Sliced tomatoes

Sliced cucumbers

From Sunshine Inn   ST. LOUIS, MISSOURI

Golden Lion Vegetarian Burgers

These yummy burgers are great to have in the freezer when you come home from work to a family of hungry folks! The same recipe makes an excellent burrito filling.

Yield: 15 burgers or burritos

Preparation Time: 45 minutes

Cooking Time: 10 minutes

2 cups soybeans

About 6 cups water for cooking the soybeans, plus $3^3/_4$ cups for cooking the millet

$3/_4$ cup millet

1 cup rolled oats

$1/_2$ cup cornmeal

$1/_4$ cup corn or vegetable oil plus 1–2 tablespoons extra for frying

$1/_2$ cup grated carrots

$1/_2$ onion, finely chopped

2 ribs celery, finely chopped

3 tablespoons tamari soy sauce (See "About Soy Sauce" on page 13.)

1 teaspoon salt

$1/_4$–$1/_2$ teaspoon cayenne pepper

1 teaspoon granulated garlic

1–2 tablespoons chili powder

1 tablespoon ground cumin

Dairy or soy cheese slices, optional

1. Place the soybeans in a large pot, and add more than enough water to cover. Soak overnight. The next day, drain and rinse the beans. Return the beans to the pot, add fresh water to cover, and cook until soft, about $1^1/_2$ hours. Drain, mash, and set aside to cool.

2. Preheat the broiler.

3. Place the millet and the remaining $3^3/_4$ cups water in a medium-sized pot. Cook over medium heat until tender, about 30 minutes. Drain, and set aside to cool.

4. While the soybeans and millet are cooking, place the oats and the cornmeal on a baking sheet. Roast under the broiler, about 30 seconds to 1 minute. Remove from the broiler, and set aside to cool.

5. In a large mixing bowl, place the mashed soybeans, oats mixture, and millet, and mix well. Add the $1/_4$ cup oil and the carrots, onion, celery, soy sauce, salt, cayenne pepper, garlic, chili powder, and cumin. Mix again.

6. Form into patties. Place the 1 to 2 tablespoons oil in a large skillet, and heat over medium-high heat. Place patties in the hot oil, and fry about 5 minutes per side. Top each burger with an optional slice of cheese, cover the pan with a lid, and allow the cheese to melt. Remove the burgers from the pan, and serve on your favorite whole grain bun with all the burger trimmings.Placed in individual plastic baggies, the uncooked burgers freeze well for up to three months. Thaw in the microwave before cooking.

To Use as a Burrito Filling:

1. Season the mixture with additional chili powder and additional cayenne to taste. Place the 1 to 2 tablespoons oil in a frying pan, and heat over medium heat. Add the filling mixture and scramble in the oil until it is thoroughly warm. Place $1/_3$ cup of the filling in a flour tortilla, top with grated dairy or soy cheese, roll up, and serve.

ABOUT THE RESTAURANT

Besides burgers, the Sunshine Inn features wok dishes, garden fresh salads with homemade dressings, soups, quiche, soy foods, seafood, poultry, whole grain breads, honey-sweetened desserts, fresh carrot juice, beers, and wines.

From The Higher Taste, Ltd.   PORTLAND, OREGON

Broccoli Burgers

A nontraditional, super-yummy veggie burger! Most burgers are ingredient-laden and labor-intensive. These burgers are a snap to make. If you want to go eggless in this recipe, an egg substitute would work better than an egg replacer. See "Alternatives to Eggs" on page 82.

1. Place the eggs (or egg substitute) in a medium-sized bowl, and beat them. Add the broccoli, mushrooms, yeast, nuts, and onion. Mix thoroughly. Add a little flour—1 tablespoon at a time—to thicken, if necessary. Form the mixture into four patties.

2. To fry the patties, place the butter (or oil) in a large sauté pan over medium heat. Add the patties to the pan, and fry until golden brown on both sides.

3. To bake the patties, preheat the oven to 350°F. Oil a baking sheet, and put the patties on the baking sheet. Place the baking sheet in the oven. Bake about 5 to 10 minutes on one side, or until the patties turn golden brown. Then turn the patties, and bake about 5 to 10 minutes on the other side.

4. Remove the burgers from the sauté pan or baking sheet, place on a toasted bun of your choice, and serve warm with your favorite condiments.

ABOUT THE RESTAURANT

The Higher Taste's Broccoli Burger, adapted from a recipe published in "Sunset Magazine," was served to Portland's mayor and received rave reviews.

Yield: *4 burgers*

Preparation Time: 20 minutes

Cooking Time: 10 minutes per burger

2 eggs or egg substitute

⅓ cup chopped broccoli

4 mushrooms, thinly sliced

1 tablespoon nutritional yeast

2 tablespoons ground raw nuts (almonds, cashews, or sunflower seeds, or a combination)

1 tablespoon chopped onion or scallion (green onion)

Flour to thicken, if necessary

1 tablespoon butter or vegetable oil

From McFoster's Natural Kind Café   OMAHA, NEBRASKA

Grilled Eggplant Sandwich

Enjoy the great taste of eggplant in this delicious sandwich.

Yield: 4 servings

Preparation Time: 20 minutes

Cooking Time: 10 minutes

1 large, firm eggplant, peeled and sliced 1/2-inch thick (8 slices)

2 tablespoons olive oil

2 tablespoons balsamic vinegar

1 large, ripe tomato, sliced into 1/2-inch rounds (4 slices)

4–8 teaspoons basil, tomato, or roasted red pepper pesto of your choice

4 toasted buns or 8 slices of bread

4 slices cheddar, Swiss, Monterey jack, or soy cheese

1. Prepare the barbecue or charbroiler for grilling.

2. Lightly brush the eggplant slices with the olive oil, and place them on the grill. Cook for 3 to 5 minutes, or until the side facing up becomes tender. Turn the slices over, and brush the grilled side of the eggplant with balsamic vinegar. Continue to cook until the second side is tender, another 3 to 5 minutes.

3. Before the eggplant is completely grilled, place the tomato slices on the grill, just long enough to heat thoroughly, about 1 minute.

4. While the veggies are grilling, toast the buns or bread. Spread 1 tablespoon of pesto sauce on each bun.

5. Remove the eggplant and tomato slices from the grill. Place a slice of eggplant on each toasted bun, layer with a grilled tomato slice, add another slice of eggplant, and top with a slice of cheese. The cheese should melt with the heat from the grilled veggies. If it doesn't, place the sandwich under the broiler for a few seconds. Top with the other half of the bun or another slice of bread, and serve hot with your favorite chips and relishes.

ABOUT THE RESTAURANT

McFoster's is one of the only natural foods restaurants you'll find between the Nebraska borders—north and south, or east and west. The owners, Tom Foster (whose name means "to nourish") and Mary McGrahaghan (whose name means "keeper of the grains"), are bringing full fruition to their names at McFoster's Natural Kind Café. The manager, Bill Lee, says of Chef Tom, "He's the best chef around. His knowledge of spices and seasoning is phenomenal; people line up around the block for his great-tasting food."

From Pyewacket Restaurant   CHAPEL HILL, NORTH CAROLINA

Barbecued Tempeh Sandwich

Discover delicious tempeh with this wonderful, casual family meal. These sandwiches are also great fun for invite-the-neighbors-over dining.

1. Place the water, salt, garlic, coriander, and chili powder in a medium-sized bowl, and stir to mix well. Add the tempeh pieces, and allow to marinate for 3 to 5 minutes. Drain the tempeh well, and set aside.

2. Heat 2 tablespoons of the vegetable oil in a medium-sized sauté pan over medium-high heat. Add the tempeh, and sauté until well browned and crispy, about 15 to 20 minutes, being careful not to let the tempeh burn.

3. Place the remaining tablespoon of vegetable oil in a small sauté over medium heat. Add the onions, and sauté until soft and lightly browned.

4. Add the onions and the barbecue sauce to the tempeh, and heat thoroughly.

5. To serve, heat the kaiser rolls in the oven until slightly crispy. Put a scoop of the tempeh mixture on the bottom bun, top with $1/3$ cup of prepared coleslaw, and finish with the top bun. Serve hot.

ABOUT THE RESTAURANT

Do you remember the name of the witch's cat in Alfred Hitchcock's movie "Bell, Book, and Candle"? Pyewacket!

Tempeh is a delicious, high-protein food made from soybeans. Tempeh usually tastes best when it is marinated before sautéeing.

Yield: *4 servings*

Preparation Time: 15 minutes

Cooking Time: 20 minutes

3 cups water

2 teaspoons salt

4 teaspoons minced garlic

2 teaspoons ground coriander

2 teaspoons chili powder

2 packages tempeh,* cut into $1/4$-inch squares or rectangles

3 tablespoons vegetable oil

2 medium yellow onions, sliced

$1/2$ cup prepared barbecue sauce

4 kaiser rolls

$1^1/3$ cups prepared coleslaw

From The Raw Carrot   AMHERST, MASSACHUSETTS

Tempeh Salad Sandwich Spread

This salad is the kind of sandwich spread you like to keep on hand for school or work lunches. It travels easily so it's also great for on-the-road meals or picnics at the park.

Yield: 4–6 servings including 2^1/$_2$ cups of mayonnaise

Preparation Time: 15 minutes for the mayonnaise; 10 minutes for the spread

Cooking Time: 10 minutes

EXCELLENT EGGLESS MAYONNAISE (from the Madison River Inn)

1 cup whole milk

^{1}/$_2$ teaspoon prepared mustard

^{1}/$_4$ cup apple cider vinegar

1 teaspoon salt

1 tablespoon honey

2 cups vegetable oil

SANDWICH SPREAD

2 tablespoons canola oil

1 clove garlic, pressed

1 pound tempeh,* chopped into ^{1}/$_2$-inch cubes

3 tablespoons tamari soy sauce (See "About Soy Sauce" on page 13.)

^{1}/$_2$–1 tablespoon dried tarragon, to taste

^{3}/$_4$ cup finely chopped scallions (green onions) or minced onions

^{3}/$_4$ cup finely chopped celery

To Make the Mayonnaise:

1. Place the milk, mustard, vinegar, salt, and honey in a blender or food processor. If you use a blender, you may need to do half of the recipe at a time. Blend or process at medium speed for about 1 minute, until the ingredients are well blended, scraping the sides if necessary.

2. Remove the blender or processor lid. With the machine turned to high speed, very slowly add the oil in a thin, steady stream. Continue to blend or process until the mixture becomes thick (about 20 to 25 minutes in a food processor).

3. Use the mayonnaise immediately, or pour it into a glass container, cover, and chill deeply in the refrigerator, about 1 hour. The mayonnaise will thicken more after chilling and will keep well in the refrigerator for one to two weeks.

To Make the Sandwich Spread:

1. Place the oil in a large sauté pan over medium heat. Add the garlic, and sauté for 1 minute.

2. Add the tempeh. Sauté for 5 to 10 minutes, or until the tempeh turns golden brown. Remove the pan from the heat, and turn the tempeh mixture into a large mixing bowl. Add the soy sauce, and mash. Set aside to cool to room temperature.

3. Season the tempeh with the tarragon, and add the scallions (or onions), celery, and 1^1/$_2$ cups of the mayonnaise. Stir to mix well. Deeply chill the tempeh salad, covered, in the refrigerator for 1 to 2 hours before using. The tempeh salad keeps well in a covered container in the refrigerator for three days.

4. Serve as a sandwich spread on your favorite whole grain, rye, or sourdough bread, or as a salad on a bed of crisp green lettuce.

ABOUT THE RESTAURANT

The Raw Carrot, a bright, cheery spot on Pleasant Street, began as a juice bar. Owner Heather Fern said that they started making sandwiches, soups, sautés, and salads when people wanted to linger longer for more of their good food!

* *Tempeh* is a delicious, high-protein food made from soybeans.

From Bagel Works   PORTLAND, MAINE

Bagel and Herb Tofu Spread Sandwich

This tasty sandwich is easy to prepare and handy to pack in lunches or for picnics. The tofu spread is great on crackers or celery, or as a veggie dip.

1. Place all the Herb Tofu Spread ingredients in a medium-sized bowl. Mash and stir well to blend the herbs with the Tofutti. Cover the bowl with plastic wrap, and chill in the refrigerator for 1 hour or longer to allow the flavor to fully develop. The spread will keep in the refrigerator in a tightly covered container for up to five days.

2. To serve, slice each bagel in half, and spread on about 2 tablespoons of the Herb Tofu Spread. Garnish with lettuce or sprouts, tomatoes, and onions. Serve with potato chips and a sliced dill pickle.

ABOUT THE RESTAURANT

The Bagel Works is the place to stop for the best fresh bagels in Portland, with sixteen varieties of bagels and all kinds of toppings, spreads, and salads.

*Tofutti is the brand name for a particular type of tofu spread that has a cream cheese-like consistency and can be found in many grocery and natural food stores.

Yield: 4 servings

Preparation Time: 5 minutes

4 fresh bagels, plain, sesame seed, pumpernickel, rye, or whole wheat

HERB TOFU SPREAD

8 ounces plain Tofutti spread*

$1/2$ teaspoon dried basil

$1/2$ teaspoon dried dill

1 teaspoon dried parsley

Pinch of salt

Pinch of pepper

Pinch of garlic powder

GARNISH

Green lettuce leaves or alfalfa sprouts

Ripe tomato slices

Slices of red or yellow onion

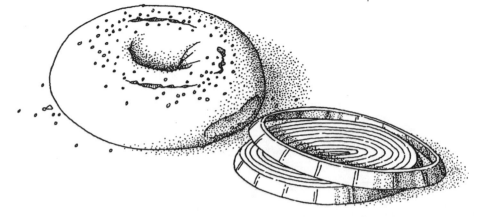

From La Méditerranée de Sodona   *SEDONA, ARIZONA*

Ful Medames

Fava beans, also known as broad beans, are popular in Mediterranean, Middle Eastern, Egyptian, and Italian cuisine.

Yield: *4 servings*

Preparation Time: 20 minutes

Cooking Time: 1 hour to cook the beans; none if using canned beans

1 cup dried fava beans or 2 cups canned

2 cloves garlic, pressed

Salt, to taste

Black pepper, to taste

Juice of 1 lemon

1 medium tomato, chopped

$1/2$ medium yellow onion, finely chopped

1–2 tablespoons olive oil

GARNISH

4 fresh mint leaves or scallion (green onion) stems

1. Place the fava beans in a medium-sized, heavy pot, and cover with water. Soak the beans overnight.

2. The next day, drain the beans, discard the water, and rinse with fresh water. Then add enough fresh water to just cover the beans. Cover the pot with a lid, and boil the beans over medium heat until tender, about 1 hour. Drain.

3. Spoon a third of the beans into a large mixing bowl, and add the garlic. Add salt and pepper to taste. Mash together until the mixture is soft but not necessarily smooth. Add the remaining beans and the lemon juice, tomato, onion, and olive oil to the mixture. Stir together until well blended and the oil is completely incorporated.

4. Spoon the Ful Medames into a serving bowl, and garnish with mint leaves or green onion. Serve warm or cold with pita bread. This dish keeps well in an airtight container in the refrigerator for several days.

ABOUT THE RESTAURANT

At La Méditerranée, where breakfast is served all day along with Greek and Turkish coffees, you'll find a wide variety of vegetarian and nonvegetarian selections, from stuffed grape leaves and falafel to New York steak and trout almandine.

Mexican Dishes

From The Old Town Café   BELLINGHAM, WASHINGTON

Veggie Enchiladas
with Creamy Homemade Sauce

Olé! Olé! This homemade sauce uses milk as a base and yields a smooth and creamy flavor your young ones will enjoy!

1. Preheat the oven to 400°F. Lightly oil a 13- by 9-inch baking pan.

2. To make the enchilada sauce, place the olive oil in a medium-sized saucepan, and heat gently over medium heat. Whisk in the flour and chili powder. Slowly add the water or stock, stirring to make a smooth paste. Slowly add the milk and soy sauce, and season with salt and pepper. Reduce the heat to low, and simmer while you prepare the enchiladas.

3. To make the vegetable filling, place the cheese and vegetables in a large bowl. Stir to mix well.

4. Place the vegetable stock in a large sauté pan over high heat until it begins to boil. Dip the corn tortillas, one at a time, in the vegetable stock to soften, turning to soften both sides. Drain each tortilla.

5. Place about $1/4$ cup of the filling in the center of a tortilla, and roll up. Place the tortilla in the prepared baking pan. Repeat with the remaining tortillas.

6. Cover the entire pan of enchiladas with the enchilada sauce, and place in the oven for 10 to 15 minutes, or until bubbly. Remove from the oven, and serve hot with rice and beans, and a green salad.

ABOUT THE RESTAURANT

The down-home atmosphere of The Old Town Café beckons you to discover the taste treats being prepared behind those big storefront windows in Old Town, Bellingham. "People in their eighties tell stories about the times they ate at The Old Town Café when they were kids," says Diane Brainard, manager. The current owner, Eugene Rietzke, has owned it for the last five years. The Old Town Café recently expanded and now connects you with the restaurant's Art Connects Gallery, where local artists display their work.

Yield: *6 servings*

Preparation Time: 30 minutes

Cooking Time: 15 minutes

ENCHILADA SAUCE

2 tablespoons olive oil

2 tablespoons flour

1–2 tablespoons chili powder, hot or mild, to taste

$1/2$ cup water or vegetable stock

4 cups milk

2 tablespoons tamari soy sauce (See "About Soy Sauce" on page 13.)

Salt, to taste

Black pepper, to taste

VEGETABLE FILLING

2 cups shredded white cheddar cheese

1 cup finely chopped onions, broccoli, or zucchini

TORTILLA PREPARATION

$1/2$ –1 cup vegetable stock

12 corn tortillas

From Seva Restaurant   ANN ARBOR, MICHIGAN

Enchiladas Calabaza
(Enchiladas with Squash)

This recipe creates one of the most unusual and incredibly delicious enchiladas you'll ever taste. The cumin, chili powder, and coriander are rendered delicate, blending with the cream cheese and squash. We found the enchiladas to be even better the day after—cold or hot!

Yield: 6–8 servings

Preparation Time: 30 minutes

Cooking Time: 15–60 minutes, depending on what kind of oven is used

Final Baking Time: 15 minutes

2 large butternut squash

$1/4$ cup corn oil or $1/4$ cup vegetable broth

3 cups chopped yellow onion (about 1 pound)

12 ounces cream cheese

2 tablespoons sliced scallions (green onions)

2 teaspoons chili powder

$1/4$ teaspoon ground cinnamon

1 teaspoon dried oregano

1 teaspoon ground coriander

1 teaspoon ground cumin

1 teaspoon salt

12 corn tortillas

1 cup vegetable broth or water

2 cups prepared tomato salsa

$1/2$–1 cup grated cheddar cheese

1. Preheat the oven to 350°F. Lightly oil a 13- by 9-inch baking pan. Fill two other 13- by 9-inch baking pans with about 1 inch of water each.

2. Cut each squash in half lengthwise, and scoop out the seeds. Place the squash, with the inside facing down, in the baking pans containing the water. Place in the oven, and bake for 45 to 60 minutes. Or cook the squash in the microwave for 15 to 30 minutes, depending on the size and voltage of your microwave. When the squash is tender, scoop out the pulp into a medium-sized bowl, mash, and set aside.

3. Place the corn oil (or vegetable broth) in a large sauté pan, and heat over medium-high heat. Add the onion, and sauté until translucent. Lower the heat to medium, and add the cream cheese. Mix until the cheese is melted. Add the squash, scallions, chili powder, cinnamon, oregano, coriander, cumin, and salt. Stir well to blend.

4. Place the 1 cup of vegetable stock or water in a large sauté pan. Heat over high heat until it begins to boil. Dip the corn tortillas, one at a time, into the stock, turning to soften both sides, for about 5 to 10 seconds. Drain each tortilla on a plate.

5. Place about $1/2$ cup of the squash filling on each corn tortilla and roll up. Place the tortillas in the oiled baking pan, and cover the enchiladas with tomato salsa. Top the enchiladas with the grated cheddar cheese.

6. Place the pan in the oven, and bake for 15 minutes to warm thoroughly. Remove the enchiladas from the oven and serve immediately with a fresh green salad and tortilla chips on the side.

ABOUT THE RESTAURANT

Some of the best Mexican food in all of Michigan is served at Seva. The impressive menu caters to vegans and vegetarians with a grand array of Mexican and Asian specialties.

From Rainbow Blossom Natural Foods & Deli   LOUISVILLE, KENTUCKY

Rainbow Ritos

Rainbow Ritos are one of the best selling items at Rainbow Blossom Natural Foods Deli. The black beans create a distinctive difference from the traditional pinto bean burrito.

1. Put the black and pinto beans together in a large pot and cover with water. Place the pot over high heat until the water comes to a boil, cover with a lid, reduce the heat to medium, and cook the beans until they are very soft, about $1^1/2$ hours. When the beans are cooked, drain the water from the pot, and reserve. Slightly mash the beans.

2. Place the olive oil in a large sauté pan, and heat over medium-high heat. Add the onion and garlic, and sauté for 2 minutes. Then add the green bell pepper, red bell pepper, and jalapeño peppers. Continue to sauté until the onions are translucent and the peppers are crisp-tender.

3. Add the green chilies, salsa, chili powder, cumin, ground coriander, fresh cilantro, salt, and black pepper to the onion mixture. Stir to mix well.

4. Add the beans to the onion mixture, and stir to blend well. Add small amounts of water or reserved bean liquid to keep the mixture soft.

5. On each tortilla, place $1/2$ cup of the bean mixture, 2 to 3 tablespoons cheddar cheese, a small handful of lettuce, 1 to 2 tablespoons black olives, and a dollop of sour cream. Roll up the tortilla. Place on a serving plate and top with more grated cheese and black olives.

ABOUT THE RESTAURANT

Your whole mind, body, and soul may blossom at Rainbow Blossom Natural Foods & Deli.

*Be careful when you are handling *jalapeños* because they can burn the skin of your hands, eyes, and mouth. It's best to wear rubber gloves. If the chilies touch your skin, wash carefully with warm (not hot or cold) soapy water to reduce the heat from the chilies.

Yield: 8–10 servings

Preparation Time: 25 minutes
Cooking Time: $1^1/2$ hours

1 cup black beans

1 cup pinto beans

2 tablespoons olive oil

1 purple onion, chopped

2 cloves garlic, minced

1 green bell pepper, chopped

$1/2$ red bell pepper, chopped

$1/2$ jalapeño pepper,* chopped

2 ounces chopped mild green chilies (canned are acceptable)

$1/3$ cup tomato salsa, hot or mild

$1^1/2$ teaspoons chili powder

$1^1/2$ teaspoons ground cumin

1 teaspoon ground coriander

1 teaspoon dried cilantro or 1 tablespoon chopped fresh cilantro

$1/2$ teaspoon salt

$1/2$ teaspoon black pepper

Water or reserved bean liquid, as needed

8–10 whole wheat or white flour tortillas

2–3 cups grated sharp cheddar cheese (6–7 ounces)

$1/2$ head Romaine lettuce, chopped

1 cup sliced black olives

1 cup sour cream, optional

From Mother Earth Natural Foods PARKERSBURG, WEST VIRGINIA

Black Bean Burritos

This recipe makes a good bunch of burritos. Freeze a few and reheat them in a jiffy when you come home and need a quick-fix dinner!

Yield: 10–12 medium burritos

Preparation Time: 20 minutes

Cooking Time: 1–1$\frac{1}{2}$ hours

2 cups black beans

2 tablespoons olive oil

1 yellow onion, chopped

2 teaspoons ground cumin

$\frac{1}{4}$ teaspoon cayenne pepper or to taste

2 teaspoons–1 tablespoon Spike, to taste (See "About Spike" on page 52.)

2–3 teaspoons garlic powder

2 tablespoons tamari soy sauce (See "About Soy Sauce" on page 13.)

1 bunch fresh cilantro (coriander), chopped

10–12 white or whole wheat flour tortillas

1$\frac{1}{2}$ cups grated cheddar cheese

2 cups chopped tomatoes

2–3 tablespoons of your favorite salsa

1. Place the beans in a medium-sized bowl, cover with water, and soak for 2 hours.

2. Drain the beans, and place in a large pot. Add 6 cups of water, cover, place over high heat, and bring to a boil. Reduce the heat to medium-low, and simmer until the beans are soft, about 1 to 1$\frac{1}{2}$ hours. Drain, mash, and set aside.

3. Place the oil in a large sauté pan, and heat over medium heat. Add the onions, and sauté until translucent. Add the cumin, cayenne pepper, Spike, and garlic powder. Stir and sauté for 1 minute more to allow the seasonings to blend.

4. Remove the pan from the heat, and add the soy sauce and cilantro.

5. Place a scoop of the black bean filling in the middle of each tortilla. Top with 1 to 2 tablespoons of the grated cheese and a few pieces of chopped tomato. Roll up the tortilla. (At this point, you may keep the burritos warm in a baking dish in the oven until ready to serve.)

6. Place the burritos on a bed of shredded lettuce on individual serving plates. Top with your favorite salsa, sprinkle with another tablespoon of grated cheese, and serve.

7. These burritos also freeze well. Wrap them individually in plastic wrap and then aluminum foil. To thaw, remove from the freezer and allow to thaw at room temperature or remove the aluminum foil and place in the microwave oven for 2 minutes to heat through.

ABOUT THE RESTAURANT

On the border between Ohio and West Virginia, you'll find the Mother Earth Natural Foods in Parkersburg. The restaurant exudes owner David Hawkins's exuberance for life and all things natural.

From The Earth Natural Foods & Deli   OKLAHOMA CITY, OKLAHOMA

Tempeh Fajitas

This recipe is about as good as you can get for a great-tasting, quick meal that the kids will love. And so will you!

1. Place the water or olive oil in a large sauté pan, and heat over medium-high heat. Crumble the tempeh burgers into the pan, and heat thoroughly.

2. Add the bell peppers, onions, garlic, cumin, and cayenne pepper. Cook until the onions are translucent, adding more water if necessary.

3. Place about 1 tablespoon of the optional grated cheese on each tortilla, and place a generous helping of the fajita mixture on top of the cheese. Top with your favorite homemade salsa, guacamole, or nonfat yogurt toppings. Roll up the tortilla, and serve immediately.

ABOUT THE RESTAURANT

You can trust that Tempie Nichols, owner of The Earth Natural Foods & Deli, will prepare a great Tempeh Fajita! She knows that the delicious difference in the foods she prepares comes from the quality of the ingredients. Only the freshest organically grown vegetables, beans, flours, and oils, as well as Lifestream carbon-filtered water, are used in the cooking. Since 1985, The Earth Natural Foods & Deli staff have been serving heart-health conscious citizens of both Oklahoma City and Norman, Oklahoma.

* *Tempeh* is a delicious, high-protein food made from soybeans.

Yield: *4 servings*

Preparation Time: 10 minutes

Cooking Time: 5–10 minutes

$1/2$ cup water or 2 tablespoons olive oil

6 prepared tempeh* burgers, found fresh or frozen in natural food stores

2 cups sliced red or green bell peppers

2 cups sliced yellow onions

4 cloves garlic, minced

$1/2$ teaspoon ground cumin

$1/2$ teaspoon cayenne pepper

$1/4$ cup grated cheddar cheese, optional

8 white flour or whole wheat tortillas

GARNISH

$1/4$–$1/2$ cup each of salsa, guacamole, sour cream, or yogurt

Mexican Layers

An enticing entrée, this meal is great for the family or for a crowd. It's best made a day ahead to allow the spices to develop to their full potential.

Yield: 6 servings

Preparation Time: 45 minutes

Cooking Time: 1 hour

2 tablespoons vegetable oil

1 medium yellow onion, finely chopped

2 medium carrots, finely chopped

2 small zucchini, finely chopped

3 small tomatoes, finely chopped

2–3 cloves garlic, minced

1–3 sliced jalapeños,* optional

1 cup sliced black olives (about 4 ounces)

1 cup chopped fresh cilantro (coriander)

1 tablespoon ground cumin

2 teaspoons ground coriander

1 tablespoon ground chili powder

$1/8$–$1/4$ teaspoon cayenne pepper, to taste

Salt, to taste

Black pepper, to taste

12 corn tortillas

1 pint sour cream

3 cups grated sharp cheddar cheese

2 large fresh tomatoes, sliced

1. Preheat the oven to 350°F. Lightly oil a 13- by 9-inch baking pan.

2. Place the 2 tablespoons of oil in a medium-sized sauté pan, and heat over medium heat. Add the onions, carrots, zucchini, tomatoes, garlic, jalapeño peppers, olives, cilantro, cumin, ground coriander, and chili powder. Season with cayenne pepper, salt, and black pepper to taste.

3. Sauté the vegetables until they are crisp-tender, and the flavors are blended, about 3 to 5 minutes. Drain the excess liquid; the mixture should not be too runny.

4. In the baking pan, use a layer of corn tortillas to completely cover the bottom. Add some of the vegetable mixture, and spread to completely cover the tortillas. Spread a thin layer of sour cream over the vegetable layer. Add a layer of the grated cheddar cheese. Place fresh tomato slices on top, closely spaced together.

5. Repeat the layers until the pan is full, ending with the tomato layer. Finally, top the tomatoes with additional grated cheese.

6. Cover the pan with foil and bake 45 minutes. Then uncover and bake an additional 15 minutes to brown the cheese. Serve hot.

ABOUT THE RESTAURANT

The paths of longtime friends Ellen Burstyn and Cloris Leachman crossed at Mickey Hornick's Chicago Diner. Their friendship dates back to their days when they studied at the Actor's Studio. Later they appeared together in "The Last Picture Show." Both actresses are vegetarians.

*Be careful when you are handling *jalapeños* because they can burn the skin of your hands, eyes, and mouth. It's best to wear rubber gloves. If the chilies touch your skin, wash carefully with warm (not hot or cold) soapy water to reduce the heat from the chilies.

From Rio Grande Mexican Restaurant   FORT COLLISON, COLORADO

Mexican Rice

The Rio Grande Ranchero Sauce is so good you'll want to scoop it up with tortilla chips before it even gets into the Mexican Rice pan!

To Prepare the Sauce:

1. Place the margarine in a large sauté pan, and heat over medium-high heat. Add the celery and onion, and cook until the onions are translucent.

2. Add the tomatoes, cilantro, and brown sugar. Bring to a full boil, and add the salt, stirring to blend well. Remove the pan from the heat.

3. Use 2 cups of the sauce for the Mexican Rice preparation. Or allow the sauce to cool, and then store it in a covered container in the refrigerator for later use. The Ranchero Sauce keeps well in the refrigerator for several days.

To Prepare the Rice:

1. Place the oil in a large pot, and heat over high heat. Stir in the rice. Sauté for 1 to 2 minutes.

2. Add 2 cups of the Ranchero Sauce. Stir to thoroughly blend.

3. Add the water, cumin, garlic, salt, and peas. Mix well.

4. Cover, bring to a boil, stir, and reduce the heat to low. Continue to cook until all the water has been absorbed and the rice is tender. Remove the rice from the heat and serve hot with your favorite Mexican dishes.

ABOUT THE RESTAURANT

Twin brothers from a family of thirteen children, owners Andre and Steve Mouton are used to feeding a crowd. Today, they are serving both traditional and upscale Yucatan-Texan-Mexican-style food to a great blend of all peoples—Colorado State University college students; business, trade, and professional people; and oodles of families. The town loves them, and they love the town.

Yield: *6 servings including 1 1/2 quarts sauce*

Preparation Time: 15 minutes for the rice; 10 minutes for the sauce

Cooking Time: 30–40 minutes for the rice; 10 minutes for the sauce

RANCHERO SAUCE

1/4 cup margarine

1 cup chopped celery

1 cup chopped onion

1 (32-ounce) can crushed tomatoes

1 bunch fresh cilantro (coriander), chopped

1 tablespoon brown sugar

1 tablespoon salt

RICE

1/4 cup vegetable oil or liquid shortening

2 cups uncooked white or brown quick-cooking rice

2 cups Ranchero Sauce

2 cups water (check the quick-cooking rice package directions)

1/2 tablespoon ground cumin

1 tablespoon chopped garlic

1 tablespoon salt

1 cup green peas

Asian Dishes

From Dara Thai   *FLAGSTAFF, ARIZONA*

Tropical Heatwave Curry

The mint leaves add a refreshing twist to this tawny golden curry. The recipe is easy, quick, and tasty.

1. In a large sauté pan, heat 3 to 4 tablespoons of the oil over medium-high heat. Place the cubed tofu in the hot oil. Deep-fry until crispy brown. Drain on paper toweling.

2. To make the curry sauce, place all the curry sauce ingredients together in a blender. Blend until smooth, and set aside.

3. Place 2 tablespoons of the vegetable oil in a large saucepan over medium heat. Add the curry sauce. Cook together for 1 minute. Add the coconut milk and paprika, and mix well.

4. Increase the heat to high, and bring the sauce to a boil. When the sauce is boiling, add the bamboo shoots, onion, bell pepper, carrot, mushrooms, and deep-fried tofu. Add the sugar, soy sauce, and optional chili pepper.

5. Cook until the sauce boils again. Simmer for 5 minutes, until the veggies are crisp-tender. Remove the pan from the heat, and add the mint leaves. Pour the curry into a serving bowl, and serve immediately with rice or noodles.

ABOUT THE RESTAURANT

If you're looking for a change of taste from traditional Southwest cooking, Dara Thai offers a great crosscultural experience with its delicious Thai food. Established in 1989 and offering a wide selection of vegetarian items, such as Veggie Rolls and tofu entrées, the staff at Dara Thai also cater to vegetarian customers by offering to prepare any of their meat dishes in a meatless variation.

Yield: 3–4 servings

Preparation Time: 15 minutes

Cooking Time: 25 minutes

5–6 tablespoons vegetable oil

14 ounces firm tofu, drained, squeezed dry, and cut into 1-inch cubes

1 (13.5-ounce) can coconut milk

1 teaspoon ground paprika

1 (8-ounce) can bamboo shoots, drained and sliced

1 medium onion, chopped

1 medium green bell pepper, cut into 1-inch pieces

1 medium carrot, sliced into $1/4$-inch rounds

6–8 medium white or brown mushrooms, cut into pieces

$3/4$ teaspoon sugar

2 teaspoons soy sauce

Dried red chili pepper or jalapeño pepper to taste, optional

10 fresh mint leaves

CURRY SAUCE

1 teaspoon dried red chili

$1/2$ teaspoon minced garlic

$1/2$ teaspoon fresh lemongrass

$3/4$ teaspoon chopped red onion

1 teaspoon salt

$1/2$ cup water

From Angelica Kitchen   NEW YORK, NEW YORK

Indian-Inspired Layered Casserole

This dish is one of the most delicious Indian recipes I have ever tasted. The flavors are subtle, rich, and distinctive, yet not at all overpowering. Although labor-intensive, this casserole is excellent for entertaining because it can be made in advance. It is perfect for a holiday dinner. Just remember to start preparing the condiments prior to baking the casserole.

Yield: 8–10 servings

Preparation Time: 1½–2 hours

Final Baking Time: 30–40 minutes

MILLET-SWEET POTATO LAYER

2 cups dried millet

1 tablespoon mustard seeds

1 tablespoon fennel seeds

½ teaspoon rice vinegar

2 pinches of salt

5 small sweet potatoes, peeled and cubed

LENTIL LAYER

2 cups green lentils

1 bay leaf

6 cups water

4 tablespoons olive oil

3 cups finely chopped onion (about ¾ pound)

2 teaspoons ground cumin

2 teaspoons ground coriander

3 tablespoons minced garlic

2 tablespoons finely minced fresh ginger

2 teaspoons salt, or to taste

Pinch of cayenne pepper

Splash of lemon juice

To Make the Millet-Sweet Potato Layer:

1. Preheat the oven to 350°F.

2. Rinse the millet in fresh water, and drain. Spread the millet on a baking sheet, and place in the oven. Bake until the millet becomes slightly golden and emits a nutty aroma, about 5 minutes. Remove the baking sheet from the oven.

3. Place the mustard and fennel seeds in a large, dry skillet over medium-high heat. Dry-roast for about 2 minutes. Remove from the heat.

4. In a two-quart saucepan, place the millet, seeds, vinegar, water, and a pinch of salt. Place over high heat, and bring to a boil. Lower the heat to low, cover, and simmer until the millet is fluffy, about 20 minutes. Remove from the heat.

5. Place the chopped, peeled sweet potatoes with just enough water to cover and a pinch of salt in a saucepan. Cover with a lid, and place on medium heat. Simmer until tender, about 20 to 30 minutes. Remove from the stove, drain the water, and mash.

6. In a large mixing bowl, place the sweet potatoes and millet, and mix together. Put the mixture into a large, deep dish casserole pan or a wide, round or oval casserole pan. Set the pan aside for the lentil layer.

To Make the Lentil Layer:

1. Place the lentils, bay leaf, and water in a four-quart pot, and cook over medium-high heat.

2. In a small sauté pan, heat 2 tablespoons of the olive oil on medium-high heat, add the onions, and cook until they are soft and beginning to brown. Add the onions to the lentils, and cook uncovered over medium heat about 30 minutes.

3. While the lentils are cooking, place the remaining 2 tablespoons of oil in another sauté pan and heat over medium heat. Add the cumin, coriander, garlic, ginger, salt, cayenne pepper, and lemon juice. Sauté for 3 minutes, stirring constantly.

4. Stir the spices into the lentils. Continue to cook the lentils until they are soft, another 20 minutes.

5. When the lentils are cooked, remove the bay leaf, pour the lentil mixture over the millet and sweet potato mixture, and spread evenly. Set aside for the chard layer.

To Make the Chard Layer:

1. Rinse the chard with fresh water, and coarsely chop. Place the chard in a pot, add 4 cups water, cover the pot, and cook over medium heat for 3 to 5 minutes, until wilted.

2. Drain the water from the pot. Sprinkle the chard with umeboshi vinegar.

3. Spread the chard over the lentil layer. Set aside for the mushroom layer.

To Make the Mushroom Layer:

1. Place the mushrooms and the olive oil in a large pot over low heat. Cook until the mushrooms have decreased in size and released their juices, about 20 to 30 minutes. Strain the mushrooms, reserving the juice, and set aside.

2. Pour the canola oil in a small, heavy sauté pan placed over medium heat. Add the flour, and stir continuously until the paste is light brown and smells toasty. Turn the heat to low. Whisk in 1 cup of the mushroom juices, and whisk until smooth. Add small amounts of water if there is not enough mushroom juice.

3. Stir the flour mixture into the mushrooms. Simmer until thick, about 5 minutes. Pour the mushroom mixture over the chard layer of the casserole. Now the casserole is ready for the oven! You can cover the casserole pan with plastic wrap and keep it in the refrigerator for 1 day until you are ready to bake.

To Bake and Serve the Casserole:

1. Preheat the oven to 350°F.

2. Cover the casserole pan loosely with aluminum foil, and bake for 15 minutes. Uncover and bake an additional 20 minutes, or until the top is brown.

3. To serve the casserole, circle each individual serving plate with 2 to 3 tablespoons of the Chutney Sauce. Place one square or scoop of the casserole in the middle of the plate. Top with 1 to 2 tablespoons of the Cucumber Raita. Surround the casserole with $1/2$ cup of the Braised Red Cabbage. Sprinkle the entire plate with 2 tablespoons of toasted almonds, and serve hot.

*Umeboshi vinegar is made from umeboshi, or Japanese pickled plum.

CHARD LAYER

$1^1/2$ pounds chard (about 2 large bunches)

4 cups water

2 teaspoons umeboshi vinegar*

MUSHROOM LAYER

$2^1/2$ pounds mushrooms, quartered

1 tablespoon olive oil

$1/4$ cup canola oil

$1/2$ cup unbleached white flour

GARNISH

Chutney Sauce (see page 170)

Cucumber Raita (see page 170)

Braised Red Cabbage (see page 171)

$1^3/4$ cups toasted almonds (See "Toasting Nuts and Seeds" on page 68.)

Chutney Sauce

Yield: 3 cups

Preparation Time: 10 minutes

Cooking Time: 15 minutes

1 tablespoon olive oil

1 cup chopped yellow onion

1 teaspoon ground ginger

1 teaspoon curry powder

$1/2$ teaspoon ground star anise*

$3^1/_2$ cups apple cider or apple juice

$1/_3$ cup chopped dried dates (about 2 ounces)

$1/_3$ cup chopped, dried apricots (about 3 ounces)

$2/_3$ cup currants

2 tablespoons apple cider vinegar

Pinch of cayenne pepper

$1/_4$ teaspoon salt

$1/_2$ cup cold water

2 tablespoons arrowroot

1. Place the olive oil in a two-quart saucepan, and heat over medium heat. Add the onions along with the ginger, curry, and star anise. Cook until the onion is translucent, about 5 to 8 minutes.

2. Add the apple cider (or juice), dates, apricots, currants, apple cider vinegar, cayenne pepper, and salt. Continue to cook over medium heat until the mixture begins to boil.

3. Place the water in a small bowl. Add the arrowroot, and stir to dissolve.

4. When the apple juice mixture comes to a boil, stir in the arrowroot mixture, stirring continuously until the juice thickens. Remove from the heat and set aside to cool. Serve with Indian-Inspired Layered Casserole (page 000), or store in a covered container in the refrigerator for up to one week.

Star anise is a small, brown star-shaped fruit containing small light brown seeds. It has a delicate aniseed flavor.

Cucumber Raita

Yield: 2 cups

Preparation Time: 10 minutes

1 pound soft tofu, drained, rinsed, and squeezed dry

$1/_4$ cup canola oil

1. Place the tofu, oil, lemon juice, umeboshi vinegar, brown rice vinegar, salt, and ground cumin seed in a food processor, and process until smooth.

2. Pour into a bowl, and fold in the mint and cucumbers.

3. If you are making this dish ahead of time, cover the bowl with plastic wrap and chill until ready to use. Remove the raita from the refrigerator and bring to room temperature. Serve with the Indian-Inspired Layered Casserole (page 000) or with rice and vegetable dishes.

¼ cup lemon juice

3 tablespoons umeboshi vinegar*

1 tablespoon brown rice vinegar

Pinch of salt

2 tablespoons toasted cumin seeds, ground (See "Toasting Nuts and Seeds" on page 68.)

⅓ cup chopped fresh mint

1 large cucumber, peeled, seeded, and chopped

Sweet & Sour Braised Cabbage

1. In a six-quart pot, place the oil and onions. Cook over medium heat until the onions are translucent.

2. Add the cabbage and apple cider. Simmer uncovered until the cabbage has completely wilted, about 40 minutes.

3. Drain the liquid, and remove the cabbage from the pot to a serving bowl. Season with umeboshi vinegar. Serve hot with the Indian-Inspired Layered Casserole or as an accompaniment to other dishes.

Yield: 8–10 servings

Preparation Time: 10 minutes

Cooking Time: 40 minutes

2 tablespoons oil

2 cups chopped yellow onion

1 head red cabbage, cored and cut into small square chunks

2 cups apple cider

3 tablespoons umeboshi vinegar*

ABOUT THE RESTAURANT

Myra Kornfeld created the Indian-Inspired Layered Casserole, which is often one of the two daily specials at Angelica Kitchen. This recipe can easily be made by one person. But if it looks too overwhelming to even consider trying, don't pass up the opportunity to get the whole family into the kitchen, or invite your friends over for a fun Saturday afternoon preparing this lovely dinner.

*Umeboshi vinegar is made from umeboshi, or Japanese pickled plum.

From Pyewacket Restaurant   CHAPEL HILL, NORTH CAROLINA

Indonesian Curried Vegetables

Fabulous! This curry sauce is especially rich and flavorful because of the of peanut butter.

Yield: 6–8 servings

Preparation Time: 20–30 minutes

Cooking Time: 45–50 minutes

CURRY SAUCE

3 tablespoons margarine

4 tablespoons pure olive oil

1½ tablespoons whole cumin seeds

3 cups chopped onions (about ¾ pounds)

3 tablespoons minced fresh ginger

1½ tablespoons minced fresh garlic

2½ teaspoons ground cumin

1½ teaspoons ground coriander

¾ teaspoon ground fenugreek*

½ teaspoon ground cinnamon

½ teaspoon ground cardamon

1 teaspoon salt

½ teaspoon turmeric

½ teaspoon crushed red pepper

⅛ teaspoon cayenne pepper

1 (28-ounce) can chopped tomatoes

½ cup water

2 tablespoons lemon juice

¼ cup peanut butter

VEGETABLE STIR-FRY

2 tablespoons vegetable oil

1 medium bunch broccoli, cut into florets

To Make the Curry Sauce:

1. Place the margarine and olive oil in a large sauté pan over high heat. Add the cumin seeds, and allow the seeds to brown for 1 to 2 minutes. Then add the onions, ginger, and garlic, sautéing for 15 minutes.

2. While the onions are cooking, combine the cumin, coriander, fenugreek, cinnamon, cardamon, salt, turmeric, red pepper, and cayenne pepper in a small bowl, and mix well. Add to the sauté mixture. Cook for 1 minute to allow the flavors to blend.

3. Add the chopped tomatoes, water, and lemon juice. Bring to a boil over medium heat, reduce the heat to low, and simmer for 25 to 35 minutes, stirring often so that the sauce will not burn on the bottom.

4. Put the peanut butter in a small mixing bowl, add some of the sauce, and mix well so that there are no lumps of peanut butter. Add the peanut butter mixture to the rest of the sauce, and cook for another 10 to 15 minutes.

To Make and Serve the Vegetable Stir-Fry:

1. In a large sauté pan, heat the oil over medium-high heat. Add the remaining ingredients. Stir-fry until the vegetables are crisp-tender.

2. Serve the vegetables over cooked brown rice. Top with the curry sauce. Sprinkle raisins, cashew pieces, and shredded, unsweetened coconut over the top. Serve with a dish of plain yogurt and wedges of lightly grilled pita bread on the side.

ABOUT THE RESTAURANT

Looking for a change of career after spending years in the contract research business, David Bacon, owner of Pyewacket Restaurant, set aside his dusty books and fountain pen for the brisk and snappy pace of a restaurant in 1977. The menu has evolved with the times too: over half of the menu selections are vegetarian, and the rest are seafood or chicken. "The changes in my career and the expansions of the restaurant have been good," remarks David. "The town and whole region have supported us, and we have appreciated that."

Fenugreek is a spicy, rather bitter herb popular in Indian and Middle Eastern cooking.

1 small head cauliflower, cut
  into florets

2 cups shredded red cabbage
  (1 small cabbage)

2 cups sliced white mushrooms
  (about ³/₄ pounds)

1 medium yellow onion, sliced

1 green bell pepper, sliced

2 medium carrots, peeled and
  thinly sliced

GARNISH

Raisins

Cashew pieces

Shredded unsweetened coconut

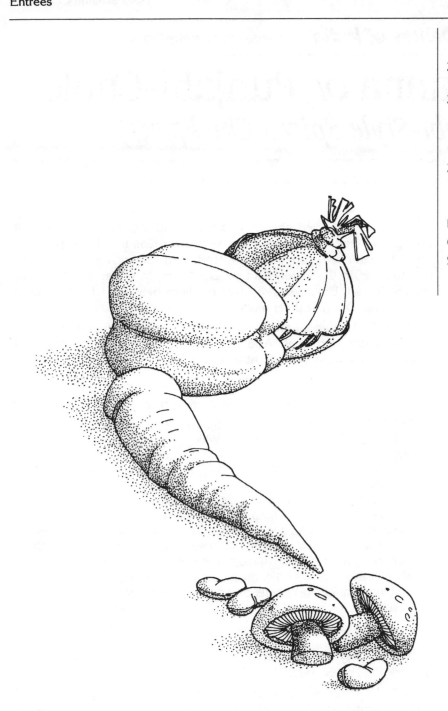

From Delites of India   MINNEAPOLIS, MINNESOTA

Pindi Channa *or* Punjabi-Chole
(Punjabi-Style Spiced Chickpeas)

The garnish of tomato, onions, ginger, and fresh cilantro (coriander) contribute to the colorful presentation of this delightful dish.

Yield: 4–6 servings

Preparation Time: 30 minutes

Cooking Time: 30 minutes with canned beans; 1½ hours with dried beans

2 cups dried chickpeas (garbanzos) or 4 cups canned (2 cans, 14½ ounces each)

3 tablespoons canola oil

½ tablespoon ghee (See "Preparing Clarified Butter.")

2 medium yellow onions, finely chopped

1 tablespoon chopped garlic

1 tablespoon chopped ginger

2 bay leaves

1 tablespoon whole cumin seeds

2 cinnamon sticks, whole

7 whole cloves

2 fresh tomatoes, chopped fine

1 tablespoon ground pomegranate pulp

2 tablespoons ground cumin

2 tablespoons ground coriander

¼ teaspoon cayenne pepper, optional

1 teaspoon ground dried mint

1 teaspoon black salt*

½ teaspoon sea salt

1 teaspoon dry mango powder*

1. Pick over the dried chickpeas for grit and stones, and rinse well until the water rinses clean. Place the chickpeas in a large pot with enough water to keep them covered, and soak overnight. In the morning, drain the water. Add enough water to cover 1 inch above the chickpeas. Boil, covered, over medium heat for 1 hour, or until very tender. Drain and set aside.

2. Place the canola oil and the ghee in a heavy saucepan, and heat over medium-high heat. Add the onions, garlic, and ginger, and sauté until the onions are light brown.

Preparing Clarified Butter

Clarified butter, called *ghee*, is used commonly as a shortening in India. Unlike whole butter, clarified butter, which is divested of its milk solids, keeps well for long periods of time. If you cannot purchase ghee at the local natural food store or Asian specialty shop, you can make your own as follows.

Cut unsalted butter into 1-inch pieces, and place in a heavy saucepan over low heat. When the butter has melted, remove the pan from the heat and let it stand for 3 to 4 minutes. Skim and discard the froth. Line a sieve with a double thickness of rinsed and squeezed cheesecloth. Pour the remaining butter through the sieve into a bowl, leaving the milky solids in the bottom of the pan. Pour the clarified butter from the bowl into a jar or crock. Store, covered, in the refrigerator. When butter is clarified, it loses about one fourth of its original volume.

---

3. Add the bay leaves, cumin seeds, cinnamon sticks, and cloves, and stir for 15 seconds.

4. Add the chopped tomatoes, ground pomegranate pulp, ground cumin, ground coriander, optional cayenne pepper, dried mint, black salt, sea salt, and dry mango powder. Cook for 5 minutes more.

* *Black salt* and *dry mango* powder, may be found in food co-ops, gourmet food markets, and the international section of grocery stores.

5. Add the chickpeas, and simmer for 15 to 20 minutes, adding up to 2 cups more water if the sauce becomes too thick.

6. Add the garam masala, turn the heat off, and cover for 10 minutes. Remove from the stove, and scoop the chickpeas onto a serving platter or individual plates. Garnish with the sliced Bermuda onion, ginger, plum tomatoes, and fresh cilantro, and add a splash of lime juice to each plate.

ABOUT THE RESTAURANT

B.K. Aurora offers his distinguished Indian cuisine at his Minneapolis location on West Lake Street.

* *Garam masala*, a mixture of spices used in Indian cooking, may be found in food co-ops, gourmet food markets, and the international section of grocery stores.

1 tablespoon garam masala*

Water, as needed (up to 2 cups)

GARNISH

1 purple Bermuda onion, thinly sliced

2 tablespoons fresh ginger, thinly sliced

4 fresh Italian plum tomatoes, cut into wedges

1 bunch fresh cilantro (coriander), finely chopped

Juice of 1 lime

Delites' Nayrattan Khumb Pulao
(Festive Vegetarian Rice)

Bright orange and snappy reds color this yummy Indian entrée. Even though the ingredient list looks complex, the recipe instructions are simple.

Yield: 6 servings

Preparation Time: 30 minutes

Cooking Time: 1 hour and 20 minutes

2 cups uncooked basmati rice*

5 cups water

3 tablespoons canola oil

2 teaspoons sea salt

1 tablespoon ghee (See "Preparing Clarified Butter" on page 174.)

6 green cardamon pods

4 bay leaves

1 cinnamon stick

1 teaspoon whole cumin seeds

6 whole cloves

12 black peppercorns

1 medium onion, sliced

1/2 teaspoon turmeric

1 teaspoon ground cumin

1 tablespoon fresh garlic paste

1/2 teaspoon curry powder

1 medium ripe tomato, coarsely chopped

1 tablespoon tomato paste

1/2 cup fresh asparagus, cut in 1-inch pieces

1/2 cup diagonally sliced baby carrots

1/2 cup small cauliflower florets

1. Preheat the oven to 325°F. Lightly spray a heavy 13- by 9-inch baking pan or a four-quart casserole with nonstick cooking spray.

2. To a four-quart saucepan, add the rice, water, 1 tablespoon of the canola oil, and 1 teaspoon of the sea salt.

3. Bring the rice to a boil over medium-high heat, and let it boil for 10 minutes, or until the water dissipates from the top surface of the rice. Cover the rice with a lid, lower the heat to low, and simmer for 10 minutes. Then turn off the heat, and let the rice stay covered for another 5 minutes. Fluff the rice with a fork, cover again, and set aside.

4. In another four-quart saucepan, place the remaining 2 tablespoons of canola oil and the ghee. Heat over medium heat, and add the green cardamon pods, bay leaves, cinnamon stick, cumin seeds, cloves, peppercorns, and sliced onion.

5. Stir for 1 to 2 minutes, until the onions are light brown. Then add the turmeric, ground cumin, garlic paste, curry powder, tomato, tomato paste, and the remaining teaspoon of sea salt. Sauté for 2 minutes.

6. Add the asparagus, carrots, cauliflower, corn, zucchini, potatoes, pearl onions, and mushrooms. Stir well, cover, and steam for 5 minutes. Then turn the heat off.

7. In the baking or casserole pan, spread a third of the cooked rice. Then add half of the cooked vegetables. Add another layer of rice. Add the rest of the vegetables. Top with a final layer of rice.

8. Sprinkle with the saffron water, raisins or currants, and garam masala. Cover the pan with aluminum foil or a tight-fitting lid. Bake for 30 to 45 minutes, or until heated thoroughly.

9. Serve the dish by fluffing the rice and vegetables together, sprinkling with the optional rose water, and garnishing with the chopped cilantro and almonds.

*Basmati rice, from India, is a particularly aromatic long-grained rice. Be sure to rinse it according to the package directions.

ABOUT THE RESTAURANT

Respectful, peaceful, loving, and warm, the atmosphere at Delites exudes the sentiments of owner B. K. Arora and his staff.

Garam masala, a mixture of spices used in Indian cooking, may be found in food co-ops, gourmet food markets, and the international section of grocery stores.

½ cup fresh or frozen corn kernels

½ cup sliced zucchini

½ cup diced baby red potatoes

½ cup peeled pearl onions

½ cup halved shiitake mushrooms (See "About Mushrooms" on page 63.)

4 strands saffron, soaked in ½ cup warm water for 10 minutes

4 tablespoons golden raisins or currants, soaked in ½ cup warm water for 10 minutes

1 teaspoon garam masala*

2–3 teaspoons rose water, optional

GARNISH

2 tablespoons chopped fresh cilantro (coriander)

4 tablespoons sliced blanched almonds

From Mela Restaurant   COLUMBIA, MARYLAND

Aloo Tikki
(Potato Patties Stuffed with Green Peas & Fresh Coconut)

This dish is delicately spiced combination of peas and potatoes. The Tamarind and Date Sauce gives this entrée an authentic Indian flavor, and it is worth taking the time to find the tamarind.

Yield: *6–8 servings including 2–3 cups of sauce*

Preparation Time: 30 minutes for the patties; 15 minutes for the sauce

Cooking Time: 20–30 minutes for the potatoes; 10–20 minutes for the patties

TAMARIND AND DATE SAUCE

1 pound dates, chopped

1/2 cup tamarind paste*

1/4 teaspoon chili powder

2 teaspoons ground coriander

1/2 teaspoon salt

PATTIES

12 medium-sized potatoes, peeled and cubed (4–5 pounds)

Salt, to taste

Black pepper, to taste

2 teaspoons vegetable oil

1/2 teaspoon cumin seeds

16 ounces fresh or 1 (16-ounce) bag frozen peas

1 teaspoon finely chopped green chilies

1 teaspoon grated fresh ginger

2 teaspoons ground coriander

To Prepare the Tamarind and Date Sauce:

1. Put the dates and tamarind paste in a blender. Add the chili powder, ground coriander, and salt to taste. Blend until the ingredients make a thick sauce, adding a little water to reach the desired consistency. Serve with the potato patties, store in a covered container in the refrigerator for up to one week, or freeze for future use.

To Prepare the Patties:

1. In a large pot, place the potatoes and enough water to cover. Boil over medium heat, covered, until tender, about 20 to 30 minutes. Drain the water, and mash the potatoes, seasoning with salt and pepper to taste. Set aside.

2. Place the oil in a large sauté pan, heat over high heat, and add the cumin seeds. Roast the seeds for about 30 seconds, or until they sizzle.

3. Add the green peas, and partially mash them with a spoon while stirring them. Add the green chilies, ginger, and salt to taste. Cover the pan, and cook for 4 to 5 minutes on medium heat.

4. Add the coriander, lemon juice, garam masala, and coconut. Stir well. Remove from the heat, and set aside to cool.

5. To form a patty, make a 2-inch ball of mashed potatoes. Flatten it with your hands to make a 3 1/2-inch round. Put 1 1/2 teaspoons of the green pea filling in the middle of the round. Fold the edges of the round to close it, making a round about 1/2 inch thick and 3 inches wide. Set aside, and continue making potato patties until all of the potatoes and filling are used.

6. Lightly brush a little oil on a flat griddle. Place the patties on the griddle over medium heat. Cook until they turn golden brown, about 3 to 5 minutes per side. Serve hot with Tamarind and Date Sauce, ketchup, or your favorite chutney. These patties also may be deep fried until they are golden brown and served hot.

*The tamarind is a tropical tree that yields a pod with a sweet, yet slightly acidic, pulp. *Tamarind paste* may be found in an Indian or a specialty grocery store.

ABOUT THE RESTAURANT

Mela means "carnival," and dining at Mela is full of delicious delight in every bite!

Garam masala is a mixture of spices used in Indian cooking, may be found in food co-ops, gourmet food markets, and the international section of grocery stores.

1 teaspoon lemon juice

1 teaspoon garam masala*

1/2 fresh coconut, grated, or 1/2 cup dried, flaked coconut

From Chiang-Mai Restaurant   HONOLULU, HAWAII

Red Vegetable Curry

The consistency of this curry will resemble a vegetable soup. A good, nourishing meal, this dish is fast and easy to make. Use vegetables of your choice—broccoli, corn, carrots, and mushrooms are all good cut into small pieces.

Yield: 4 servings

Preparation Time: 15 minutes

Cooking Time: 20 minutes

1³/₄ cups water

1³/₄ cups coconut milk

4 kaffir leaves (See "About Thai Ingredients" on page 62.)

4 teaspoons red curry paste

2 teaspoons sugar

1 teaspoon salt

1 pound steamed mixed vegetables (See "Steaming Vegetables" on page 31.)

1 pound tofu, cubed, optional

5 fresh basil leaves or 1 teaspoon dried basil

1. In a large soup pot, place the water and coconut milk. Cook over medium-high heat until the mixture is hot, but not boiling. Add the kaffir leaves and red curry paste to the milk mixture, and stir to blend thoroughly. Then add the sugar and salt, and stir until the salt and sugar are completely dissolved.

2. Add the steamed, mixed vegetables and optional tofu, and simmer on low heat. For the final seasoning, after 10 minutes of simmering, add the basil.

3. Pour the curry into individual serving bowls over rice or noodles.

ABOUT THE RESTAURANT

You'll find this pleasant little restaurant on King Street near the University of Honolulu. It offers an abundant selection of vegetarian entrées.

From Mela Restaurant   COLUMBIA, MARYLAND

Patiala Sabzi (Vegetable Sauté)

This sweet vegetable entrée has hints of cinnamon and coriander.

1. Place the garlic and ginger in a blender, add 3 tablespoons of the water, and blend until a paste-like consistency is achieved. Set the garlic paste aside.

2. Put the cauliflower, carrots, green pepper, and peas into a medium saucepan, and add just enough water to cover. Bring to a boil over medium-high heat. Simmer until just tender, about 10 minutes. Drain and set aside.

3. Place the ghee in a large sauté pan, and heat over medium heat. Add the onions, and gently sauté for 3 minutes. While the onions are cooking, mix the garlic paste in a small bowl with 2 tablespoons of the water and add to the onions. Add the turmeric, and continue to cook until the onions are soft.

4. Add the cooked vegetables, green chili, milk, sugar, and cinnamon. Season with salt, and heat thoroughly.

5. Place the corn flour in another small bowl, and add the remaining 2 tablespoons of water. Mix well, and add to the vegetables. Cook for 2 to 3 minutes, transfer to a serving dish, sprinkle the top with the cilantro, and serve at once.

ABOUT THE RESTAURANT

Already the owners of three Indian fast-food centers in the Maryland and Georgetown areas, husband and wife owners Jawahar and Doler Shah opened their small Indian restaurant in Columbia in 1993. Dining at Mela is an experience of delicious delight at a leisurely pace.

Yield: 3–4 servings

Preparation Time: 15 minutes

Cooking Time: 25 minutes

3 garlic cloves, peeled

1/2-inch piece ginger, peeled

1/4 cup plus 3 tablespoons water

1 cup small cauliflower florets

1/2 cup chopped carrots

1/2 cup chopped green bell pepper

2/3 cup green peas, fresh or frozen

1 tablespoon ghee (See "Preparing Clarified Butter" on page 174.)

1 medium onion, finely chopped

1/4 teaspoon turmeric

1 green chili, finely chopped

1/2 cup milk

1/2 teaspoon sugar

1/4 teaspoon ground cinnamon

Salt, to taste

1 teaspoon corn flour

GARNISH

1 teaspoon finely chopped fresh cilantro (coriander)

From Chicago Diner CHICAGO, ILLINOIS

Gado Gado

In this recipe, a savory combination of spices blends with the vegetables and tempeh to yield a complete and satisfying meal.

Yield: 6–8 servings

Preparation Time: 20 minutes

Cooking Time: 40–45 minutes

1 package tempeh*

Tamari soy sauce, to taste (See "About Soy Sauce" on page 13.)

3 medium red potatoes, diced

2 medium sweet potatoes, peeled and diced

$^3/_4$ cup peanut butter

1 small can whole tomatoes, drained with juice reserved

1 teaspoon sea salt

1 teaspoon ground cinnamon

$^1/_2$ teaspoon ground nutmeg

$^1/_4$–$^1/_2$ teaspoon cayenne pepper or to taste

$^1/_4$ teaspoon ground fenugreek*

2 tablespoons soy oil

1 medium yellow onion, sliced

2 medium carrots, cut in $^1/_2$-inch rounds

3 cloves garlic, minced

2 cups white mushrooms, halved (about 8 ounces)

1 large green bell pepper, cut into large dice

1 large red bell pepper, cut into large dice

1 large yellow pepper, cut into large dice

1. Start the grill or preheat the broiler. Oil a grill or baking sheet.

2. Cut the tempeh lengthwise into two thin layers. Then cut each layer into triangles measuring 1 inch on each side.

3. Lay the triangles on the grill or baking sheet, sprinkle with the soy sauce, and grill or broil on both sides until golden brown. Remove the tempeh from the grill or broiler, and set aside.

4. In a large pot of water, place the red and sweet potatoes. Add water to cover. Boil over medium-high heat until almost cooked. Drain and set aside.

5. In a blender, place the peanut butter, drained tomatoes, sea salt, cinnamon, nutmeg, cayenne pepper, and fenugreek. Season with a splash of soy sauce. Blend until smooth. Set aside.

6. Place the soy oil in a large sauté pan, and heat over medium heat. Add the onion, carrots, and garlic, and cook until they are half cooked, about 2 to 3 minutes. Add the mushrooms and bell peppers, and sauté a few minutes more.

7. Add the peanut butter mixture to the mushroom mixture. Bring to a simmer. Add the grilled tempeh, potatoes, and tomato wedges. Continue to simmer until the flavors blend, about 10 to 15 minutes.

8. Add the reserved tomato juice and the vegetable broth for additional liquid. The tomato wedges should retain their shape.

9. Turn the mixture into a large bowl, sprinkle with the chopped peanuts and chopped spinach, and serve with basmati rice and pita bread.

ABOUT THE RESTAURANT

Mickey Hornick, the owner of the Chicago Diner, has traveled extensively, gathering recipes to add to the restaurant's eclectic assortment of international vegetarian fare.

Tempeh is a delicious, high-protein food made from soybeans. *Fenugreek* is a spicy, rather bitter herb popular in Indian and Middle Eastern cooking.

3 medium tomatoes, cut into wedges

$\frac{1}{2}$ cup vegetable broth

2–3 tablespoons chopped peanuts

1 cup chopped fresh spinach (See "Preparing Fresh Spinach" on page 29.)

From Indian Paradise   NEWPORT BEACH, CALIFORNIA

Gobi Aloo (Cauliflower and Potatoes)

An excellent dish, this recipe is easy to prepare and can be spiced to suit individual tastes. Adding small tofu cubes turns this dish into a complete protein meal.

Yield: *4 servings*

Preparation Time: 15 minutes

Cooking Time: 20–30 minutes

2 tablespoons vegetable oil

1 medium onion, chopped

2 medium potatoes, diced

1 medium cauliflower, separated into florets

1 tomato, chopped

1-inch piece of ginger, peeled and grated, or to taste

$\frac{1}{2}$ teaspoon coriander powder, or to taste

$\frac{1}{2}$ teaspoon cumin powder, or to taste

1 small (5 ounce) can diced green chilies, or to taste

Salt, to taste

1 pound firm tofu, squeezed dry and cut into $\frac{1}{2}$-inch cubes, optional

Fresh cilantro (coriander), chopped, to taste

1. Place the oil in a large sauté pan, and heat over medium-high heat. Add the onion. Cook until the onion turns golden to brown in color, about 5 to 10 minutes.

2. Add the potatoes and cauliflower, stirring to mix well. Lower the temperature to medium. Add the tomato and ginger. Add the coriander powder, cumin powder, green chilies, and salt to taste. Stir to blend well. Add the optional tofu.

3. Cover the pan, and cook until tender and soft, about 20 to 30 minutes. Add the cilantro just before serving, and serve hot.

ABOUT THE RESTAURANT

This Indian restaurant, which opened in 1994, is easily reached from the Pacific Coast Highway in Newport Beach. Sodi Dhami, the owner, remains faithful to his Indian traditions of preparing the most authentic Indian food possible.

From Delites of India   MINNEAPOLIS, MINNESOTA

Dal Pak (Lentils with Spinach)

Yellow lentils are smaller than red or green lentils and have a much more delicate flavor than the green variety. Easy to prepare, this dal offers a taste of India that is easy to fall in love with.

1. Pick over the dal for grit or other foreign matter. Rinse the dal three or four times, or until the water becomes clear. Place the dal in a heavy nonstick saucepan. Add the water, the turmeric, and 1 teaspoon of the canola oil. Boil the dal over medium-high heat until tender, about 30 minutes.

2. Remove the pan from the heat, and add the sea salt and spinach. Return to medium heat, and simmer for 5 minutes. You should have a thick mixture. Check the salt, and adjust the seasoning to taste.

3. In a large sauté pan, place the ghee and the remaining 5 teaspoons of canola oil, and heat over medium-high heat. Add the onions, cumin seeds, and fresh garlic paste. Sauté for 2 minutes. Turn the heat off, and add the ginger and garam masala. Mix together. This mixture is known as *tarka*. Remove half of the tarka, and set aside to use as a garnish.

4. Add the remainder of the tarka to the cooked dal mixture. Spoon onto individual serving plates. Garnish with the remaining tarka, fresh cilantro (coriander), lime juice, and lemon and lime wedges. Serve with basmati rice or puris (page 83).

ABOUT THE RESTAURANT

Books on Indian philosophy, yoga, and vegetarian cooking line the walls. They are available for perusal or purchase, along with Indian food products and teas, at Delites of India.

*Dal is an Indian word that refers to a wide variety of dried legumes. *Moong dal* may be purchased at Indian and Asian specialty stores. *Garam masala* is a combination of spices used in Indian cooking.

Yield: 4 servings

Preparation Time: 15 minutes

Cooking Time: 30 minutes

$1\frac{1}{2}$ cups moong dal* (yellow lentils), washed

$4\frac{1}{2}$ cups water

1 teaspoon turmeric

2 tablespoons (6 teaspoons) canola oil

$1\frac{1}{2}$ teaspoons sea salt

1 bunch spinach, chopped (See "Preparing Fresh Spinach" on page 29.)

1 tablespoon ghee (See "Preparing Clarified Butter" on page 174.)

2 medium purple onions, thinly sliced, optional

1 teaspoon whole cumin seeds

1 teaspoon fresh garlic paste, optional

1 tablespoon fresh grated ginger

1 teaspoon garam masala*

GARNISH

2 tablespoons chopped fresh cilantro (coriander) or 1 teaspoon ground coriander

1 tablespoon lime juice

1 lemon, cut into 4 wedges

1 lime, cut into 4 wedges

From Extra Sensory   PROVIDENCE, RHODE ISLAND

Harissa Chutney with Couscous

A traditional accompaniment for couscous, harissa chutney will perk up your favorite grain and bean dishes. This variation is nicely spiced and low-fat.

Yield: 6 servings

Preparation Time: 10 minutes

Cooking Time: 20–25 minutes

HARISSA

3 cups fresh, diced carrots (about 6 carrots)

1$\frac{1}{2}$ cups water

1$\frac{1}{2}$ teaspoons fresh, minced garlic

$\frac{1}{2}$ teaspoon hot pepper flakes, or to taste

2 tablespoons extra virgin olive oil

4 teaspoons ground cumin

$\frac{1}{2}$ teaspoon ground caraway

$\frac{1}{2}$ teaspoon ground coriander

5 teaspoons fresh lemon juice

Sea salt

$\frac{1}{2}$ cup unsulphured dried apricots

COUSCOUS

6 cups water

1 tablespoon Vegebase or other vegetable broth seasoning

3 cups uncooked couscous

To Make the Harissa:

1. Place the carrots and the water in a medium-sized saucepan over medium high heat. Cook until tender. Drain, and reserve the water.

2. Place the garlic, hot pepper flakes, oil, cumin, caraway, coriander, lemon juice, and salt in a food processor. Add 1 cup of the reserved water from the carrots, and process for 30 seconds. (If you do not have enough carrot water, add plain water to make 1 cup.) Turn the mixture into a medium-sized bowl, and set aside.

3. Put the apricots in a small bowl, and cover with hot water to soften for 1 minute. Drain the water, and chop the apricots into small pieces. Add the apricots to the puréed mixture, and mix well. If you are not going to serve the harissa chutney right away, cover the bowl and refrigerate for up to two days. Remove the harissa chutney from the refrigerator an hour ahead of serving time to allow it to come to room temperature. Then pour into your favorite serving bowl.

To Prepare the Couscous:

1. Bring the water to boil in a large saucepan over high heat. Add the Vegebase (or other vegetable-based seasoning) and the couscous. Stir once, cover, and remove from the heat. Let stand for 5 minutes. Then fluff with a fork. Scoop onto individual serving plates, or place in a large serving bowl. Serve hot with the harissa chutney.

ABOUT THE RESTAURANT

Extra Sensory turns the ordinary to extra-ordinary!

From Joy Meadow   REDWOOD CITY, CALIFORNIA

Enchanted Forest

Once you've stocked your pantry with Asian ingredients, recipes such as this one are not the least bit intimidating and add wonderful new dimensions to your cooking repertoire. Although the recipe calls for marinating the tofu for 1 hour, I have made this entrée by marinating the tofu for 5 to 10 minutes for a quick dinner, and it was still delicious.

1. To make the marinade, place the hoisin sauce, plum sauce, tomato sauce, soy sauce, garlic, and salt together in a large bowl. Stir to blend well.

2. Add the sliced tofu, turning gently to completely cover the tofu with the marinade. Cover the bowl with plastic wrap, and refrigerate for 1 hour.

3. When the marinade has been in the refrigerator for 45 minutes, put the vegetable stock in a large pot, add the broccoli, and cook the broccoli until it is tender-crisp, about 5 to 10 minutes. Remove the broccoli from the stock, arrange on the individual serving plates, and sprinkle with soy sauce.

4. While the broccoli is cooking, pour the olive oil into a large sauté pan and heat over medium-high heat. Add the tofu and the marinade to the olive oil, and add additional vegetable stock, if necessary, to prevent the tofu from sticking. Stir and heat thoroughly.

5. Remove the tofu from the heat, and spoon the tofu and marinade over the broccoli. Serve hot with rice on the side.

ABOUT THE RESTAURANT

Next door to the Joy Meadow is the restaurant's Harmony Bookshop, where you can browse to your heart's delight through all the new-age books and specialty goods.

*Hoisin sauce, a very thick, dark brown sauce used in Asian cooking, is made from soybeans, garlic, sugar, and chilies. *Plum sauce* is a blend of plum purée, sugar, water, and vinegar. It has a slightly sweet and sour flavor and is used in Asian cooking as a dipping sauce and as a glaze.

Yield: 4 servings

Preparation Time: 10 minutes; 1 hour to marinate the tofu

Cooking Time: 10–15 minutes

1 tablespoon hoisin sauce*

1 teaspoon plum sauce*

1 teaspoon tomato sauce

2 teaspoons soy sauce plus additional sauce to taste (See "About Soy Sauce" on page 13.)

1 teaspoon crushed garlic

1 teaspoon salt

1 pound firm tofu, drained, rinsed and cut into rectangular slices

4 cups vegetable stock

1 pound broccoli florets (about 3 cups)

1 tablespoon olive oil

From Lucky Creation Vegetarian Restaurant
SAN FRANCISCO, CALIFORNIA

Sautéed Bean Curd Rolls with Broccoli

This absolutely delicious dish is easier to make than you might think!

Yield: 2 servings

Preparation Time: 20–30 minutes plus 30 minutes for soaking the mushrooms

Cooking Time: 2 minutes per roll

FILLING

$2/3$ cup dried Chinese black mushrooms (See "About Mushrooms" on page 63.)

1 tablespoon vegetable oil

$1^1/3$ cups finely chopped or shredded carrot

$1^1/3$ cups finely chopped or shredded celery

$1^1/3$ cups bean sprouts

$1^1/2$ teaspoons sugar

1 teaspoon light soy sauce (See "About Soy Sauce" on page 13.)

2 teaspoons cornstarch

1 tablespoon water

PASTE AND WRAPPERS

2 teaspoons flour

1 tablespoon water

10–12 pieces of (5- by 7-inch) bean curd sheets or spring roll wrappers*

2 cups oil, approximately

To Make the Filling:

1. Place the Chinese black mushrooms in a medium-sized bowl, cover with hot water, and set aside to soak for 30 minutes. Remove from the water, and chop finely.

2. In a large sauté pan or wok, place the oil and heat over high heat. Add the mushrooms, carrots, celery, and bean sprouts, and stir-fry for 2 minutes.

3. In a small bowl place the sugar, soy sauce, cornstarch, and water. Whisk together.

4. Briskly stir the soy sauce mixture into the stir-fry mixture. Cook for an additional minute. Drain the excess liquid, and set aside to cool.

To Fill the Rolls:

1. Preheat the oven to 200°F.

2. Place the flour and water for the paste in a small bowl, and combine.

3. Remove a spring roll wrapper from the pack of wrappers. Keep the remaining wrappers covered to prevent them from drying out.

4. Place 1 to 2 tablespoons of the filling on the wrapper. Roll up as illustrated on page 9. Use the paste to seal the edges together. Set aside the roll until all the filling has been used to make rolls.

5. Place vegetable oil to a depth of 2 inches in a large frying pan or deep fryer, and heat to 400°F. Deep fry each roll in the oil for about 1 minute, until it turns golden brown. Depending on the size of your pan, you may be able to fry more than one roll at a time. Remove the rolls from the oil, and allow to drain on several thicknesses of paper towels. Then place the rolls on a baking sheet and place in the oven while you prepare the broccoli.

*Spring roll wrappers are found in the refrigerated case in the produce section of most grocery stores. There are twenty wrappers in a 1-pound package.

To Finish and Serve the Dish:

1. Place enough water to cover the broccoli in a large pot. Bring to the boil over medium-high heat. Add the broccoli, return water to the boil, and cook for 3 minutes over high heat. Remove the broccoli from the boiling water, and drain on paper towels.

2. While the broccoli is cooking, prepare the dark soy sauce mixture. Place the sugar and dark soy sauce in a small saucepan. Cook over medium-high heat until warm. In a small bowl, mix the cornstarch with the water. Add the cornstarch mixture to the pan, stirring constantly until the sauce thickens slightly. Remove the sauce from the heat.

3. To serve, place shredded lettuce on individual plates. Remove the rolls from the oven, and place on the lettuce. Decorate the edges of each plate with several pieces of broccoli. Drizzle the dark soy sauce mixture over the rolls and broccoli, and serve hot.

DARK SOY SAUCE MIXTURE AND GARNISH

1 pound finely chopped broccoli

1$\frac{1}{2}$ teaspoons sugar

$\frac{1}{2}$ teaspoon dark soy sauce

1 teaspoon cornstarch

$\frac{1}{4}$ cup water

4 cups shredded iceberg lettuce (1 medium head)

ABOUT THE RESTAURANT

Owner Hin Kwong Mak and his partners started in the restaurant business in Hong Kong in the 1970, before emigrating to California and opening Lucky Creation in 1988. Their all-vegetarian menu includes over twenty-five tantalizing entrées.

From Cherry Street Chinese Vegetarian   PHILADELPHIA, PENNSYLVANIA

Steamed Rainbow Bean Curd

Tofu dances to a colorful tune in this medley of veggies.

Yield: 4 servings

Preparation Time: 30 minutes

Cooking Time: 10 minutes

10 dried Chinese black mushrooms (See "About Mushrooms" on page 63.)

2 pounds of tofu

10 slices vegetarian ham, optional

4 carrots, peeled and cut into thin, round slices

KALE GARNISH

12 whole Chinese (or regular) green kale leaves

1 teaspoon vegetable oil for boiling kale

Pinch of salt for boiling kale

SAUCE

2 tablespoons cornstarch or arrowroot

$1/4$ cup water

2 teaspoons vegetable oil

2 teaspoons minced garlic

2 teaspoons fermented black beans,* minced

2 cups vegetable stock or water

1 teaspoon salt, optional

1. Place the mushrooms in a bowl of hot water, and soak for 30 minutes while you prepare the rest of the ingredients. Drain and place on a paper towel to dry. Then cut the mushrooms into four pieces each.

2. Steam or boil the kale in a large pot, about 5 to 10 minutes until crisp, but tender. If you boil the kale, add the 1 teaspoon of vegetable oil and pinch of salt to the water to retain the vivid color of the kale. If softer kale is desired, steam or boil longer. Drain the kale, and arrange it in the middle of and on the two longer sides of one large rectangular or oval platter. Or arrange the kale around the perimeter of four individual plates.

3. Cut the bean curd and the mock ham each into forty 3-inch by $1/2$-inch strips, allowing ten strips each of tofu and mock ham for each person.

4. In a steamer, arrange the carrot rounds, mock ham strips, mushrooms, and tofu strips in that order, overlapping in the steamer. Place over high heat for 5 minutes. Remove from the steamer. Drain on several thicknesses of paper towel, and save the water used for steaming. There should be $1/2$ to 1 cup of water.

5. Preheat the oven to warm. To arrange the steamed ingredients on the serving platter or plate garnished with the kale leaves, alternate one strip of bean curd, one slice of carrot, one strip of mock ham, and one piece of Chinese mushroom, until you have used ten slices of each ingredient per person. You may form two or three rows of the ingredients, depending on the size of the platter. Place the platter or individual plates in the warm oven while you prepare the sauce.

To Prepare the Sauce and Serve:

1. Place the cornstarch (or arrowroot) and water in a small bowl, and stir with a fork or whisk until well blended.

* *Vegetarian ham* is a product found in most natural food stores. It is usually made from a soy-based or other vegetable protein that is combined with spices to yield a cholesterol-free, low-fat, flavorful alternative to a traditional meat product. *Fermented black beans* are very small beans that are preserved in salt. They are found in the Asian foods section of most supermarkets or in Asian grocery stores. Be sure to rinse them well before using.

2. Heat the oil in a medium-sized pot over medium-high heat, and add the garlic, black bean, stock (or water), salt, and the reserved steaming water used to steam the tofu. Bring this mixture to a boil.

3. Pour the cornstarch mixture slowly into the sauce, stirring constantly with a whisk as you pour and the sauce thickens.

4. Pour the sauce evenly on top of the bean curd, mock ham, carrot, and Chinese mushroom arrangement. Serve immediately with white or brown rice.

ABOUT THE RESTAURANT

"The genuine joy of the owners has been caught by everybody on the staff and is quickly passed on to the customers. Almost every entrée comes out of the kitchen with flower decorations made from vegetables: a flower pot with flowers carved from a carrot, a chrysanthemum made of daikon, a crane of carrot with daikon wings bringing a sprig of dill to build a nest," comments Jim Quinn in his August 18, 1991, review in Lifefood.

"People think vegetarian cooking is nothing special," says Raymond Fung, owner-chef of Chinese Street Vegetarian, *"and we try to show that vegetarian food can be delicious and beautiful."*

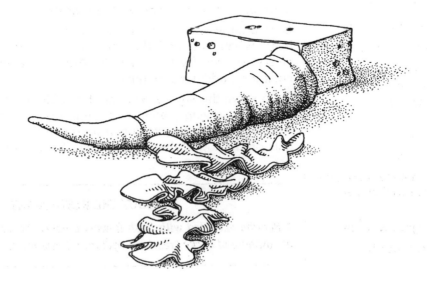

From Lucky Creation Vegetarian Restaurant
SAN FRANCISCO, CALIFORNIA

Diced Mushrooms with Cashew Nuts

I found that our local supermarket had everything I needed to make this simply exquisite entrée.

Yield: 4 servings

Preparation Time: 10 minutes plus 30 minutes for soaking the mushrooms

Cooking Time: 10 minutes

4 ounces dried Chinese black mushrooms (See "About Mushrooms" on page 63.)

1 cup plus 1 teaspoon vegetable oil

2 cups raw cashew nuts

1 pound cauliflower florets (about 3 cups)

1 cup canned button mushrooms or fresh white mushrooms

1 cup straw mushrooms

4 carrots, sliced into rounds

1 cup chopped green bell pepper

1 cup chopped celery

SAUCE

1 teaspoon salt

3 teaspoons sugar

2 teaspoons dark soy sauce (See "About Soy Sauce" on page 13.)

4 teaspoons light soy sauce

2 teaspoons cornstarch

1. In a medium-sized bowl, soak the Chinese black mushrooms for 30 minutes in enough warm water to generously cover the mushrooms. Drain, and chop into small pieces.

2. Place 1 cup of the oil in a deep fryer and heat to 400°F. Deep-fry the cashews just slightly golden brown. Or place a large sauté pan over medium-high heat, and add 1 tablespoon of the oil. When the oil is hot, place the cashews in the oil, and quickly sauté them for 1 minute. Remove the nuts from the pan with a slotted spoon, and drain on several thicknesses of paper towel.

3. Place enough water to cover the cauliflower in a large pot. Bring to the boil over medium-high heat. Add the florets, return water to the boil, and cook for 3 minutes. Remove the cauliflower from the boiling water, drain, and set aside.

4. In the same pot, in the same manner as you did the cauliflower, blanch together for 1 minute the chopped black mushrooms, the button (or white) mushrooms, the straw mushrooms, the carrots, the green bell pepper, and the celery. Drain, and set aside.

5. To make the sauce, place all the sauce ingredients in a small bowl, and whisk to blend well. Set aside.

6. In a large sauté pan or wok, place 1 teaspoon of oil over high heat. When hot, add the mushrooms, carrots, bell pepper, and celery, and stir-fry for 1 minute. Add the sauce to the stir-fry, and cook for 1 additional minute.

7. To serve the stir-fry, arrange the cauliflower around the edges of individual serving plates or the edge of one large serving platter. Mound the other vegetables in the center, and sprinkle the cashew nuts on the top of the finished dish. Serve hot with white or brown rice.

ABOUT THE RESTAURANT

A Buddha encircled with fresh flowers creates the simple, exquisite Chinese atmosphere of Lucky Creation Vegetarian Restaurant.

From Tipps Thai Cuisine   VENTURA, CALIFORNIA

Pad Thai Tofu
(Thai-Style Noodles with Tofu)

This traditional Thai dish has a subtle hint of peanut.

1. Place the oil in a wok or sauté pan, and heat over high heat. Add the tofu, and stir until well browned.

2. Add the optional eggs, and stir with the tofu to scramble the eggs.

3. Add the rice noodles, and continue to stir. Sometimes the noodles require additional oil to keep them soft, or you may add water instead of oil.

4. Add the soy sauce, vinegar, sugar, and paprika. Stir well for 3 to 4 minutes to prevent the noodles from sticking.

5. Add the scallions, bean sprouts, and 2 tablespoons of the crushed peanuts. Mix well over high heat.

6. Transfer to individual serving plates, garnish with more bean sprouts, and the remaining crushed peanuts, and serve.

ABOUT THE RESTAURANT

Tipps has always been a busy spot for the active crowd. Tipps keeps pace with their discriminating clientele with over twenty entrée selections for vegetarians.

Yield: *4 servings*

Preparation Time: 10 minutes

Cooking Time: 10 minutes

3 tablespoons vegetable oil

1$\frac{1}{2}$ pounds tofu, diced into 1-inch cubes

2 eggs, optional

8–10 ounces soft rice noodles (or dry rice noodles soaked in water for 25 minutes to soften; see "About Thai Ingredients" on page 62.)

$\frac{1}{4}$ cup Thai thin soy sauce

$\frac{1}{4}$ cup cider vinegar

1 tablespoon sugar

Paprika, to taste

4 scallions (green onions), cut into 1-inch lengths

$\frac{1}{2}$ cup bean sprouts plus bean sprouts for garnish

4 tablespoons crushed raw peanuts

From Alisan Restaurant   ANAHEIM, CALIFORNIA

Four Threads Sautéed

Asian cuisine has created an amazing expansion of vegetarian cooking with the addition of gluten. This versatile ingredient gives substance and protein to vegetarian dishes. Gluten is especially helpful for those people who are making a transition from a meat diet to a vegetarian diet because it resembles meat in appearance, texture, and taste.

Yield: *4 servings*

Preparation Time: 20 minutes

Cooking Time: 5 minutes

1 tablespoon vegetable oil

3 pieces dried Chinese black mushrooms, soaked in water until soft, finely chopped

12 ounces gluten, finely chopped (premade, or see page 196.)

2–3 thick slices of vegetarian ham,* finely chopped, optional

8 ounces extra firm tofu, drained and patted dry, cut into small pieces

2 medium celery stalks, finely chopped

2 medium carrots, finely chopped

2 tablespoons soy sauce (See "About Soy Sauce" on page 13.)

2 teaspoons sugar

2 tablespoons sesame oil

1. Place the vegetable oil in a large sauté pan over medium-high heat. Add the mushrooms, and stir-fry by quickly tossing, stirring, and mixing over high heat for about 10 seconds.

2. Add the gluten, vegetarian ham, tofu, celery, and carrots. Continue to stir-fry.

3. In a small bowl, place the soy sauce and sugar, and whisk together. Add to the stir-fry mixture. Stir-fry for 5 minutes.

4. Add the sesame oil, mix, and serve hot with white rice.

ABOUT THE RESTAURANT

Specializing in unique and interesting vegetarian dishes, Alisan Restaurant lists more than twenty-five vegetarian selections on its menu.

Vegetarian ham is a product found in most natural food stores. It is usually made from a soy-based or other vegetable protein that is combined with spices to yield a cholesterol-free, low-fat, flavorful alternative to a traditional meat product.

From Doe Bay Café   OLGA, WASHINGTON

Buddha's Noodles

This traditional-tasting Asian dish has a sauce you can count on to be delicious!

To Prepare the Sauce:

1. Place all the sauce ingredients in a small saucepan. Cook over low heat until well blended, about 10 minutes. Remove from the heat.

To Prepare the Noodles:

1. Place water and the salt in a large pot. Cover and bring to a boil over high heat. Add the pasta, and cook al dente (until done but not soft).

2. While the pasta is cooking, place the sesame oil in a large sauté pan, and heat over medium-high heat. Add the sesame seeds, and stir.

3. Add the tofu cubes, and sauté until they begin to turn golden.

4. Add the mixed vegetables and the sauce. Cook until the veggies are bright in color, or tender-crisp.

5. Drain the pasta, and place on a serving platter or individual serving plates. Spoon the vegetables over the top, and serve.

ABOUT THE RESTAURANT

Crisp mornings invite you to warm yourself around the wood-burning stove in the Doe Bay Café, where it stays cozy all day. Serving breakfasts, lunches, and dinners to guests who come for just a meal or an overnight stay in the cabins, Doe Bay Café is one of those relaxed places where "hanging out" and enjoying the view or canoeing in the bay are the main events of the day.

Yield: *4 servings*

Preparation Time: 15 minutes

Cooking Time: 15 minutes

BUDDHA'S SAUCE

1/2 cup tamari soy sauce (See "About Soy Sauce" on page 13.)

2 tablespoons freshly grated ginger

1 tablespoon apple cider vinegar

2 tablespoons honey

Dash cayenne pepper

2 teaspoons five-spice powder

BUDDHA'S NOODLES

1 teaspoon sea salt

2 pounds fresh pasta (buckwheat or rice noodles are best)

2 tablespoons sesame oil

1/4 cup sesame seeds

1 pound firm tofu, cubed

2 pounds mixed seasonal veggies (such as broccoli, onions, carrots, cauliflower, mushrooms, and red pepper), chopped

From Alisan Restaurant   ANAHEIM, CALIFORNIA

Sweet and Sour Gluten

This gluten recipe, which has a tangy, slightly sweet flavor, may be fixed quickly with prepared gluten. If you have not worked with gluten before, you may want to purchase the prepared gluten, so you'll know what taste, texture, and appearance to expect. After you are familiar with the product, you may enjoy experimenting by making your own. To turn the gluten into seitan, simmer the gluten in stock seasoned with tamari soy sauce. Seiten can be sliced, cubed, or ground for use in burgers, chili, casseroles, or sauces.

Yield: *4 servings including 4 cups gluten*

Preparation Time: for the gluten: 15 minutes for the dough, 2 hours to soak; for the final recipe: 5 minutes

Cooking Time: 30 minutes for the gluten: 5–10 minutes for the final recipe

BASIC GLUTEN

Method 1

2 cups vital wheat gluten powder

3 cups room-temperature water

Method 2

8 cups unbleached all-purpose flour

2 tablespoons salt

4½ cups room-temperature water

SWEET AND SOUR GLUTEN

2–4 tablespoons vegetable oil

5 slices peeled fresh ginger

2 tablespoons soy sauce for the final recipe (See "About Soy Sauce" on page 13.)

4 tablespoons sugar

Basic Gluten Method 1:

1. Mix the gluten powder with the water, and stir until the powder is fully dissolved. The mixture should look like dough.

2. Submerge the ball of dough in a large bowl filled with water, and allow to rest for 2 hours.

3. Place the dough in a large plastic strainer or colander. Knead and rinse the dough under a stream of running tap water, allowing the milky starch to rinse off. Continue to rinse the dough until the water becomes almost clear.

4. Divide the dough into four equal parts, roll and pat into small balls, and boil or steam the dough until it is cooked, about 30 minutes. Test for doneness by gently making a slice with a knife in one small dough ball. The dough should be firm but somewhat porous. If the gluten has not cooked enough, the dough will be sticky.

Basic Gluten Method 2:

1. Place the flour and salt in a large mixing bowl, and mix. Slowly stir in the water until the flour is fully dissolved. The mixture should look like dough. Cover with plastic wrap, and let rest 6 to 8 hours or overnight.

2. The next day, place the dough in a large plastic strainer. Rinse with tap water, allowing the milky starch to rinse off until the water becomes almost clear.

3. Divide the dough into 4 equal balls, and boil or steam until cooked, about 30 minutes.

To Prepare the Sweet and Sour Gluten:

1. Over medium heat in a wok or small sauté pan, place the vegetable oil and ginger, and stir-fry for 1 minute.

2. Add the soy sauce, sugar, vinegar (or lemon juice), water, and tomato sauce. Bring to a boil.

3. When the mixture is boiling, add the gluten. Simmer over medium heat until the liquid is reduced so that the gluten is almost dry. Add the sesame oil, stirring to blend evenly.

4. Transfer to a serving bowl, and serve immediately with white rice.

2 tablespoons vinegar or lemon juice

2 cups water

2 tablespoons tomato sauce

24 ounces gluten, diced into small pieces

1 1/2 tablespoons sesame oil

ABOUT THE RESTAURANT

Ken Su, owner of Alisan Restaurant, has been serving the Anaheim area since 1980. The chefs at Alisan continue to experiment, intending to make all of their entrées low-fat or nonfat and entirely vegetarian.

"Eating less meat builds a kinder heart," comments the manager, Wayne Su, on the restaurant's commitment to educate people. "We aim to educate people so that they know they can eat well, be healthy, and promote life on the planet." Wayne Su says that his mother's very thorough, meticulous hands carefully craft the gluten used in many of the Alisan Restaurant dishes.

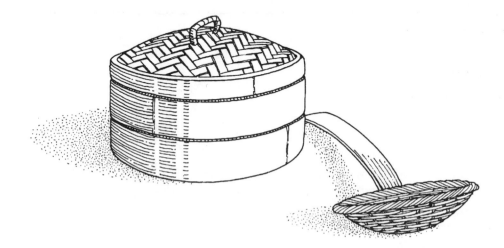

From Cornucopia Restaurant   LAWRENCE, KANSAS

Fried Brown Rice

Adding sautéed tofu or tempeh, or a legume such as beans, lentils, or peas, to this savory rice dish adds extra protein for a nutritionally complete, one-dish meal.

Yield: 6–8 servings

Preparation Time: 20–30 minutes

Cooking Time: 30 minutes

3 cups uncooked brown rice

6 cups water

1 tablespoon butter

1¼ cups chopped celery

1¼ cups chopped mushrooms (about 6 ounces)

1 cup chopped green bell pepper

½ cup chopped scallion (green onion)

⅓ cup sesame seeds

⅓ cup sunflower seeds

½ cup tamari soy sauce (See "About Soy Sauce" on page 13.)

GARNISH

Slices of fresh fruit, in season

1. Steam the rice and water in a pressure cooker for 25 minutes. Or place the rice and water in a large saucepan, cover, and bring to a boil over high heat. Reduce the heat to low, and simmer until done, about 30 minutes.

2. Place the butter in a large sauté pan, and melt over medium heat. Add the celery and mushrooms, and sauté until they are soft. Set aside.

3. When the rice is done, drain any excess water from the pan and rinse in fresh, warm water to remove the starch. Turn the rice into a large mixing bowl, and add the ingredients from the sauté pan. Then add the green bell pepper, scallion, sesame seeds, sunflower seeds, and soy sauce. Stir well to mix all the ingredients.

4. Transfer the fried rice to a large serving bowl or platter or to individual plates. Garnish with fresh fruit slices.

ABOUT THE RESTAURANT

The Cornucopia Restaurant has served many customers in its twenty years in business in Lawrence.

From Kingsbury House   BELFAST, MAINE

Holiday Rice with Cranberry Sauce

This festive mélange of rices is accented by a lovely, deep red cranberry sauce.

To Prepare the Cranberry Sauce:

1. To roast the pecans, preheat the oven to 350°F. Spread the pecans on a baking sheet, and place in the oven for 10 minutes. Stir the pecans and roast another 1 to 2 minutes. Remove from the oven, and allow to cool. Coarsely chop before using.

2. Place the cranberries, orange pieces, apple juice, and agar-agar in a large saucepan. Bring to a boil over medium-high heat. Reduce the heat to low, cover, and simmer for 20 minutes, stirring occasionally until slightly thickened.

3. Remove the pan from the heat, add the pecans, and pour into a 9- by 9-inch pan or mold. Allow to become cool and firm in the refrigerator, about 30 to 40 minutes.

To Prepare the Rice:

1. Place the brown rice, basmati rice, and wild rice in a large saucepan or pressure cooker, and add the water. Add the water chestnuts, bring to a boil over high heat, and add the sea salt. Cover the pan, lower the heat to low, and simmer for 40 to 50 minutes, or until the rice is tender and all the water is absorbed. If you use a pressure cooker, it may take 35 to 45 minutes to cook the rice.

2. Remove the pan from the heat. Gently fluff and mix the rice with a fork. Then transfer to a serving bowl, and garnish with roasted pumpkin seeds. Serve warm with the Kingsbury House Holiday Cranberry Sauce.

ABOUT THE RESTAURANT

Kingsbury House, a small bed-and-breakfast inn, offers only macrobiotic meals to its fortunate clientele.

*A combination of certain sea vegetables, *agar-agar* is a white, powdered jelling agent used in some gelatin desserts, aspics, and glazes. It may be found in most natural food stores. *Basmati rice*, from India, is a particularly aromatic long-grained rice. Be sure to rinse it according to the package directions.

Yield: 8 *servings*

Preparation Time: 10 minutes for the rice; 10 minutes for the cranberry sauce

Cooking Time: 40–50 minutes for the rice; 20 minutes for the cranberry sauce plus 30–40 minutes for chilling

CRANBERRY SAUCE

1/4–1/2 cup pecans

2 cups whole cranberries

1 medium orange, peeled, quartered, and seeded

2 cups apple juice

4–6 tablespoons agar-agar*

RICE

2 cups short-grain brown rice

1 cup basmati rice*

1/2 cup wild rice

6 cups water

1 cup chopped water chestnuts

Pinch of sea salt

GARNISH

Roasted pumpkin seeds

From Café Chimes   NORTH CONWAY, NEW HAMPSHIRE

Herbed Brown Rice Carousel Casserole

This casserole features a colorful array of vegetables. Leftovers make a superb fried rice.

Yield: *8 servings*

Preparation Time: 20 minutes

Cooking Time: 50 minutes

3 cups short-grain brown rice, washed

4 cups water

2 pinches of sea salt

2 cups chopped kale

1 teaspoon vegetable oil

1 cup thinly sliced red cabbage

1/4 cup tamari soy sauce (See "About Soy Sauce" on page 13.)

1 tablespoon sesame oil

2 tablespoons olive oil

1/2 cup roasted sesame seeds

1 tablespoon dried basil

1 tablespoon garlic powder

1/2 teaspoon ground cinnamon

1/2 cup dried parsley

1/2–1 teaspoon Herbamere* to taste

1 cup grated carrots

1/2 cup diced red bell pepper

1/4 cup presoaked arame*

1. Lightly oil a three- or four-quart round or square casserole pan.

2. Place the brown rice, 4 cups of water, and a pinch of the sea salt in a medium-sized pot. Bring to a boil over high heat. Cover, turn the heat to low, and simmer for 50 minutes.

3. While the rice is cooking, put the kale in a large pot, and add enough water to cover. Add the vegetable oil and the remaining pinch of salt. Cover the pot with a lid, and place on high heat until the water starts to boil. Lower the heat to medium, and continue to cook until tender, about 30 to 40 minutes.

4. Place the red cabbage in a medium-sized pan, and add enough water to cover. Place on medium-high heat, cover, and bring to a boil. Allow the cabbage to boil gently for 20 minutes, until it is tender and cooked. Set aside.

5. Check the rice to be sure all the water has been absorbed and the rice is tender. Transfer the rice to a large mixing bowl, if the pan is not large enough to mix in. Then add the soy sauce, sesame oil, olive oil, sesame seeds, basil, garlic powder, cinnamon, parsley, and Herbamere. Toss well, check for taste, and season accordingly. Place the rice in the prepared casserole dish. Preheat the oven to 350°F.

6. Arrange the vegetables in circles on top of the rice. Begin with the kale on the outside row, next add the cooked red cabbage, then the grated carrot, then the red bell pepper, and finally end with the arame in the center. The design should resemble the circular motion of a carousel. Cover with a lid or with aluminum foil.

7 Place the casserole in the oven for 15 minutes to warm thoroughly. Remove from the oven and serve immediately. To store the leftovers, separate the veggies from the rice and place each in separate refrigerator containers with lids. The rice holds well in the refrigerator for several days and freezes well, too.

ABOUT THE RESTAURANT

Kathleen Etter, owner of Café Chimes, states, "We specialize in cooking with intuition, with the seasons, and with a joyful attitude. We began this way and shall remain this way, yet held together by the constant change for growth."

Herbamere is an herb seasoning salt. *Arame seaweed* is a sea vegetable found at most natural food stores or Asian grocery stores.

Brunch Dishes

From Madison River Inn THREE FORKS, MONTANA

Sour Cream Breakfast Cake

This moist, rich coffee cake is wonderful to have on hand for any breakfast or brunch occasion. You can easily double the recipe for a large group, too. If you want to skip the eggs, you may substitute 2 tablespoons tofu blended with 2 tablespoons plain or vanilla yogurt. See "Alternatives to Eggs" on page 82.

1. Preheat the oven to 350°F. Lightly grease and flour a 9- by 9-inch baking pan.

2. In a medium-sized mixing bowl, sift together the flour, baking powder, baking soda, and salt.

3. In a large mixing bowl, cream together the butter (or margarine), sugar, vanilla extract, and eggs (or egg replacer).

4. Add about a third of the flour mixture to the butter mixture, and blend in. Then add about a third of the sour cream to the butter mixture, and blend in. Continue alternating additions of the flour and the sour cream until all ingredients are blended together.

5. To make the topping, place all the topping ingredients in a small bowl, and combine.

6. Spread half the batter on the bottom of the prepared baking pan. Then, sprinkle half the topping mixture on the batter on the pan. Spread the remaining batter on top, and sprinkle the remaining topping to cover the batter.

7. Place in the oven, and bake for 30 to 40 minutes. Remove from the oven, and allow to rest for 5 minutes on a wire cooling rack before cutting into squares and serving warm.

ABOUT THE RESTAURANT

You can sip freshly ground and brewed coffee and enjoy this delicious coffee cake, which is frequently featured at the Madison River Inn breakfast buffet, as you sit on the natural stone steps overlooking the Madison River.

Yield: *6–8 servings*

Preparation Time: 20 minutes

Cooking Time: 30–40 minutes

2 cups flour

1 teaspoon baking powder

1 teaspoon baking soda

1/2 teaspoon salt

1/2 cup butter or margarine

1 cup sugar

1 teaspoon vanilla extract

2 eggs or egg replacer

1 cup sour cream

TOPPING

1/4 cup melted butter

1 cup pecans

1/4 cup sugar

1/3 cup brown sugar

1 teaspoon ground cinnamon

From Paradise Café LAWRENCE, KANSAS

Blue Corn Pancakes

Sensational pancakes! Try putting cottage cheese or vanilla yogurt and sliced bananas drizzled with maple syrup on top for a truly pleasurable breakfast treat.

Yield: *4 pancakes; 1$\frac{1}{2}$ cups of syrup*

Preparation Time: 3 minutes for the syrup; 5 minutes for the pancakes

Cooking Time: 5 minutes for the syrup; 10–20 minutes for the pancakes

HOMEMADE MAPLE-FLAVORED SYRUP
(from the Madison River Inn)

1 cup water

2 cups white sugar

$\frac{1}{2}$–1 teaspoon maple flavoring (such as Crescent Mapeleine)

PANCAKES

2 eggs or $\frac{1}{2}$ cup yogurt (See "Alternatives to Eggs" on page 82.)

$\frac{1}{4}$ cup brown sugar

$\frac{1}{4}$ cup vegetable oil (Use 2–3 tablespoons for a great low-fat version.)

1 teaspoon salt

2 cups buttermilk, as needed for thinning batter

2 tablespoons baking powder

1$\frac{1}{2}$ cups blue corn flour

1 cup unbleached white flour

To Make the Syrup:

1. Place the water in a small saucepan, and bring to a boil over high heat. Add the sugar, stirring until it is completely dissolved.

2. Remove from the heat, add the maple flavoring, and stir to blend.

3. Pour the syrup into a serving pitcher and serve warm, or pour into a glass container and allow to cool before covering. Store in the refrigerator for several weeks.

To Make and Serve the Pancakes:

1. Lightly brush a pancake griddle or skillet with oil, and preheat to 400°F.

2. Place the eggs or yogurt, brown sugar, vegetable oil, and salt in a large mixing bowl. Beat with an electric beater or wire whisk until thoroughly blended.

3. Add the 2 cups of buttermilk and the baking powder, and mix well. Beat in the blue corn flour and the white flour. Mix until all the lumps disappear. If needed, blend in additional buttermilk until the batter reaches the consistency of sour cream.

4. Pour $\frac{1}{3}$ cup to $\frac{1}{2}$ cup of batter onto the hot griddle for each pancake. Allow the pancakes to cook for 1 to 2 minutes on each side. Remove the pancakes from the griddle, and serve immediately with fresh butter and warm syrup.

ABOUT THE RESTAURANT

An eclectic bunch gathers in the booths at The Paradise Café. The early-risin' "biscuit boys" are the first to arrive, ready for their cup of freshly ground coffee and a plate of warm, homemade biscuits or almost-too-good-to-be-true blue corn pancakes. The discriminating dinner customers know they're assured of a wonderful evening of food and fun. And many students from the University of Kansas and Haskell Jr. College—which just happens to be host to a large diversity of Native American tribes—impress their parents with a night on the town that begins at The Paradise Café.

From The Old Town Café   BELLINGHAM, WASHINGTON

Flanagan French Toast

The cheese–and–fruit filling in this recipe is so good, you'll be tempted to eat it all by itself! This luscious and sensual treat is a great way to start a Sunday morning. You may use either all fruit (such as raspberries, blueberries, and peaches) or all nuts (such as pecans, walnuts, and sunflower seeds) or a combination for this filling. The fruit may be fresh or frozen. Fruit with a peel, such as apples and peaches, should be peeled before use.

To Make the Syrup:

1. Place the water in a small saucepan, and bring to a boil. Then lower the heat and add the brown sugar, stirring to dissolve completely.

2. Remove the pan from the heat. Add the maple flavoring, and mix together.

3. Pour into a serving pitcher and serve warm, or allow to cool and store in a covered container for up to several weeks in the refrigerator.

To Make and Serve the French Toast:

1. Place 1 to 2 tablespoons of butter (or oil) in a large skillet, and melt over medium heat. Remove from the heat, and set aside until the bread is ready to be grilled.

2. Place the cream cheese, ricotta cheese, honey (or maple syrup), and 2 teaspoons of the vanilla extract in a medium-sized bowl, and whip together with an electric beater. Gently stir in the fruit and nuts.

3. In another medium-sized bowl, place the milk, cinnamon, and optional eggs or yogurt, and the remaining 2 teaspoons of vanilla extract. Whip together with the electric beater.

4. Return the skillet with the melted butter (or oil) to medium heat. For each serving, spread about 2 tablespoons of the cheese-and-fruit filling between 2 slices of bread. Press the slices together. Then lightly immerse the sandwich in the milk mixture.

5. Place the sandwich in the skillet, and grill the bread until it turns golden brown and the filling is warm in the center. Remove the Flanagan French Toast from the skillet, and serve immediately with butter and warm syrup.

ABOUT THE RESTAURANT

Yahoo! The Old Town Café serves breakfast all day!

Yield: *6 servings, including 2 cups of syrup*

Preparation Time: 3 minutes for the syrup; 30 minutes for the French toast

Cooking Time: 5 minutes for the syrup; 10 minutes for the French toast

GOLDEN MAPLE-FLAVORED SYRUP
(from the Madison River Inn)

1 cup water

2 1/2 cups brown sugar

1/2–1 teaspoon maple flavoring (such as Crescent Mapeleine)

FRENCH TOAST

1–2 tablespoons butter or vegetable oil

16 ounces cream cheese, softened

1/2 cup ricotta cheese

1/4 cup honey or maple syrup

4 teaspoons vanilla extract

2 cups fruit and nuts

2 cups milk

1 teaspoon cinnamon

6 eggs or 1/2 cup yogurt, optional (See "Alternatives to Eggs" on page 82.)

12 slices sourdough or whole wheat bread

From The Community Food Co-op   BOZEMAN, MONTANA

Tofu Quiche

Absolutely scrumptious—anytime! For those who like quiche but don't want to eat eggs, this recipe is a great replacement for traditional recipes that are laden with eggs.

Yield: *6 servings*

Preparation Time: 30 minutes

Cooking Time: 55 minutes

CRUST

2 cups oats

$^1\!/_2$ cup walnuts, halves or pieces

$^1\!/_3$–$^2\!/_3$ cup water

TOFU FILLING

1 pound firm tofu

$^1\!/_4$ cup canola or safflower oil

1 cup sliced fresh mushrooms

FRENCH ONION ESSENCE

1–2 tablespoons vegetable oil

1 medium yellow onion, finely chopped

1 tablespoon chopped garlic

$^1\!/_2$ cup shredded carrots

1 red bell pepper, chopped

$^1\!/_4$ cup liquid aminos or tamari soy sauce

3 scallions (green onions), chopped

GARNISH

Sprinkle of paprika

To Prepare the Crust:

1. Preheat the oven to 350°F.

2. Place the oats and walnuts in a food processor or blender, and process until crumbly. Turn the mixture into a medium-sized mixing bowl. Working the mixture with your hands or a fork to blend well, and add enough water to moisten and hold the ingredients together.

3. Press the crust mixture into a 9-inch pie pan, and place in the oven to bake for 10 minutes, until lightly browned. When the crust is cooked, remove it from the oven and place on a wire rack while you prepare the filling. Reset the oven temperature to 450°F.

To Prepare the Filling:

1. In the food processor or blender, place $^1\!/_2$ pound of the tofu and all the oil. Blend until smooth.

2. Turn the mixture into a medium-sized bowl, and crumble in the rest of the tofu. Add the mushrooms, mix well, and set aside.

To Prepare the French Onion Essence:

1. Heat a large sauté pan over medium heat, and add the vegetable oil. Add the onions and garlic, and sauté until the onions are translucent.

2. Add the carrots and red bell pepper, and sauté the veggies until they are crisp-tender.

3. Add the soy sauce and the scallions. Stir to blend well, and remove from the heat.

To Prepare and Bake the Quiche:

1. Place the onion essence in a medium-sized mixing bowl, and add the tofu filling, mixing well to blend.

2. Spoon the quiche mixture into the crust, sprinkle with paprika, and place in the oven to bake for 45 minutes. The top will turn golden brown.

3. Remove the quiche from the oven, and allow to rest for 5 minutes before cutting. Serve hot with your favorite green salad, fresh fruit slices, and multigrain rolls.

ABOUT THE RESTAURANT

The deli of the Community Food Co-op is one of the coziest meeting spots around town.

From Hyatt Regency Westshore *TAMPA, FLORIDA*

Tofu Scramble

This alternative to an omelette is sublime and simply delicious.

1. Place the butter in a medium-sized sauté pan, and melt over medium heat. Add the chopped onions. Allow the onions to cook until they are translucent.

2. Add the chopped red and green peppers, and sauté for 1 to 2 minutes.

3. Add the tofu, and stir gently to heat the tofu thoroughly. Season the mixture with salt and white pepper to taste.

4. Remove the sauté pan from the heat, and spoon the tofu scramble into a medium-sized serving bowl or onto individual serving plates. Serve hot garnished with a few sprigs of fresh parsley, fresh tomato slices, and a hot muffin, biscuit, or toast on the side.

ABOUT THE RESTAURANT

Chef Hans Hickel, a native of Austria, is an expert in the culinary arts. His creative genius transforms an ordinary dish into an entrée of simplicity and elegant distinction.

Yield: 4 servings

Preparation Time: 10 minutes

Cooking Time: 10 minutes

2 tablespoons butter

1 small yellow onion, finely chopped

1 medium red bell pepper, chopped

1 medium green bell pepper, chopped

1 pound firm tofu, cubed

Salt, to taste

White pepper, to taste

GARNISH

Sprigs of fresh parsley

Fresh tomato slices

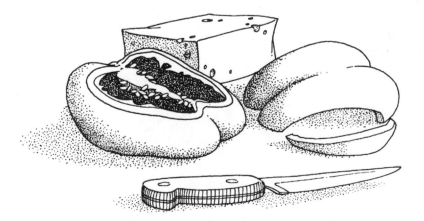

From Madison River Inn   THREE FORKS, MONTANA

Scrambled Tofu

Simplicity of ingredients, ease of preparation, and a hint of thyme make this tofu scramble great for a breakfast or dinner entrée. And the leftover scramble makes a great sandwich filling for lunch.

Yield: 4 servings

Preparation Time: 10 minutes

Cooking Time: 10 minutes

1–2 tablespoons vegetable oil

3 scallions (green onions), chopped

3/4 cup sliced white mushrooms, optional

16 ounces firm tofu, drained and squeezed dry

1/4 teaspoon dried thyme

1/2 teaspoon turmeric

2 tablespoons tamari soy sauce (See "About Soy Sauce" on page 13.)

2 tablespoons sesame seeds, optional

OPTIONAL ADDITIONS

10 ounces fresh spinach, chopped (See "Preparing Fresh Spinach" on page 29.)

1 cup grated cheddar and Monterey jack cheeses (about 3 ounces total)

1. Place the oil in a large sauté pan, and heat over medium heat. Add the scallions and optional mushrooms. Sauté until the mushrooms are soft, about 3 minutes.

2. Crumble the tofu into the pan. Add the thyme, turmeric, and soy sauce, stirring well to blend. Add the optional spinach and cheese, if desired.

3. Heat the tofu thoroughly, remove the pan from the heat, and scoop the tofu onto individual serving plates. Sprinkle with the optional sesame seeds, and serve hot with your favorite breakfast muffins, scones, biscuits, or toast.

ABOUT THE RESTAURANT

Healthy and hearty breakfasts of scrambled tofu, quiche dishes, granola, fruits, or waffles start the day at the Madison River Inn.

From Madison River Inn   THREE FORKS, MONTANA

Indian-Style Scrambled Tofu

A wonderful blend of East and West, this recipe offers a rich, smooth, and creamy tofu scramble. Thank you Linda Kaholokai for this recipe!

1. Place the ghee in a large sauté pan, and heat over medium-high heat. Add the mustard and cumin seeds, and heat until the seeds begin to pop. Add the turmeric, salt, and pepper. Stir to blend well.

2. Add the whole piece of tofu to the sauté pan, and mash into small pieces in the pan using a fork.

3. Add the cream cheese, and allow it to melt. Mix thoroughly. Continue to cook until the scrambled tofu is warmed completely.

4. Serve hot with whole grain toast, fresh creamery butter, and your favorite homemade preserves.

ABOUT THE RESTAURANT

The Madison River Inn offers traditional egg casseroles and quiches as well as nontraditional fare, such as this recipe provides.

Yield: 4 servings

Preparation Time: 10 minutes

Cooking Time: 10 minutes

1 tablespoon ghee (clarified butter; see "Preparing Clarified Butter" on page 174.)

1/4 teaspoon mustard seeds

1/4 teaspoon whole cumin seeds

1/2 teaspoon turmeric

1/2 teaspoon sea salt

1/2 teaspoon black pepper

16 ounces firm tofu, drained and squeezed dry

8 ounces cream cheese

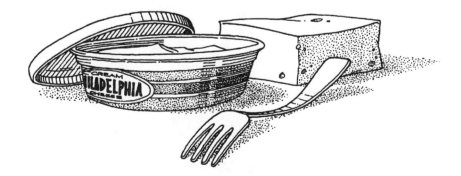

From Everybody's Natural Foods   LEXINGTON, KENTUCKY

Purple Hank Breakfast Drink

This creamy, thick smoothie breakfast drink is a delicious way to start your day.

Yield: 2 servings

Preparation Time: 5 minutes

1 cup unsweetened pineapple
juice

1 cup unsweetened coconut
milk

1 cup frozen blueberries (about
4 ounces)

1 cup frozen banana (about 1
large banana)

1. Place all the ingredients in a blender. Blend at high speed until the mixture is liquified. Pour into two tall glasses, and serve.

ABOUT THE RESTAURANT

Leave it to owner-chef Hetty Carriero at Everybody's to serve a colorful, crowd-pleasing drink for Sunday brunch.

Desserts

From Adam's Mountain Café MANITOU SPRINGS, COLORADO

Almond Cake with Caramelized Pears

If you want to go eggless with this one, you can use a combination of egg replacers, according to your preferences. For instance, a blend of yogurt and tofu plus Ener G brand egg replacer is a successful combination (see "Alternatives to Eggs" on page 82).

To Make the Cake:

1. Preheat the oven to 325°. Butter and flour a bundt cake pan.

2. In a large mixing bowl, place the almond paste, butter, and sugar. Cream with an electric mixer until smooth. Add the eggs or egg replacer, one at a time, beating well after each addition. Add the almond and vanilla extracts, and blend well.

3. Mix together the milk and liqueur, and add to the batter. Slowly add the flour and baking powder in small amounts, stirring gently after each addition. Fold in the ground almonds, and stir well. The batter will be thick, almost like a dough. Pour the batter into the prepared bundt pan.

4. Place the pan in the oven to bake for $1^1/2$ hours, or until the tester inserted in the center comes out clean. Remove the bundt pan from the oven, and slide a knife around the inside edges of the pan. Remove the cake from the pan, and place on a wire rack to cool.

To Make the Pears:

1. Place the butter in a large sauté pan, and melt over medium heat. Add the pears. Sauté the pears until they are completely warmed, about 5 minutes.

2. Put the water and brown sugar in a small saucepan, and place the pan over medium-high heat. Bring the mixture to a boil, and continue to boil gently until thickened, about 5 minutes. Remove the sauce from the heat, and pour over the pears. Allow to cool.

3. When the pears have cooled, add the liqueur, and gently stir.

To Serve the Cake:

1. Place a slice of cake on an individual serving plate. Ladle a few pear slices and some sauce over the cake. Add a dollop of whipped cream, and serve.

ABOUT THE RESTAURANT

At the foot of Pikes Peak, with the majestic Rocky Mountains "peaking out" along the skyline, every view from Adam's Mountain Café is glorious.

Yield: *10–12 servings*

Preparation Time: 15 minutes for the cake; 10 minutes for the pears

Cooking Time: $1^1/2$ hours for the cake; 10 minutes for the pears

ALMOND CAKE

7 ounces almond paste

$1^2/3$ cups soft butter

2 cups turbinado sugar

5 eggs or egg replacer

1 teaspoon almond extract

1 teaspoon vanilla extract

$2/3$ cup milk

$1/4$ cup amaretto liqueur

$1^2/3$ cups unbleached white flour

$1^3/4$ teaspoons baking powder

$1^2/3$ cups ground, toasted almonds (See "Toasting Nuts and Seeds" on page 68.)

CARAMELIZED PEARS

4 teaspoons butter

4 pears, peeled, cored, and thinly sliced

$1/2$ cup water

$3/4$ cup brown sugar

$1/4$ cup amaretto liqueur

Gingerbread with Lemon Sauce

Gingerbread is so warm and nourishing as hot summer days fade into cool, crisp fall afternoons. The lemon sauce transforms this moist, rich gingerbread into an elegant gourmet dessert. Any unsweetened cocoa will do nicely, but Pernignotto cocoa from Italy (sold by Williams-Sonoma) lends a silky richness to this gingerbread. If you use salted butter for the sauce, you may omit the salt.

Yield: 6 servings

Preparation Time: 20 minutes for the cake; 5 minutes for the sauce

Cooking Time: 25–30 minutes for the cake; 10 minutes for the sauce

GINGERBREAD

$1/2$ cup unsalted butter

$1 1/2$ teaspoons ground ginger

1 tablespoon unsweetened cocoa

$1 1/2$ teaspoons ginger juice,* optional

$1/2$ cup light molasses

$1/4$ cup pure maple syrup

$1/2$ cup plain yogurt

2 eggs, beaten (See "Alternative to Eggs" on page 82.)

$1/2$ cup unbleached white flour

$3/4$ cup whole wheat pastry flour

1 teaspoon baking powder

$1/2$ teaspoon baking soda

Scant $1/2$ teaspoon salt

1 teaspoon ground cinnamon

$1/8$ teaspoon ground cloves

$1/8$ teaspoon ground nutmeg

$1/4$ cup chopped pecans or walnuts, optional

To Prepare the Gingerbread:

1. Preheat the oven to 350°F. Butter an 8-inch square pan.

2. Place the butter in a medium-sized saucepan, and melt over low heat. Add the ginger and cocoa, and stir to blend well. Add the optional ginger juice, and remove the pan from the heat.

3. Add the molasses and maple syrup, and let cool to lukewarm. Whisk in the yogurt and eggs (or egg replacer).

4. Place the white flour, whole wheat flour, baking powder, baking soda, salt, cinnamon, cloves, and nutmeg into a large bowl. Whisk the dry ingredients together.

5. Pour the liquid mixture over the dry ingredients, and whisk only until smooth. Pour the batter into the buttered pan. Sprinkle the optional chopped nuts on top of the batter.

6. Bake the gingerbread on the middle rack of the oven until the cake springs back when pressed gently, 25 to 30 minutes.

To Prepare the Lemon Sauce:

1. Place the maple syrup and water in a small saucepan, and bring to a boil over medium-high heat.

2. Reduce the heat to low, and add the salt and dissolved arrowroot. Continue to cook until the mixture thickens and becomes translucent, stirring gently, about 2 to 3 minutes.

3. Add the butter, lemon zest, and lemon juice. Cook only until the butter is melted. Remove the pan from the heat.

4. Use the sauce hot or at room temperature. The sauce will keep up to several days covered in the refrigerator, but may lose its thickness when reheated.

*To make *ginger juice*, put slices of ginger in a garlic press and squeeze, catching the juice in a small bowl.

To Serve the Gingerbread:

1. Remove the pan from the oven to a wire rack. To serve the cake whole on a platter, let it cool in the pan for 10 minutes, loosen the edges with a knife, and then invert the cake onto another rack. Cover the inverted cake with the first rack and invert it again. Or you may let the cake cool completely in the pan, and then cut it into squares. Serve warm with the lemon sauce, or cover and keep unrefrigerated for up to one day.

ABOUT THE RESTAURANT

The Natural Café elevates natural foods to gourmet status with Chef Lynn Walters' marvelously spiced, exquisitely prepared cuisine. Fortunately, her innovative recipes are available in her cookbook, "Cooking at the Natural Café in Sante Fe."

LEMON SAUCE

1/2 cup pure maple syrup

1/3 cup water

Pinch of salt

2 teaspoons arrowroot, dissolved in 1/4 cup water

2 tablespoons unsalted butter

3/4 teaspoon grated lemon zest

1/3 cup lemon juice

From Angelica Kitchen   NEW YORK, NEW YORK

Strawberry Shortcake
with Strawberry Sauce and Vanilla Tofu Cream

Not a traditional white shortcake, this recipe uses whole wheat pastry flour to yield a rich, moist, tan-colored cake that blends superbly with the strawberries and the tofu cream. The cream itself is a perfect alternative to whipped cream with a considerably lower fat content. No refined sugar, less fat . . . simply delicious!

Yield: *12 servings*

Preparation Time: 15–20
  minutes for the cake;
  5 minutes for the sauce;
  5 minutes for the cream plus 1
  hour chilling time

Cooking Time: 25 minutes for
the cake

CAKE

2 cups whole wheat pastry flour

2 cups unbleached white flour

1 tablespoon plus 1 teaspoon
  baking powder

2 teaspoons baking soda

2/3 cup canola oil

1 1/2 cups maple syrup

1 1/2 cups water

2 teaspoons apple cider vinegar

1 teaspoon salt

2 teaspoons vanilla extract

STRAWBERRY SAUCE

1 pint fresh or frozen
  strawberries, hulled and
  stemmed

1/2 teaspoon lemon juice

1/4 teaspoon vanilla extract

1 tablespoon maple syrup

Pinch of salt

To Make the Cake:

1. Preheat the oven to 350°F. Line a 12- by 18-inch jelly roll pan with waxed or parchment paper.

2. Sift the whole wheat flour, white flour, baking powder, and baking soda together into a medium-sized bowl.

3. Place the oil, maple syrup, water, vinegar, salt, and vanilla in a large bowl, and whisk together.

4. Stir the dry ingredients into the wet ingredients, blending well. Pour the batter into the prepared jelly roll pan.

5. Bake for 25 to 30 minutes, or until the tester comes out clean and the cake is golden brown. Remove the cake from the oven, and allow it to cool in the pan.

To Prepare the Strawberry Sauce:

1. Place all ingredients in a food processor, and process until smooth.

To Prepare the Tofu Cream:

1. Place, tofu, oil, maple syrup, lemon juice, and salt in a food processor, and set aside.

2. In a heavy-bottomed saucepan, place the agar-agar and cold water. Stir frequently over medium heat until the mixture reaches a boil, about 3 to 5 minutes.

3. While the agar-agar is cooking, in a separate bowl blend the arrowroot, soy milk, and vanilla. Add to the boiling agar-agar mixture. Cook, stirring continuously, until the mixture begins to bubble. Remove the pan from the heat.

4. Add the hot mixture to the food processor containing the tofu, and process until smooth.

5. Pour the cream into a container, and refrigerate for 1 hour, or until well chilled.

To Serve the Shortcake:

1. Cut the cooled cake into 12 or 24 squares.

2. Place 1 square of the cake on an individual serving plate. Place a dollop of the tofu cream on the cake, and top with a second square of cake. (For a smaller serving, use only 1 square of cake for the bottom layer and omit the top layer of cake.) Ladle strawberry sauce over the cake, and top with additional dollop of tofu cream. Garnish with fresh mint and halved strawberries. Repeat for each serving.

ABOUT THE RESTAURANT

Angelica Kitchen features its strawberry shortcake quite often in the summertime, when local farmers bring in the biggest, juiciest strawberries.

*A combination of certain sea vegetables, *agar-agar* is a white, powdered jelling agent used in some gelatin desserts, aspics, and glazes. It may be found in most natural food stores.

VANILLA TOFU CREAM

16 ounces silken or soft tofu, drained

1/2 cup canola oil

1/2 cup maple syrup

1 tablespoon lemon juice

1/4 teaspoon salt

3/4 teaspoon agar-agar powder*

1 cup cold water

1/4 cup arrowroot powder

1 cup soy milk

1/4 cup vanilla extract

GARNISH

Fresh mint leaves

1 pint strawberries, hulled and halved

From Madison River Inn   THREE FORKS, MONTANA

Poppy Seed Cake

Deliciously rich, moist, and bakery-perfect, this cake is simple to prepare and a real crowd pleaser! To make an orange or a lemon glaze, you may add 1 teaspoon grated orange or lemon peel and substitute orange or lemon juice for the vanilla and water.

Yield: 8–10 servings

Preparation Time: 20 minutes for the cake; 5 minutes for the glaze

Cooking Time: 50 minutes

CAKE

1 package yellow cake mix

1/4 cup cornstarch

1/4 cup sugar

4 eggs (or 3 teaspoons Ener G Egg Replacer combined with 1/4 cup plain or vanilla yogurt; see "Alternatives to Eggs" on page 82.)

1 cup water

1/2 cup oil

1/4 cup poppy seeds

CREAMY GLAZE

1/4 cup butter

2 cups powdered sugar

2 teaspoons vanilla

2–4 tablespoons hot water

To Make the Cake:

1. Preheat the oven to 350°F. Lightly grease and flour a bundt pan.

2. Place the cake mix, cornstarch, sugar, eggs or egg replacer, water, and oil in a large mixing bowl. Mix with a mixer on medium speed for 5 minutes. Be sure to beat the mixture for a full 5 minutes so that the batter will incorporate as much air as possible.

3. Add the poppy seeds, and gently combine them with the cake batter. Pour the batter into the prepared bundt pan.

4. Place the pan on the middle rack of the oven to bake for 50 minutes. Insert a wooden pick or knife into the cake to test for doneness. Remove from the oven to a wire rack to cool for 5 minutes.

5. Gently slide a knife around the inside edges of the pan before removing the cake from the pan. Cool completely before glazing.

To Prepare the Glaze:

1. Place the butter in a medium-sized saucepan, and heat until melted. Stir in the powdered sugar and vanilla.

2. Stir in the water 1 tablespoon at a time, until the glaze reaches the desired consistency. Remove from the heat.

To Serve the Cake:

1. Pour the warm glaze on the cooled cake. Spread gently to cover the surface of the cake and allow to drizzle down the sides.

ABOUT THE RESTAURANT

Catering to weddings, anniversaries, birthdays, and other special events, the Madison River Inn provides a lovely setting for any romantic rendezvous.

From Sunshine Inn ST. LOUIS, MISSOURI

Carrot Cake

This deliciously moist and rich cake sports a creamy-smooth icing that contains no refined sugar.

To Make the Cake:

1. Preheat the oven to 350°F. Oil and flour a 9- by 13-inch baking pan.

2. Place the oil, honey, eggs, and molasses in a large mixing bowl, and beat with an electric mixer for 2 minutes.

3. Into another bowl, sift together the flour, baking powder, baking soda, salt, cinnamon, nutmeg, and cloves. Add to the honey and oil mixture.

4. Stir in the walnuts, raisins, and carrots, being careful not to overmix.

5. Pour the cake batter into the prepared baking pan. Bake for 40 to 50 minutes.

6. Remove the pan from the oven, and allow to cool for 5 minutes on a wire rack. Slip the edge of a knife around the inside edges of the cake, and invert on the wire rack. Placing another wire rack over the top, invert the cake again to cool right side up.

To Make the Icing and Frost the Cake:

1. Place the cream cheese and hot water in a medium-sized bowl, and blend until smooth. Add the honey, lemon juice, and vanilla extract. Blend again until smooth. Using a spatula, spread icing on the top and then the sides of the cooled cake. Cover leftover cake with plastic wrap, and store in the refrigerator for up to 3 days.

ABOUT THE RESTAURANT

Sunday brunch at the Sunshine Inn features omelettes, multigrain pancakes with pure maple syrup, potato pancakes, fresh fruit platters, fresh juices, and desserts like this luscious carrot cake.

Yield: 10–12 servings

Preparation Time: 25 minutes

Cooking Time: 40–50 minutes

CAKE

1 cup vegetable oil

$2/3$ cup honey

4 eggs (See "Alternatives to Eggs" on page 82.)

$2/3$ cup molasses

$1^3/4$ cups whole wheat flour

$1^1/2$ teaspoons baking powder

$1^1/2$ teaspoons baking soda

$1/2$ teaspoon salt

1 teaspoon ground cinnamon

$1/2$ teaspoon ground nutmeg

Scant $1/2$ teaspoon ground cloves

$1/2$ cup chopped walnuts

$1/2$ cup raisins

3 cups grated carrots (about 6 carrots)

CREAM CHEESE ICING

16 ounces cream cheese

1 tablespoon hot water

$1/3$ cup honey

1 tablespoon lemon juice

2 teaspoons vanilla extract

From Adam's Mountain Café   MANITOU SPRINGS, COLORADO

Carrot Cake
with Coconut Filling & Frosting

Can a dessert really be both good and good for you? This carrot cake uses honey in place of sugar and is a wonderfully rich and not-too-sweet cake. Filled with luscious fruits and nuts, Adam's Mountain Café Carrot Cake makes a stunning three-layer presentation.

Yield: 10–12 servings

Preparation Time: 30–40 minutes for the cake; 5 minutes for the filling; 5 minutes for the frosting

Cooking Time: 25–30 minutes for the cake; 15–20 minutes for the filling

CAKE

1 cup plus 1 tablespoon soft butter or margarine

1 cup plus 1 tablespoon honey

4 eggs (See "Alternatives to Eggs" on page 82.)

1 teaspoon vanilla extract

3 cups grated carrots (about 6 carrots)

$3/4$ cup crushed pineapple (an 8-ounce can, with as much juice squeezed out as possible)

$3/4$ cup shredded coconut

$3/4$ cup chopped walnuts or 1 cup raisins

$1^1/2$ cups unbleached white flour

$3/4$ cup whole wheat flour

$1/2$ teaspoon ground cloves

$3/4$ teaspoon ground ginger

$1^1/2$ teaspoons ground cinnamon

$3/4$ teaspoon baking soda

To Make the Cake:

1. Preheat the oven to 325°F. Butter and flour three 9-inch round cake pans.

2. In a large mixing bowl, place the butter and honey, and beat together until smooth, either by hand or with an electric beater.

3. Add the eggs (or egg replacer) one at a time, beating well after each addition. Add the vanilla, and beat well.

4. Gently fold in the carrots, pineapple, coconut, and walnuts or raisins.

5. In a separate medium-sized bowl, sift together the white flour and whole wheat flour. Add the cloves, ginger, cinnamon, baking soda, baking powder, and salt. Mix well.

6. Add the flour mixture to the carrot batter, and lightly mix.

7. Pour the batter evenly into the cake pans, and place in the oven. Bake for 25 to 30 minutes, or until the tester comes out clean when inserted into the middle of the cake. Remove the pans from the oven, and invert the cakes onto a wire rack to cool.

To Make the Filling:

1. In a medium-sized saucepan, place the milk, butter, honey, vanilla, and egg yolks. Cook over medium heat until thick. Remove the mixture from the heat, add the coconut and walnuts, and mix.

To Make the Frosting:

1. Place the cream cheese, honey, butter, and vanilla in a medium-sized mixing bowl, and cream together until smooth.

To Assemble the Cake:

1. Place one the cooled cakes on a serving plate, and spread half of the filling on the top. Then place the second cake on the bottom layer, and spread the remaining filling on top. Add the third cake to the other two cakes.

2. Using a spatula, spread the frosting on the top and then the sides of the cooled cake. Top with toasted coconut.

ABOUT THE RESTAURANT

Antique wooden furniture, beamed ceilings, chandeliers, leaded-glass windows, original watercolors, fresh flowers, and old-fashioned wallpaper define the Victorian-style decor of Adam's Mountain Café. Since moving to its current location at 110 Cannon Avenue in Manitou Springs, this charming café offers more seating and the same wonderful food.

1 1/2 teaspoons baking powder

Scant 1/2 teaspoon sea salt

FILLING

3/4 cup evaporated milk

3 ounces butter

1/2 cup honey

1 teaspoon vanilla extract

3 egg yolks

1/3 cup coconut

1/3 cup chopped walnuts

CREAM CHEESE FROSTING

12 ounces cream cheese

1/3 cup honey

1/2 cup butter

1 teaspoon vanilla extract

GARNISH

Toasted coconut (See "Toasting Nuts and Seeds" on page 68.)

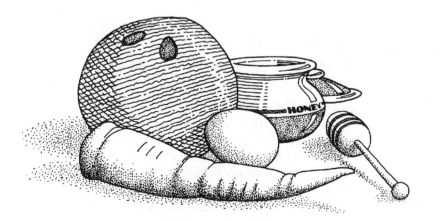

From Bloodroot   BRIDGEPORT, CONNECTICUT

Sourdough Chocolate Devastation Cake

For sourdough lovers, here's an opportunity to have that uniquely distinct sourdough flavor in chocolate form! The sourdough, vinegar, and baking soda combination causes the cake to rise nicely without eggs. The rich, dark chocolate flavor blends well with the slightly sweet raspberry filling.

Yield: 8–10 servings

Preparation Time: 20 minutes for the cake; 10 minutes for the glaze

Cooking Time: 25–30 minutes for the cake; 5 minutes for the glaze

1/4 cup plus 1 tablespoon unsweetened cocoa

1 1/2 cups Sucanat* or 2 cups white sugar

3 cups unbleached white flour

2 teaspoons baking soda

1/2 teaspoon salt

2 tablespoons grain coffee powder (such as Caffix or Pero) or instant coffee powder, optional

1/2 teaspoon ground cinnamon

1 cup sourdough starter (See "Preparing Sourdough Starter.")

1 2/3 cups water

2 tablespoons cider vinegar

1 cup vegetable oil

1 teaspoon vanilla extract

1 (10-ounce) jar "fruit only" raspberry preserve, preferably without seeds

To Make and Fill the Cake:

1. Preheat the oven to 350°F. Lightly oil two 9-inch round cake pans, and line the bottoms of the pans with waxed paper.

2. Place the cocoa, Sucanat (or sugar), flour, baking soda, salt, coffee, and cinnamon in a medium-sized bowl, and whisk to blend thoroughly.

3. In a large bowl, place the sourdough starter, water, vinegar, oil, and vanilla, stirring with a whisk or fork.

4. Using a wooden spoon, fold the dry ingredients into the wet ingredients with as few strokes as possible to blend. Then pour the batter evenly into the two pans.

5. Place on the middle rack of the oven. Bake for 25 to 30 minutes, until just done and a tester or toothpick inserted near the center of the cakes comes out clean.

6. Remove the pans from the oven, and allow the cakes to cool for 5 minutes in the pans on a wire cooling rack. Then loosen the edges of the cake from the pan by sliding a knife around the inside perimeter of the pan. Invert the cakes onto the cooling racks. Peel off and discard the waxed paper, and let the cakes cool thoroughly.

7. Spread the tops of both cakes with the raspberry preserve. Stack the cakes on top of each other on a serving plate, and set aside.

To Make the Glaze and Serve the Cake:

1. In a medium-sized saucepan, place the water, cocoa, maple syrup, coffee, salt, and kudzu.

2. Bring the mixture to a boil over medium-high heat, stirring constantly with a wire whisk, and cook until thickened. Remove the pan from the heat, and stir in the vanilla, and additional kudzu if the glaze is not thick enough.

3. Immediately drizzle the glaze on slices of the cake, pouring additional chocolate glaze on the side of each plate to make a little chocolate pool. Add a mint leaf for a final finishing touch.

*Sucanat is sugar cane juice that has been allowed to evaporate into granules. It tastes similar to brown sugar.

Preparing Sourdough Starter

You can purchase sourdough starter from your local bakery or food co-op, or you can make your own: Mix 1 cup water with 2 cups unbleached white flour. (If you use whole wheat flour, you will have an even more "sour" sourdough taste.) Place the mixture in a glass jar or plastic container, and cover loosely with plastic wrap. It is not advisable to cover with a cloth, which would be too porous. Keep the starter at room temperature for four to five days, stirring it each day. You may add a little more water or a little more flour to reach the desired consistency. The starter will keep indefinitely in a covered container in the refrigerator.

ABOUT THE RESTAURANT

"Nonmeat eaters from Baltimore to Rhode Island flock to Bloodroot, a vegetarian restaurant and bookstore, in Bridgeport's almost-gentrified Black Rock section," reports The New York Times.

*Kudzu is a warm-climate vine, the root of which is ground into a powder and used as a thickener. Cornstarch, arrowroot, or potato starch can be used instead.

GLAZE

1 cup water

1/3 cup unsweetened cocoa

2 1/2 –5 tablespoons maple syrup, depending on the level of sweetness you prefer

2 1/2 tablespoons grain coffee powder (such as Caffix or Pero) or instant coffee powder

Dash of salt

1/2 –1 1/2 tablespoons kudzu,* optional

3/4 teaspoon vanilla extract

GARNISH

Fresh mint leaves

From Black Dog Café   MISSOULA, MONTANA

Chocolate Chocolate Chip Pound Cake

Chocolate lovers watch out! You may have just met your match in this densely rich, luscious, oh-so-chocolaty cake.

Yield: 8–10 servings

Preparation Time: 20 minutes

Cooking Time: 50–60 minutes

CAKE

2¹/₂ cups whole wheat pastry flour (or 1¹/₄ cups unbleached white and 1¹/₄ cups whole wheat pastry flour)

1 cup unsweetened cocoa

2 teaspoons baking soda

1 teaspoon salt

2 cups unsweetened applesauce

1 cup cold water

³/₄ cup light vegetable oil

1¹/₂ teaspoons vanilla extract

2 tablespoons cider vinegar

1¹/₂ cups turbinado sugar or 2 cups white sugar

1 cup mini semisweet chocolate chips (about 6 ounces)

GLAZE

¹/₂ cup safflower oil margarine

1 cup unsweetened cocoa

1 cup powdered sugar

1 teaspoon vanilla extract

¹/₂ cup brewed coffee

To Make the Cake:

1. Preheat the oven to 350°F. Lightly butter and flour a fluted bundt pan.

2. Into a medium-sized bowl, sift together the flour, cocoa, baking soda, and salt.

3. In a large bowl, place the applesauce, water, oil, vanilla, and vinegar. Blend together well.

4. Slowly add the sifted dry ingredients to the applesauce mixture, stirring gently with each addition.

5. Add the sugar and mini chocolate chips, and mix or whisk the entire mixture until the batter is thoroughly blended.

6. Pour the batter into the bundt pan. Bake until a tester comes out clean, about 50 to 60 minutes.

7. Remove the cake from the oven, and cool for 10 minutes before removing from the pan. Allow the cake to cool completely before glazing.

To Prepare the Glaze and Serve the Cake:

1. Place all the glaze ingredients in a food processor or blender, and blend until smooth.

2. Place the cake on a serving dish. Pour the glaze over the cooled cake, or ladle a small amount of glaze over slices of cake on individual plates.

ABOUT THE RESTAURANT

"At Black Dog Café we believe in chocolate, so much so that we sometimes have to remind ourselves that dessert doesn't always equal chocolate and make some other yummy treat. This cake has been a constant on our menu almost since we opened. It is delicious, very popular, and contains no eggs or dairy products. Though not quite as rich as the majority of our other desserts, it seems to satisfy most urges for something sweet and chocolaty," says Nancy Randazzo, co-owner of the Black Dog Café.

From Madison River Inn   THREE FORKS, MONTANA

Chocolate Crazy Cake

This recipe makes a traditional, very moist, and rich chocolate cake—with a traditional cream cheese frosting. The easy-to-make recipe calls for mixing the ingredients right in the baking pan. If you prefer to use round cake pans and remove the cake from the pans to frost all sides of the cake, you will need to grease and flour the cake pans and prepare the batter in a separate mixing bowl.

To Prepare the Cake:

1. Preheat the oven to 350°F.

2. Into a 13- by 9-inch ungreased baking pan, sift together the flour, cocoa, salt, sugar, and baking soda. Mix together.

3. Make three holes in the flour mixture. Place into the three holes about one third each of the vanilla, vinegar, and oil. Pour the water over all of the mixture, and blend together gently with a fork until just mixed.

4. Place the pan in the oven, and bake for 25 to 30 minutes, until a tester inserted into the center comes out clean. Remove the cake from the oven, and allow it to cool on a wire rack.

To Prepare the Frosting and Serve the Cake:

1. In a medium-sized mixing bowl, place the cream cheese, milk (or cream), and vanilla, and cream together. Slowly beat in the powdered sugar, adding more if necessary to reach the desired consistency.

2. Using a spatula, frost the top and sides of the cooled cake. Slice and serve.

ABOUT THE RESTAURANT

The Georgian-style mansion with Italian marble fireplaces in every room is a picture of grace and luxury on the Montana landscape.

Yield: *10–12 servings*

Preparation Time: 20 minutes for the cake; 10 minutes for the frosting

Cooking Time: 25–30 minutes

CAKE

3 cups unbleached white flour

1/4 cup unsweetened cocoa

1 teaspoon salt

2 cups sugar

2 teaspoons baking soda

1 teaspoon vanilla extract

1 tablespoon apple cider vinegar

3/4 cup vegetable oil

2 cups water

FROSTING

8 ounces cream cheese

3–4 tablespoons milk or cream

1 teaspoon vanilla extract

2 cups powdered sugar

From Marx Bros. Café   ANCHORAGE, ALASKA

Marx Bros. Cheesecake

Excellent! The roasted nuts in the cheesecake crust enhance the flavor of this traditional cheesecake.

Yield: 8–10 servings

Preparation Time: 30 minutes

Cooking Time: 1 1/2 hours

1 tablespoon soft butter

1/2 cup ground roasted hazelnuts or almonds (See "Toasting Nuts and Seeds" on page 68.)

1/4 cup chilled butter, cut into small pieces

2 cups graham cracker crumbs

3 pounds cream cheese (six 8-ounce packages), at room temperature

2 eggs

2 egg yolks

2 cups sugar

1/2 cup sour cream

1 tablespoon vanilla extract

3 tablespoons flour

1. Preheat the oven to 250°F.

2. Rub the soft butter on the bottom and sides of a 10-inch springform pan. Coat the sides and bottom with the ground hazelnuts or almonds.

3. In a mixer, using a flat paddle, place the chilled butter and graham cracker crumbs. Combine until well blended. If your mixer does not have a flat paddle, you may want to mix by hand, using the back of a wooden spoon or your fingers. Press the graham cracker mixture into the bottom of the pan. Set aside.

4. Place the cream cheese in the mixer, and mix on low speed until soft. Scrape down the sides of the bowl, and add the eggs and egg yolks. Mix again until thoroughly blended and soft. Add the sugar, and mix for several minutes more. Scrape down the sides of the bowl, and add the sour cream, vanilla, and flour. Mix again.

5. Pour the cream cheese mixture into the prepared pan, and place the pan in the oven. Bake for 1 1/2 hours. Turn the oven off, and allow the pan to stand in the oven 15 minutes longer.

6. Remove the cheesecake from the oven, and allow to cool to room temperature. Refrigerate overnight. Release the pan sides, and transfer the cheesecake to a serving platter. Cut into slices and serve.

ABOUT THE RESTAURANT

Why the name the Marx Bros.? "In 1979, the trio's [owners Jack Amon, Van Hale, and Ken Brown] previous restaurant was sold and the buyers were of the opinion their purchase included all the restaurant equipment. On the night of April 1st—April Fool's Day—the three served their last dinners to a house full of friends. As each plate was washed and each chair vacated, it was whisked away and loaded into a waiting vehicle. The cops were called and after examining the papers concluded the partners were entitled to remove the equipment and keep it. One observer commented that the chaos 'looked like a Marx Brothers movie,'" according to "Bon Appétit" magazine. And thus, the name was born.

From The Higher Taste, Ltd. *PORTLAND, OREGON*

Apple Raspberry Almond Crisp

The raspberries and almonds give a new twist to the traditional crisp!

1. Preheat the oven to 350°F.

2. To prepare the filling, place the apples and raspberries in a large bowl, and toss. In a small bowl, place the flour, sugar, cinnamon, and nutmeg. Combine, and sprinkle over the fruit mixture. Place the mixture in an ungreased 8-inch-square baking dish. Dot the top with the butter slices.

3. To prepare the topping, place the flour, sugar, and cinnamon in a medium-sized bowl, and mix. With your hands, work the butter into the flour mixture until it forms crumbs. The longer you mix it with your fingers, the crumblier it gets—10 minutes is best. If you don't want to work the butter in with your fingers, use a fork. Add the almonds to the flour mixture, and toss gently.

4. Sprinkle the topping over the fruit filling. Place the pan in the oven, and bake for 50 minutes. Remove the pan from the oven and place on a wire rack to cool. Serve warm or at room temperature with vanilla ice cream.

ABOUT THE RESTAURANT

Owners Hans and Rhonda Wrobel met at a party in New York, and the magic began. They have been cooking and preparing exciting gourmet vegetarian food ever since.

Yield: 6–8 servings

Preparation Time: 20 minutes

Cooking Time: 50 minutes

FILLING

6 cooking apples, peeled and sliced (Granny Smiths, Gravensteins, or Romes)

1 1/2 cups fresh or thawed frozen raspberries

2 tablespoons unbleached white flour

1/4 cup sugar

1/2 teaspoon ground cinnamon

Dash of nutmeg

4 thin slices of butter

TOPPING

1 cup unbleached white flour

1/2 cup granulated sugar

1/4 teaspoon ground cinnamon

1 stick unsalted butter, at room temperature

1/4 cup sliced almonds

From The Higher Taste, Ltd. PORTLAND, OREGON

Sculptured Orange Baskets

These orange baskets filled with cranberry sauce make a beautiful presentation on your holiday table.

Yield: *8 servings*

Preparation Time: 1 hour

Cooking Time: 10 minutes

8 large navel oranges

CRANBERRY ORANGE SAUCE

1 (12-ounce) bag fresh cranberries

1 cup diced, fresh orange pieces, reserved from making the baskets

To Prepare the Baskets:

1. Set the "belly button" of each orange on the cutting surface. If the orange doesn't stand up, slice a thin piece from the bottom to level it.

2. To begin forming the handle, use a sharp knife to make two cuts one inch apart from the top of the orange to the middle. Then on each side, cut the orange around the middle from handle base to handle base. (See the diagram.)

3. Carefully peel the orange rind immediately around the handle. With a teaspoon, very carefully peel out the remaining fruit, lifting it out over a bowl to collect the juice and pieces of fruit for the sauce.

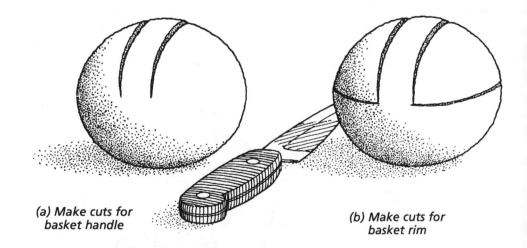

(a) Make cuts for basket handle

(b) Make cuts for basket rim

Making an Orange Basket

To Make the Sauce:

1. Wash the cranberries, and place the cranberries, orange pieces, water, and honey in a medium-sized saucepan.

2. Bring the mixture to a boil, and cook until the cranberry skins pop, about 10 minutes. Remove the pan from the heat, and skim off the white froth. Allow to cool.

To Fill and Serve the Baskets:

Fill the center of each orange basket with the cooled cranberry orange sauce. Refrigerate until time to serve. Garnish with sprigs of fresh mint. The sauce will keep for several days in an airtight container in the refrigerator.

¼ cup water

¾ cup honey

GARNISH

Fresh mint leaves

ABOUT THE RESTAURANT

Hans Wrobel learned to cook at his parents' bed and breakfast businesses in the United States and abroad. From there, he trained at a culinary school in Berlin and worked in several European restaurants before coming to the United States in 1979. Rhonda, his wife and partner in The Higher Taste, was raised in New York, where her family owned a produce business. She developed an eye for fresh ingredients and an understanding of their importance. Together, they traveled to India, where they indulged in Indian cuisine. The natural foods they prepare reflect a wonderful blend of international cultures.

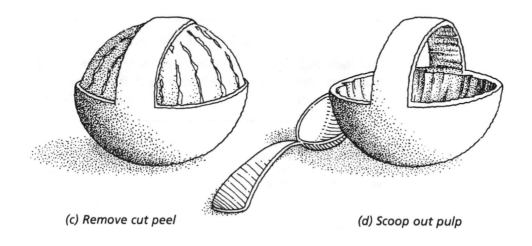

(c) Remove cut peel   *(d) Scoop out pulp*

From Hyatt Regency Westshore   TAMPA, FLORIDA

Chocolate Mousse

Eating this dessert is like floating on a cloud on a summer day. You'll love this heavenly delight!

Yield: 6 servings

Preparation Time: 30 minutes

Chilling Time: 1 hour

1 pound Baker's semisweet chocolate

1/4 cup water

1 ounce Knox (or other) unflavored gelatin, agar-agar,* or kudzu*

1 quart heavy cream

GARNISH

Chocolate shavings

1. Break the chocolate into small bits, and place in a medium-sized saucepan over low heat. Allow the chocolate to melt, stirring frequently to make sure it doesn't burn. Remove the chocolate from the heat, and set aside to cool.

2. In a small pan, bring the water to a boil. Remove the pan from the heat, and dissolve the gelatin, agar-agar, or kudzu in the water, stirring carefully.

3. Place the heavy cream in a large bowl, and whip with a wire whisk or an electric beater until the cream reaches soft peaks.

4. Reserve about $1/2$ cup of the whipped cream for a garnish. Fold the melted chocolate into the remaining whipped cream.

5. Spoon a third of the chocolate whipped cream into another bowl, and add the gelatin mixture to it. Gently fold the gelatin-chocolate mixture back into the remaining chocolate whipped cream until well blended.

6. Spoon the chocolate mousse into one large serving bowl or individual parfait glasses. Chill in the refrigerator for 1 hour before serving. Garnish with a dollop of the reserved whipped cream and chocolate shavings on top.

ABOUT THE RESTAURANT

Chef Hans Hickel prepares exquisite culinary creations for two of Hyatt restaurants—Armani's and the Oystercatcher. Plus, he serves as co-chairperson of Share our Strength in Tampa, which provides food for the hungry.

*A combination of certain sea vegetables, *agar-agar* is a white, powdered jelling agent used in some gelatin desserts, aspics, and glazes. It may be found in most natural food stores. *Kudzu* is a warm-climate vine, the root of which is ground into a powder and used as a thickener.

From Artichoke Café   ALBUQUERQUE, NEW MEXICO

Toasted Piñon-Maple Mousse

Pure maple syrup is Pat Keene's secret for this easy, light, and fluffy dessert. For a really decadent treat, you might like to try a small dollop of the mousse on gingerbread.

1. Place the maple syrup, egg yolks, and salt in the top of a double boiler, and combine. Place the top of the double boiler in boiling water. Heat the mixture over medium-high heat, whisking until the mixture is thick and the color goes from a dark brown to a light tan, or about 7 minutes.

2. Remove the egg mixture from the stove, and stir in the orange peel. Place the mixture in a bowl, and cool in the refrigerator for 30 minutes.

3. Place the cream in a medium-sized bowl, and whip until the cream holds its shape.

4. Fold in the cooled custard mixture, and then the toasted nuts.

5. Pour the mousse into dessert dishes, garnish with crushed nuts on top, and refrigerate until ready to serve.

ABOUT THE RESTAURANT

Nestled in the heart of downtown Albuquerque, the Artichoke Café is the perfect place to discuss business proposals over lunch or to linger over a romantic dinner for two.

Yield: 6–8 servings

Preparation Time: 30 minutes

Cooking Time: 7 minutes

Chilling Time: 30 minutes

1 cup real maple syrup

6 egg yolks

Pinch of salt

2–4 teaspoons grated orange peel

2 cups heavy cream

1/2 cup toasted piñon nuts (See "Toasting Nuts and Seeds" on page 68.)

GARNISH

1/4 cup crushed, toasted piñon nuts

From Café For All Seasons   SAN FRANCISCO, CALIFORNIA

Sweet Cream
with Raspberry Sauce & Fresh Summer Berries

This wonderful dessert celebrates any season in grand style. A perfect ending to an exquisite dinner party, it is light and luscious and easily prepared in advance.

Yield: 8 servings

Preparation Time: 20 minutes plus 3 hours chilling time

SWEET CREAM

1/4 cup cold water

1 tablespoon unflavored gelatin, agar-agar powder, or kudzu*

1 cup heavy whipping cream

2/3 cup sugar

1 3/4 cups sour cream

6 ounces cream cheese, broken into pieces

3/4 teaspoon vanilla extract

RASPBERRY SAUCE

1 cup fresh or frozen raspberries

1 teaspoon freshly squeezed lemon juice

2 tablespoons sugar

OPTIONAL GARNISH

1–2 cups cleaned, fresh mixed berries (Peaches and nectarines also may be used.)

Fresh mint leaves

To Prepare the Sweet Cream:

1. Pour the water in a small bowl. Sprinkle in the gelatin (or agar-agar or kudzu), and set aside.

2. In the top of a double boiler, place the whipping cream, sugar, sour cream, and cream cheese, and combine. Place the top of the double boiler, but over (not in), boiling water. Cook over high heat, mixing with a wire whisk until the cream is very warm.

3. Stir the dissolved gelatin into the cream, and continue to stir until the gelatin is well dissolved and smooth. Do not let the cream boil.

4. Remove the double boiler from the heat, and stir in the vanilla.

5. Pour the cream mixture into a 1 1/2-quart glass serving bowl. Place in the refrigerator to chill for 3 hours.

To Make the Raspberry Sauce:

1. Place the raspberries, lemon juice, and sugar in a food processor or blender, and blend until smooth. Strain the seeds through a wire mesh strainer, if you desire.

To Serve:

1. Spoon the cream from the serving bowl onto individual dessert plates. Ladle the sauce on top of and around the cream. Surround with the optional fresh mixed berries. Garnish with fresh mint leaves.

ABOUT THE RESTAURANT

Café For All Seasons is an elegant place without pretense. Clean design lines and original photographs are accentuated by soft lighting. As in co-owner Frank Katzl's neighborhood markets in his earlier days, fresh produce is on display in glass cases. Photographs that line the walls showcase James Beard and Marion Cunningham—the culinary mentors of co-owner and executive chef Donna Katzl—as well as the Katzls' dining tours in restaurants around the world.

*A combination of certain sea vegetables, *agar-agar* is a white, powdered jelling agent. *Kudzu* is a thickener.

Tartufo Dessert

This dessert is great for dinner parties, as you can make it in advance. The ice cream, robed in white chocolate, rests on a beautiful red raspberry sauce or a dark chocolate pool—or a combination of both! A touch of green mint makes for a very pretty plate.

To Make the Ice Cream Ball:

1. Allow the ice cream to soften slightly. With an ice cream scoop, roll the ice cream into one ball the size of a tennis ball or two balls the size of golf balls.

2. Place the white chocolate shavings in a small bowl, and roll the ice cream ball in the white chocolate to completely cover the ball.

3. Wrap the ice cream ball in plastic wrap, and return it to the freezer until ready to serve.

To Make the Raspberry Sauce:

1. Preheat the oven to 550°F.

2. Place the jelly, raspberries, and sugar together in a large casserole pan that can be used in the oven. Mix well, and place the pan in the oven to cook for 10 to 15 minutes.

3. Remove the pan from the oven, and stir to blend. Chill well in the pan.

To Make the Chocolate Sauce:

1. Place all the chocolate sauce ingredients together in a large bowl. Mix until the sauce reaches a smooth and creamy consistency.

To Serve the Ice Cream Ball:

1. Ladle 3 to 4 tablespoons of the raspberry sauce or the chocolate sauce, or a combination of both, onto an individual dessert plate.

2. Unwrap the ice cream, and place it on the sauce. Ladle a small amount of sauce on top of the ice cream, and sprinkle with white chocolate shavings. Serve with a sprig of fresh mint on the side.

ABOUT THE RESTAURANT

The Pizza Kitchen's atmosphere is lively and upbeat. Lots of college students, families, and business and professional people enjoy the fun and good humor of the Pizza crew.

Yield: *1 serving ice cream; 2¹/₂ cups of each sauce*

Preparation Time: 10 minutes for ice cream; 10 minutes for raspberry sauce; 10 minutes for the chocolate sauce

Cooking Time: 10–15 minutes for raspberry sauce

ICE CREAM BALL

8–10 ounces French vanilla ice cream

2 ounces white chocolate, grated

RASPBERRY SAUCE

1¹/₂ cups red currant jelly

1 cup frozen raspberries, thawed

¹/₄–¹/₂ cup sugar

CHOCOLATE SAUCE

1 can hot fudge sauce, or Homemade Hot Fudge Sauce (see page 232.)

2 tablespoons hot coffee (half espresso and half regular brew or decaffeinated)

1 cup Hershey's chocolate syrup

From Madison River Inn   THREE FORKS, MONTANA

Homemade Hot Fudge Sauce
with Ice Cream

My sister, Jerri Balsam, gave this recipe to me years ago and it is decidedly one of the best, most reliable hot fudge sauces I have ever made. Thank you, Jerri! Don't be surprised to find your family sneaking into the refrigerator to dip into the jar for a big, gooey lick!

Yield: *4 servings, including 2^1/$_2$ cups sauce*

Preparation Time: 10 minutes

Cooking Time: 15 minutes

1 quart vanilla, peppermint, or your favorite flavor ice cream

SAUCE

1 cup unsweetened cocoa

^{3}/$_4$ cup sugar

^{1}/$_2$ cup packed brown sugar

^{1}/$_8$ teaspoon salt

1 cup heavy cream

^{1}/$_2$ cup butter, cut into pieces

1 teaspoon vanilla extract

GARNISH

Mint Leaves

Small flowers

To Make the Sauce:

1. In a medium-sized saucepan, place the cocoa, sugar, brown sugar, and salt, and stir. Add the cream and butter, and place over medium heat, stirring constantly.

2. Bring the mixture to a boil, and boil for 1 minute, stirring constantly. Remove the pan from the heat, and allow the sauce to cool for 5 minutes in the pan. Stir in the vanilla, and mix well. Serve hot.

3. To store, pour the sauce into a glass container with a tightly fitting lid and place in the refrigerator, where it will keep for up to one month. To reheat, spoon the desired amount into a microwave bowl and heat in the microwave, or spoon into a saucepan and reheat over low heat.

To Serve:

1. Place one large or two small scoops of ice cream in each dish. Top with several tablespoonfuls of the warm sauce, and garnish with the mint leaves and small flowers.

ABOUT THE RESTAURANT

Gaze at the big blue sky and watch puffy white clouds drift by at the Madison River Inn.

Banana Ice Cream
in Sweet Almond Pastry Shells

This dessert—more a sorbet than an ice cream—is a wonderful nondairy alternative to ice cream.

1. Peel the bananas, cut them in half, and wrap in plastic wrap.

2. Freeze for 1 to 2 hours, or until frozen solid. While bananas are freezing, prepare the pastry shells.

To Make the Pastry Shells:

1. Preheat the oven to 275°F. Lightly coat six muffin cups with vegetable oil.

2. Place almonds and oatmeal together in blender or food processor, and grind to a fine powder. Add flour and salt, and briefly blend to mix.

3. Pour the mixture into a medium-sized bowl. Stir in the honey, water, and almond extract with a wooden spoon or fork to make a soft dough.

4. Turn the dough onto a lightly floured surface. With your fingers, pat the dough into a large round circle, about $1/4$-inch thick. With a rolling pin, roll out the dough as thin as possible, about $1/16$- to $1/8$-inch thick. Then, using a knife, cut the dough into six to eight 5-inch circles.

5. Line each ungreased muffin cup with a dough circle, leaving enough extra pastry to crimp or flute the edges.

6. Place the muffin pan on the middle rack of the oven, and bake for 10 to 20 minutes, until crisp and golden. Remove the pan from the oven, and allow to cool before removing the pastry. These shells keep well when frozen in a tightly sealed container and for several weeks at room temperature in a dry, well-sealed container. If necessary, re-crisp them in a warm (250°F) oven for 10 minutes before serving.

To Fill the Pastry Shells and Serve:

1. Place the frozen banana pieces, one at a time, in a blender or food processor. Blend, adding just enough soy or nut milk to bring the bananas to a puréed consistency, similar to that of soft frozen yogurt or ice cream.

2. Spoon the banana ice cream into the pastry shells (or into frosted dessert bowls), add a fresh mint leaf, and serve.

ABOUT THE RESTAURANT

Gourmet vegan cuisine is served at the High Noon Café.

Yield: 6 servings

Preparation Time: 1–2 hours to freeze the fruit; 10 minutes for the ice cream; 20 minutes for the pastry shells

Cooking Time: 20 minutes for the pastry shells

8 ripe bananas

$1/4$–$1/2$ cup nut milk or soy milk

SWEET ALMOND PASTRY SHELLS

$1 1/3$ cups almonds

$1 1/2$ cups uncooked oatmeal

1 cup plus 2 tablespoons unbleached white flour

$3/4$ teaspoon salt

$1/2$ cup honey

$1/4$ cup water

2 teaspoons almond extract

GARNISH

Fresh mint leaves

From Café For All Seasons   SAN FRANCISCO, CALIFORNIA

Pecan Pumpkin Pie
with Caramel Sauce

Donna Katzl of Café For All Seasons says the packaged cake mix "gives the traditional pumpkin pie a delightful and delicious new variation." You may substitute egg replacer plus 1 teaspoon agar-agar, available in natural food stores, for the eggs. See "Alternatives to Eggs" on page 82.)

Yield: *Two 9-inch pies (including 2 cups each whipped cream and caramel sauce)*

Preparation Time: 20 minutes for the pie; 5 minutes for the whipped cream; 5 minutes for caramel sauce

Cooking Time: 35–45 minutes; 5–10 minutes for caramel sauce

PECAN PUMPKIN PIE

1 (29-ounce) can pumpkin or 3 cups fresh, puréed pumpkin

1 (5-ounce) can evaporated milk

1 cup sugar

3 eggs, lightly beaten

$1/2$ teaspoon salt

2 teaspoons cinnamon

1 package Pillsbury Plus yellow cake mix with pudding

$1^1/2$ cups chopped pecans

1 cup butter, melted and slightly cooled

CARAMEL SAUCE

1 cup sweet butter

2 cups light brown sugar

1 cup heavy cream

WHIPPED CREAM

2 cups heavy whipping cream

3 tablespoons powdered sugar

$1^1/2$ teaspoons vanilla extract

To Make the Pies:

1. Preheat the oven to 350°F. Line the bottom and sides of two 9-inch pie pans with waxed paper, and lightly oil the waxed paper.

2. In a large mixing bowl, place the pumpkin, milk, sugar, eggs (or egg replacer and agar-agar), salt, and cinnamon. Mix together with a wire whisk. Pour the mixture into the pie pans.

3. Sprinkle the yellow cake mix over tops of both pies. Distribute pecans over tops, and drizzle the melted butter over all.

4. Place the pie pans in the oven to bake for 35 to 45 minutes. A knife inserted in the center should come out clean. Remove the pies from the oven, allow to cool, and then chill deeply in the refrigerator before cutting into wedges.

To Make the Caramel Sauce:

1. Cut the butter into pieces, and place in a small, heavy-bottomed saucepan. Stir in the brown sugar and cream. Cook over very low heat, stirring constantly. Whisking the sauce helps to blend it together.

2. Heat the sauce until warm and well blended. Serve warm. Refrigerate the remaining sauce in a covered container. Reheat on low heat to serve again.

To Make the Whipped Cream:

1. Pour the whipping cream into a medium-sized chilled bowl. Begin beating the cream with an electric beater or wire whisk for 1 minute. Then add the powdered sugar and vanilla, and continue to beat until the cream has formed soft peaks. Serve right away.

To Serve the Pie:

1. Place a wedge of pie on each plate, drizzle the warm caramel sauce over the top, and top with a dollop of whipped cream.

ABOUT THE RESTAURANT

Co-owners Donna and Frank Katzl have taught by their example the rich, warm pleasures of cooking and dining to their two daughters, Cathy Ann and Lisa, who are currently managers at the restaurant.

From John Bozeman's Bistro   BOZEMAN, MONTANA

Harvest Pie

Autumn splendor in a pie!

To Prepare the Pie Crust:

1. In a large bowl, combine the flour, sugar, and salt. Cut in the butter and shortening a tablespoon at a time with a pastry cutter. Or place the flour mixture, butter, and shortening in a food processor, and pulse until the ingredients are pea-sized pieces.

2. Add the water, and gently form the dough into two balls. Wrap the dough in plastic wrap, and chill for 1 hour.

To Prepare the Filling and Glaze, and Bake the Pie:

1. Preheat the oven to 375°F.

2. Put the peach concentrate in a medium-sized saucepan, add the sugar, and bring to the boil over medium heat. Reduce the amount of liquid to about half.

3. Place a small amount of the hot concentrate mixture in a small bowl. Add the cornstarch, and stir with a fork to blend well. Add the cornstarch-concentrate mixture to the rest of the peach concentrate in the pan, and continue to heat until the mixture is very thick.

4. In a large bowl, place the peaches, apples, raisins, and currants. Add the thickened syrup to the fruit, and mix well.

5. Remove the dough from the refrigerator, and roll out one ball of dough on a lightly floured surface. The sheet of dough should be large enough to overlap the pan by 1/2 inch. Place on the bottom of a 9-inch pie pan. In the same way, roll out the second ball of dough as the top crust.

6. Pour the filling into the prepared pie shell. Lay the other pie crust on top of the filling, and pinch the crust together along the edges to seal.

7. To make the optional glaze, place the egg and sugar in a bowl, and whisk together. Brush the glaze on the top pie crust, or brush with milk.

8. Place the pie in the oven, and bake until golden brown, about 45 minutes. Serve warm with vanilla ice cream.

ABOUT THE RESTAURANT

Creativity, imagination, and a flair for putting together just the right ingredients are what it takes to create a new variation on an old theme. The chefs at The Bistro accomplish this task with ease.

Yield: *One 9-inch pie*

Preparation Time: 45 minutes plus 1 hour for chilling the dough

Cooking Time: 45 minutes for the pie; 10 minutes for the filling

PIE CRUST

2–2 1/2 cups unbleached white flour

2 teaspoons sugar

1 teaspoon salt

1/2 cup unsalted butter

1/4 cup plus 2 tablespoons shortening

1/4 cup plus 1 tablespoon ice water

FILLING

1 can peach concentrate

1 cup brown sugar

2 tablespoons cornstarch

2 cups fresh or frozen peaches (not too ripe, if fresh)

2 cups Granny Smith, Rome, MacIntosh, or other baking apples, peeled and sliced

1/2 cup raisins

1/2 cup currants

OPTIONAL GLAZE

1 egg

2 tablespoons granulated white sugar

From Restaurant Keffi   SANTA CRUZ, CALIFORNIA

Banana Cream Pie

This is a wonderful dessert recipe for those who do not eat dairy products or white sugar. However, if you would like to make this pie with white granulated sugar and dairy milk, you will still get the same tasty results.

Yield: 8 servings

Preparation Time: 15 minutes for the pie crust; 20 minutes for the filling

Cooking Time: 15–20 minutes for the pie crust

Chilling Time: 30 minutes for the filling; 1 hour for the completed pie

10 whole graham crackers, ground into fine crumbs

1 teaspoon ground cinnamon

1/2 cup melted soy or dairy margarine

3/4 cup fructose, turbinado, or white sugar

1/4 cup plus 1 tablespoon cornstarch

1 1/2 cups soy or dairy milk

1/2 teaspoon salt

1 teaspoon vanilla extract

8 ounces soft tofu

2 large bananas

1/3 cup coarsely chopped, toasted almonds (See "Toasting Nuts and Seeds" on page 68.)

1. Preheat the oven to 350°F.

2. In a medium-sized bowl, place the graham cracker crumbs, the cinnamon, and 6 tablespoons of the melted margarine. Stir with a fork until completely mixed. Press the mixture into the bottom and along the sides of a 9-inch pie pan.

3. Place the crust in the oven, and bake until lightly toasted, about 20 minutes. Remove the pan from the oven, and let cool on a wire cooling rack while you prepare the filling.

4. Place the sugar and cornstarch in a large bowl. Add the soy milk, salt, and vanilla, and whisk until well blended. Add the remaining 2 tablespoons of melted margarine. Place the mixture in a double boiler over, but not in, boiling water.

5. Cook the mixture over medium heat, stirring frequently, until very thick. Leaving the mixture in the pan, place it, uncovered, in the refrigerator.

6. Refrigerate until chilled, about 30 to 45 minutes, stirring occasionally. Then pour the mixture into a food processor or blender, add the tofu, and blend until smooth and creamy.

7. Peel and slice the bananas in rounds. Arrange over the cooled crust. Pour the custard mixture on top of the bananas, and sprinkle with the chopped toasted almonds. Cover the top of the pie loosely with plastic wrap and refrigerate until firm, at least 1 hour. Serve chilled.

ABOUT THE RESTAURANT

At Restaurant Keffi, there's no end to the ways to create keffi, a good feeling. This pie is a sure way to make a grand finale to a dinner or an after-the-theater party on a sweet spring night.

From Delites of India   MINNEAPOLIS, MINNESOTA

Kheer (Indian Rice Pudding)

This pudding is an excellent dessert to accompany any dinner, especially Indian entrées.

1. Place the rice and the water in a bowl, and soak for as long as it takes to bring the milk to the boil in the next step.

2. Place the milk in a large, heavy, nonstick saucepan, and bring to a boil over medium-high heat. Add the rice and the water it was soaking in. Cook over medium heat until the rice is soft and the mixture is reduced to three-fourths of the original volume.

3. Add the sugar, raisins, and cardamon, and the milk with the soaked saffron threads. Reduce the heat to low, and continue to simmer until the pudding becomes thick, stirring to avoid scorching.

4. Remove the pan from the heat, and stir in the sliced almonds and rose water. Allow the kheer to cool to room temperature.

5. Pour into individual serving bowls. Garnish each bowl with a silver leaf and sprinkle with sliced pistachio nuts. Serve at room temperature or refrigerate, covered, until well chilled, about 1 to 2 hours.

ABOUT THE RESTAURANT

About this rice pudding, B. K. Arora says, "Next to ambrosia nectar, it's the God's food." Need more be said?

---

*Basmati rice, from India, is a particularly aromatic long-grained rice. Be sure to rinse it according to the package directions. Rose water, which is made by steeping rose petals in water, and silver leaves may be bought at Indian or specialty food markets.

Yield: 4 cups

Preparation Time: 10 minutes

Cooking Time: 30–50 minutes

4 tablespoons basmati rice*

1/2 cup water

5 cups 2 percent milk (For creamier pudding, use whole milk.)

1/4 cup plus 1 tablespoon sugar

1/4 cup golden raisins, softened in 1 cup water

1/2 teaspoon ground cardamon

3–4 saffron threads, soaked in 2 tablespoons milk and ground with the back of a spoon

2 tablespoons sliced blanched almonds

2 tablespoons rose water,* optional

2 tablespoons sliced unsalted pistachio nuts

8 silver leaves,* optional

Rice Pudding

This rice pudding makes a delicious wholesome dessert or a nutritious breakfast entrée.

Yield: 6 servings

Preparation Time: 10 minutes

Cooking Time: 20–30 minutes

2 cups soy or dairy milk

1 tablespoon arrowroot

2 cups cooked brown or
   basmati rice*

16 ounces soft tofu, drained

1/4 cup plus 2 tablespoons
   honey

1/2 teaspoon ground cinnamon

1/2 teaspoon ground nutmeg

1/2 cup raisins

1/2 teaspoon vanilla extract

1. Place the milk in a small bowl with the arrowroot, and stir to mix well. Pour the milk into a large saucepan. Add the rice, tofu, honey, cinnamon, nutmeg, and raisins to the saucepan.

2. Cook over low heat until the mixture becomes thick. It will thicken more once it cools.

3. Remove the pudding from the heat, and add the vanilla. Spoon into a large serving bowl or individual serving bowls, and serve warm or cold.

ABOUT THE RESTAURANT

The Chicago Diner is dedicated to promoting healthy eating for the sake of humans, animals, and the planet. The owners are the hub for the animal rights movement in the Midwest.

*Basmati rice, from India, is a particularly aromatic long-grained rice. Be sure to rinse it according to the package directions.

From High Noon Café   JACKSON, MISSISSIPPI

Peach Bread Pudding

In this satisfying, low-fat dessert, the flaxseed takes the place of eggs. Ground flaxseed is a good egg substitute for other cake recipes as well. You may substitute 3/4 cup water plus 1/4 cup soy supreme or 1 cup dairy milk for the soy milk.

1. Preheat the oven to 350°F. Lightly oil a 13- by 9-inch baking pan.

2. Place the flaxseed in a small grinder, and grind for 1 minute, to a smooth powder. Transfer the flaxseed powder to a food processor or blender.

3. Add the milk, apple juice concentrate, salt, cardamon, coriander, and vanilla to the processor or blender. Process for several minutes until all the ingredients are well blended.

4. In a large bowl, place the bread cubes, nuts, and peaches. Add the liquid mixture to the bread cube mixture, and stir lightly, just to mix.

5. Pour the bread mixture into the prepared baking pan, and place in the oven. Bake for 45 minutes, or until lightly browned.

6. Remove the pudding from the oven, and place on a wire cooling rack. You may serve it either warm or at room temperature with High Noon Café Banana Ice Cream (see page 233), your favorite whipped topping, or ice cream.

ABOUT THE RESTAURANT

The High Noon Café keeps pace with the trends in vegan cuisine and offers other great recipes in Regina Glass's cookbook, "The Basics of Vegetarian Cooking," which is available from Harvestime Farm, P.O. 39, Puckett, MS 39151.

Yield: 8 servings

Preparation Time: 20 minutes

Cooking Time: 45 minutes

3 tablespoons flaxseed

1 cup soy milk

1 can frozen apple juice concentrate

$1/4$ teaspoon salt

$1/4$ teaspoon ground cardamon

$1/2$ teaspoon ground coriander

2 teaspoons vanilla extract

5–6 cups fresh bread cubes

$1/2$ cup chopped nuts (walnuts or pecans)

3 cups diced fresh (3 large) or canned peaches

From Dairy Hollow House Country Inn and Restuarant
EUREKA SPRINGS, ARKANSAS

Fresh Ginger Snaps

Yummers! This ginger snap is made with fresh ginger!

Yield: 3¹/₂ dozen cookies

Preparation Time: 20 minutes

Cooking Time: 8–10 minutes

³/₄ cup butter, at room
   temperature

³/₄ cup margarine

1¹/₂ cups sugar

2 eggs (See "Alternatives to
   Eggs" on page 82.)

¹/₂ cup dark molasses

2–4 tablespoons fresh ginger,
   peeled and chopped finely

4¹/₂ cups unbleached white
   flour

2 teaspoons ground cinnamon

¹/₄ teaspoon ground cloves

¹/₄ teaspoon ground or freshly
   grated nutmeg

¹/₂ teaspoon salt

1 tablespoon plus 1 teaspoon
   baking soda

1. Preheat the oven to 350°F. Lightly oil two baking sheets.

2. Place the butter, margarine, and sugar in a large bowl, and cream together. Add the eggs (or egg substitute), molasses, and fresh ginger. Beat until well incorporated.

3. Into a medium-sized bowl, sift together the flour, cinnamon, cloves, nutmeg, salt, and baking soda.

4. Add the flour mixture to the creamed mixture, and mix gently make a dough. The dough should be stiff enough so that you can easily roll it into small, pecan-size balls. If it is not, you may need to add more flour.

5. After you shape the dough into balls, roll each ball in additional granulated sugar, place on the oiled baking sheet, and flatten slightly with your hand. Bake 8 to 10 minutes, or until lightly browned and crinkled. Be careful not to overbake, or they will turn too hard when cooled.

ABOUT THE RESTAURANT

Crescent Dragonwagon, co-owner of Dairy Hollow House and author of "The Dairy Hollow House Cookbook" and "Dairy Hollow House Soup & Bread: A Country Inn Cookbook," conducts writing workshops and poetry readings at this cozy, comfy inn.

From Creative Vegetarian Café BOULDER, COLORADO

Peanut Butter Chocolate (or Carob) Cookies

This rich, moist cookie combines peanut butter with a smooth chocolate flavor the kids will rave about. If you are using white sugar, you may need more milk, about 3/4 cup.

1. Preheat the oven to 350°F. Lightly oil two baking sheets.

2. Place the margarine, Sucanat (or sugar), and vanilla in a large bowl, and cream with an electric beater. Add the peanut butter, and blend well.

3. In a small bowl, place the water and arrowroot, and mix. Add to the peanut butter mixture. Stir to blend.

4. Put the flour, baking soda, and salt in a medium-sized bowl, and blend together. Add to the creamed peanut butter mixture. Lightly blend just until the flour mixture is no longer visible. Add the chocolate or carob chips, being careful not to overmix.

5. Add enough milk to soften the mixture so that when a ball of dough is pressed, the outside edge does not crack or break apart. Form into balls, place on the baking sheets, and press with a fork.

6. Place in the oven, and bake for 8 to 10 minutes. Remove the cookies from the oven. Using a spatula, place the cookies on a wire rack or paper toweling to cool. To store, place in an airtight container.

ABOUT THE RESTAURANT

When asked for one of their recipes, the chef remarked, "Oh, so many of our recipes are truly done creatively—without any recipe. We just intuitively put ingredients together and by mixing a little of this, adding a little of that, and tasting to see what else it needs, we create some of our tastiest dishes." This is a way of cooking we might all aspire to. Fortunately for this cookbook, the chefs translated this delight into a recipe!

*Sucanat is sugarcane juice that has been allowed to evaporate into granules. It tastes similar to brown sugar.

Yield: 3 dozen cookies

Preparation Time: 20 minutes

Cooking Time 8–10 minutes

1/2 cup vegan or dairy margarine

2 cups Sucanat* or white sugar

1 teaspoon vanilla extract

2 cups peanut butter

2 teaspoons water

2 teaspoons arrowroot

3 cups unbleached white flour

1 1/2 teaspoons baking soda

1 teaspoon sea salt

Splash of soy, rice, nut, or dairy milk, as needed

12 ounces chocolate or carob chips

From The Higher Taste, Ltd.   PORTLAND, OREGON

Coconut Kisses

Easy, easy, easy! These kisses are after-school treats that your kids will have fun making!

Yield: *2 dozen cookies*

Preparation Time: 10 minutes

Cooking Time: 8–10 minutes

1/2 cup honey

1/2 cup peanut butter

1/4 cup nonfat dry milk

1 teaspoon vanilla extract

2 cups unsweetened coconut

1. Preheat the oven to 300°F. Lightly oil a baking sheet.

2. In a large bowl, place the honey, peanut butter, dry milk, and vanilla. Stir well to blend. Fold in the coconut, mixing well. The dough will be very stiff.

3. Drop the cookie batter by teaspoons onto the baking sheet. Place in the oven to bake for 8 to 10 minutes.

4. Remove the pan from the oven, and allow to cool on a wire rack. Then serve to your precious little munchkins!

ABOUT THE RESTAURANT

With four children of their own, owners Hans and Rhonda Wrobel know exactly what makes a big hit on the home front.

Power Snacks

Trail mix in a cookie form, these power bars are rich in fruit and nut goodies that make a delicious snack whether you're on the trail, at the office, or at home and you need a yummy, good-for-you boost!

1. Preheat the oven to 350°F. Lightly oil or butter an 11- by 17-inch baking pan.

2. Place all the ingredients for the crust in a large bowl, and stir to mix well. Press into the bottom and sides of the pan, and set aside.

3. Place all the ingredients for the topping in a large bowl. Stir to mix well. Pour the topping mixture over the crust, and spread evenly.

4. Place the pan in the oven, and bake for 20 minutes. Remove the pan from the oven, and allow to cool on a wire rack before cutting into squares.

ABOUT THE RESTAURANT

Local artwork and luscious gardens, tantalizing entrées and dangerous desserts—that's Honest Ozzie's Café and Desert Oasis.

Yield: 24 squares

Preparation Time: 20 minutes

Cooking Time: 20 minutes

CRUST

1 cup butter, softened

1 cup brown sugar

1 cup rolled oats

2 cups whole wheat pastry flour

1/2 cup wheat germ

1–2 teaspoons orange zest

TOPPING

1 cup chopped almonds

1 cup chocolate chips, optional

1 cup raisins

1/2 cup chopped dried apricots

1/2 cup chopped dates or papaya

1/2 cup shredded coconut

1/2 cup raw sunflower seeds

1/2 cup brown sugar

1/4 cup sesame seeds

4 eggs, beaten (See "Alternatives to Eggs" on page 82.)

From The Body Guard   YANKTON, SOUTH DAKOTA

Sunflower-Rye Bars

These bars may also be made with wheat flour. They are great little treats whether you eat wheat or not!

Yield: 15 bars

Preparation Time: 20 minutes

Cooking Time: 25–30 minutes

1/2 cup rye flour

1/2 cup rolled quick oats

1/2 cup chopped walnuts

1/4 cup sunflower seeds

1/2 teaspoon baking powder

1/2 teaspoon salt

2 eggs or egg replacer (See "Alternatives to Eggs" on page 82.)

1 cup packed brown sugar

1/3 cup vegetable oil

1 teaspoon vanilla extract

1. Preheat the oven to 350°F. Grease the bottom of an 8-inch square baking pan.

2. In a medium-sized mixing bowl, place the flour, oats, walnuts, seeds, baking powder, and salt, and set aside.

3. In a large mixing bowl, place the eggs (or egg replacer), brown sugar, vegetable oil, and vanilla, and beat until smooth, about 3 minutes. Gradually stir in the flour mixture, blending well.

4. Spoon the dough into the baking pan, spreading evenly. Bake until the mixture is brown and it springs back when touched in the center, about 25 to 30 minutes.

5. Remove the pan from the oven, and place on a wire rack to cool. Cut into bars in the pan. These bars store well in an airtight container.

ABOUT THE RESTAURANT

The Body Guard, located in Yankton on the South Dakota-Nebraska border, provides a one-stop body shop for its clientele, offering a sandwich counter, vitamins and other health care products, tanning beds, and massage therapy.

Metric Conversion Tables

Common Liquid Conversions

Measurement	=	Milliliters
$1/4$ teaspoon	=	1.25 milliliters
$1/2$ teaspoon	=	2.50 milliliters
$3/4$ teaspoon	=	3.75 milliliters
1 teaspoon	=	5.00 milliliters
$1\,1/4$ teaspoons	=	6.25 milliliters
$1\,1/2$ teaspoons	=	7.50 milliliters
$1\,3/4$ teaspoons	=	8.75 milliliters
2 teaspoons	=	10.0 milliliters
1 tablespoon	=	15.0 milliliters
2 tablespoons	=	30.0 milliliters

Measurement	=	Liters
$1/4$ cup	=	0.06 liters
$1/2$ cup	=	0.12 liters
$3/4$ cup	=	0.18 liters
1 cup	=	0.24 liters
$1\,1/4$ cups	=	0.30 liters
$1\,1/2$ cups	=	0.36 liters
2 cups	=	0.48 liters
$2\,1/2$ cups	=	0.60 liters
3 cups	=	0.72 liters
$3\,1/2$ cups	=	0.84 liters
4 cups	=	0.96 liters
$4\,1/2$ cups	=	1.08 liters
5 cups	=	1.20 liters
$5\,1/2$ cups	=	1.32 liters

Converting Fahrenheit to Celsius

Fahrenheit	=	Celsius
200—205	=	95
220—225	=	105
245—250	=	120
275	=	135
300—305	=	150
325—330	=	165
345—350	=	175
370—375	=	190
400—405	=	205
425—430	=	220
445—450	=	230
470—475	=	245
500	=	260

Conversion Formulas

LIQUID When You Know	Multiply By	To Determine
teaspoons	5.0	milliliters
tablespoons	15.0	milliliters
fluid ounces	30.0	milliliters
cups	0.24	liters
pints	0.47	liters
quarts	0.95	liters

WEIGHT When You Know	Multiply By	To Determine
ounces	28.0	grams
pounds	0.45	kilograms

Index